As I Was Sayi

T0167976

PATRICIA BEER was born in Exmouth, Devon, into a Plymouth Brethren family she vividly described in her autobiography, *Mrs Beer's House* (1969). She studied at Exeter University and at Oxford, and taught English Literature in Italy and at Goldsmiths College, London, before becoming a full-time writer in 1968. From the 1970s onwards, she reviewed regularly for a number of periodicals, including the *Listener*, the *Times Literary Supplement*, the *London Review of Books* and *PN Review*. Her books include *Reader I Married Him*, a study of four nineteenth-century women writers, as well as *Driving West* (1975), *The Lie of the Land* (1983), *Collected Poems* (1988), *Moon's Ottery* (1988), and *Autumn* (1997). She died in Devon in 1999.

SARAH RIGBY was born in 1972, and read English at Oxford. She worked for the *London Review of Books* for five years, and has reviewed for the *LRB* and for the *Times Literary Supplement*. She now works for Carcanet Press.

MARY-KAY WILMERS is the editor of the *London Review of Books*.

Also by Patricia Beer:

Poetry:
The Loss of the Magyar (1959)
The Survivors (1963)
Just Like the Resurrection (1967)
The Estuary (1971)
Driving West (1975)
Selected Poems (1979)
The Lie of the Land (1983)
Collected Poems (1988)
Friend of Heraclitus (1993)
Autumn (1997)

Prose:
An Introduction to the Metaphysical Poets (1968)
Mrs Beer's House (1969)
Reader, I Married Him (1974)
Wessex: A National Trust Book (Photographs by Fay Godwin) (1985)
Moon's Ottery (1988)

PATRICIA BEER

As I Was Saying Yesterday

Selected Essays and Reviews

Edited with an introduction by Sarah Rigby
Preface by Mary-Kay Wilmers

CARCANET

This edition first published in Great Britain
in 2002 by
Carcanet Press Limited
4th Floor, Conavon Court
12–16 Blackfriars Street
Manchester M3 5BQ

A CIP catalogue record for this book
is available from the British Library

ISBN 1 85754 057 3

The publisher acknowledges financial
assistance from the Arts Council of England

Typeset in Monotype Bembo by XL Publishing Services, Tiverton
Printed and bound in England by SRP Ltd, Exeter

Contents

On New Fiction

On New Poetry

On Religion

On Place

On Literature and Criticism

On Lives

On Society

Preface

In a long essay about Rebecca West, written for the *London Review of Books* and included here, Patricia Beer described a review by West as 'cheerfully serious'; it was, she said, 'a good thwacking piece'. (The subject was Mrs Humphry Ward.) 'Cheerfully serious' is an almost perfect description of her own reviews – many of which were also memorably thwacking.

'I was well into Giles Gordon's *Aren't We Due a Royalty Statement?* before I noticed that other readers were taking the book seriously.'

'The Duchess [of Windsor] seems to defy any description which is simultaneously favourable, interesting and convincing.'

'The way in which Tillyard writes about the rebellion recalls Simon Schama's remark about "chaotic authenticity". I am not qualified to speak of the authenticity of Tillyard's treatment of the situation but I can vouch for its being chaotic.'

Writers don't always sound pleased when you ring up to ask whether they'd like to review a book or a film or a play. They're too busy finishing a novel or preparing a lecture; they might say: 'my wife would kill me if I took on any other assignments'; or: 'the book in question is published by the same firm that publishes my books'; or: 'you only pay peanuts so it wouldn't be fair to my agent.' Literary journalism is an extension of social life and it's easy for an editor to feel snubbed. Patricia Beer wasn't like that; she didn't snub people and she didn't suck up to them. She was a plain speaker; and like many people who say what they think, she enjoyed it.

'One reviewer comments approvingly that Esther Freud writes about what she knows; well, let us hope we all do that.'

'Tillyard's kind of sustained instruction can have a weird effect. When

I was reading her description of the birth of one of Emily's children, with full details naturally (the accoucheur, the expectant wet-nurse, the caudle the attendants were drinking, with recipe, all kinds of obstetric theory and speculations as to what room the Duke of Leinster, Emily's husband, might be in, waiting for the news), I could not rid myself of the notion that she was about to tell us where babies come from.'

'When people try to sound caring they usually sound soulful and so too often does she. This is a pity – we have several reminders of how wonderfully uncaring she can be.'

I first met Patricia in the late 1960s, when she wrote radio and book reviews for the *Listener*. Derwent May was the literary editor but I looked after the other reviews and I would sometimes phone her to suggest one or two minor changes to her radio piece. She was always patient, always willing to listen (I was quite young and quite nervous), but she was the only reviewer I've ever known who insisted that the new sentence be read out to her over the phone – so that she could be sure the 'rhythm' was right. At the time I thought that was very odd, though it's plain enough to me now that many writers, even journalists, hear their sentences in their heads as they write them (which is why in many cases you get their meaning only by mimicking the author's own intonation). Patricia was a patriotic Devonian and proud of what remained of her Devon accent. T.S. Eliot, she said in a piece about regional accents written for the *Listener* in January 1971, pointed out that 'all poets, major and minor, write in the terms of their own voices. Somebody,' she went on to suggest, 'should read "Ode to a Nightingale" aloud with a Cockney accent', adding: 'and perhaps somebody has'. I expect that somebody has read Patricia Beer's poems out loud in a Devon accent; it has probably been done many times. Only Patricia herself took the same trouble with her journalism.

After the *Listener* I went to work at the *Times Literary Supplement*, where I looked after the novels (I commissioned the piece about Louisa M. Alcott's thrillers included here); but it was at the *LRB* that I was most often in touch with her. In the past few days I've been re-reading some of the reviews she wrote for the paper as well as *Mrs Beer's House*, a memoir of her childhood that she published in 1968 (and which Carcanet hopes to reissue in 2003). What strikes me most as I look at it all is Patricia's strength of character and how much she herself (rightly) valued it. At a very early age she determined that one day she would be both rich and famous and – oxymoronically – a poet. The conviction stayed with her throughout her childhood so, for example, when the family had their first ride in a motor car (she would have been five or six) and her mother asked her, '"Are you going to have a big car like this when you're grown up?"' she was not in any doubt. '"Much bigger," I said firmly, not meaning to be rude, but, since asked, ready to state a fact.'

That's what she did: she stated the facts. At the end of her life when she had trouble with her head (I can't now remember the physiological cause) she was intrigued by what was happening to her and told us on the phone, believing it to be both true and untrue, that her mother – who died when she was fourteen – was downstairs in the kitchen. 'Sixty years dead my mother is chattering downstairs,' she would later write in a poem entitled 'Post-Operative Confusion'. On another occasion, she talked about the brain scans she'd been subjected to and how sometimes she hadn't been sure whether she was lying in her coffin or the scanning machine, or which was which. Her manner didn't change in all this. She was as alert as she was confused, as matter of fact as she was deluded. And when some months before her death she recovered, she looked back on the whole episode in her usual unruffled way.

She wasn't a writer who lived to the side of her lines or her sentences. Reviewing a memoir by William Trevor, she says: 'In the way we all take through the dark wood William Trevor is one of the few who can look round at the past without bumping into a tree.' William Trevor is an excellent writer but more admirable in my eyes, as well as more fun, is someone like Patricia who takes the bumps and collisions, her own and other people's, in her stride.

Mary-Kay Wilmers, 2002

Introduction

In 1968 Patricia Beer gave up her job at Goldsmiths College, London, in order to become a full-time writer. It was a pragmatic decision: she had by then already published three collections of poetry, *The Loss of the Magyar* (1959), *The Survivors* (1963) and *Just Like the Resurrection* (1967), but with fewer constraints upon her time, she was able to write more prolifically in the years that followed, and for the first time, her output included a significant amount of prose.

In 1969 she produced *Mrs Beer's House*, an autobiographical account of her childhood experiences as a member of the Plymouth Brethren, and this was followed by a new collection of poems in 1971. *Reader, I Married Him*, a study of four nineteenth-century women novelists, appeared in 1974, and Beer also began to write fiction and to review regularly for a number of literary magazines and journals, including the *Listener*, the *Times Literary Supplement*, and, later, the *London Review of Books* and *PN Review*.

The essays in this book span the thirty years in which Patricia Beer reviewed, and include the last long essay she wrote (on Elaine Feinstein's *Pushkin*), which was published in the *London Review of Books* a few months before she died. Though she saw herself predominantly as a poet, the subjects Beer wrote about were diverse, including the countryside (she spent a large proportion of her time in her native Devon from 1968 onwards) and religion, as well as new poetry, fiction and criticism. As she began to be seen as a comic writer (or at any rate as a writer who could raise a laugh out of even the most mundane material) she was also asked to cover books she could send up. To some extent she seemed to relish this: she wrote some very funny articles on non-literary books, including those on the Duchess of Windsor and on debutantes, but her strongest pieces tend to be those which deal with subjects she knew a great deal about, and in which close analysis is mixed with her distinctively disarming and unexpected asides.

With one exception, the essays printed here have never been published in book form before, and I have thought of the selection as a 'best of'; as a means of rescuing some of Patricia Beer's strongest articles from piles of now long-backdated magazines. The sheer number of reviews she wrote has made the selection difficult, but one of my main concerns in choosing the essays has been to represent the breadth of her interests and areas of expertise.

Putting the book together more than thirty years after some of the earliest reviews were written, I have also tried to include articles in which the subject matter is still interesting in its own right – either because it concerns 'big' books or writers, which are still discussed; or because it opens up an area about which Beer was unusually knowledgeable.

I have also tried to include some of Beer's funniest pieces; her casual, almost gossipy tone, her caustic humour and her attentiveness to odd (but searingly illustrative) details of a book were an integral part of the way she wrote and thought about literature, and I have tried to show the extent of this. I have also included a substantial number of longer pieces: though the short reviews Beer wrote retain her distinctive tone, the longer essays allowed her to analyse (or play with) her subjects more thoroughly, and gave her naturally digressive, allusive style the kind of scope that suited it best.

Although Beer wrote so many articles in the course of her career, they are surprisingly unformulaic. Her method, in as much as she had one, was to explain, as simply as possible, what she thought of a particular book, regardless of other reviewers' previous reactions to it, or the esteem in which its writer was supposed to be held.

Sometimes this meant that she found herself arguing her point against the tide of accepted opinion. Reviewing *Nazi Lady: The Diaries of Elisabeth von Stahlenberg* in the *Listener*, for example, she noted that 'the book reads like an inept novel in diary form or a diary titivated by hindsight'. The book, which had been marketed as a genuine memoir (a claim which had not been challenged by other reviewers) was soon afterwards revealed to be a fake, and an article quoting Patricia Beer's comments about it was published in the *Evening Standard*. Once she had formed an opinion, she was dogged: no one would shake her confidence in it.

The tone of this confidence was often irreverent. In frivolous mode, she begins her 1993 article on Giles Gordon's autobiography in the *LRB* with the comment that 'I was well into Giles Gordon's *Aren't We Due a Royalty Statement?* before I noticed that other readers were taking the book seriously. Up to then, I had assumed it had set out to be an ingenious spoof,' before going on light-heartedly to savage the book, disingenuously throwing up such questions along the way as, 'Is he lampooning people who talk like that, or is he talking like that?'

Though Beer was in many ways a generous reviewer, she was also scrupulously honest about the books she discussed, and her judgements tend to be made baldly, in a tone of absolute clarity and certainty. 'Half the last sentence, perhaps the whole of it, is unnecessary,' she says bluntly in an otherwise favourable review of Alice Munro's *Lives of Girls and Women*; and, in an article in *PN Review*, '*The Faber Book of Blue Verse* is quite a stylish title in itself. Unfortunately, it is not accurate.'

Beer was never self-consciously conciliatory or literary: she didn't use jargon or theory, or go out of her way to sound learned. Instead, by lightly establishing comparisons and nudging at association, personal experience and half forgotten fact, she situated precisely her own experience of reading a new book, and vividly established a context for it.

The results are evocative. Comparing Dickens's Mrs Jellyby to 'Mum' in a review of Esther Freud's first novel, for instance, she says, 'Yet whereas Dickens, his co-narrator, most of his characters and probably all his readers thought [Mrs Jellyby] was dreadful, readers of *Hideous Kinky* who cannot help feeling that Mum is absurd and potentially dangerous may well be worrying that they could be small-minded, elderly and overly maternal. That is clever. That is how the Sixties used to make you feel.' In the same way, Peter Porter is compared to Hardy; Philip Toynbee to de Quincey; the *Faber Book of Blue Verse* to afternoons spent behind a school bicycle shed. The comparisons are unexpected, but immediately lucid.

Beer's approach to criticism is, above all, logical. Each stage of her discussion is worked through rationally and she explains her reasons for taking a particular line in sensible, sometimes almost bemused tones, wondering, for example, why Stella Tillyard's *Aristocrats* quotes 'substantial parts of the marriage service, the best-known parts, including "I will"' when a family wedding takes place, musing that 'there can be few of her readers who are not familiar ... with a traditional Anglican church wedding or who have not at least watched one on TV'.

The parts of a book which strike Beer as being particularly interesting – the use of the entire wedding service in *Aristocrats*; or a particular sentence in a Beryl Bainbridge novel; or the fact that Randall Jarrell, though he described himself as 'not gregarious' seemed always to be surrounded by large numbers of people – are never predictable. Often, they are small details which initially seem almost irrelevant, but which, when Beer pursues them, start to reveal something different and unexpected about the book under consideration.

Her reactions to the larger questions some books raise are equally unpredictable, and sometimes include a number of contradictions. Though she was a feminist, for instance, she refused to defer to contemporary feminist ideology, and, in a review of *The Penguin Book of Women's Poetry*, openly denounced positive discrimination, attacking the logic which had led to the book's having been commissioned. She refused to be tribalised. Instead, her voice is that of the common-sense observer on the sidelines – shouting her encouragement, decisively taking sides with the characters, or voicing her rage. So a character in a Beryl Bainbridge novel is enthusiastically described as a 'sadistic phoney'; and A. Alvarez's complaint in his memoirs that his wife did not reply to something he said is caustically quoted. 'Well, she has now,' Beer says with almost personal feeling as she goes on to quote a recent article about the book by his ex-wife.

Though she didn't hold back where she suspected hypocrisy or duplicity, Beer's honesty also included an empathetic openness to new work. Repeatedly, within the essays, she puts forward a best-case scenario in defence of a new or partially successful writer, or tries to explain and account for what she sees as a book's failings. When she admires a particular quality in a book, she is equally articulate. Above all, she brings a sense of life to the books she discusses, and the reviews are worth reading almost as much for the fun she seems to have had in writing them, and for her infectious sense of humour, as for the knowledge she stealthily imparts in them.

The breadth of her scholarship is clear, and her critical pieces are based on logical discussion and impressively close analysis (of sentence construction in Emyr Humphrey's prose, for instance; or Marilyn Hacker's use of rhythm; or Robert Lowell's use of imagery). But Beer's best articles are rooted in a personal, almost unruly energy, and even in her most serious pieces, she can rarely resist pointing out something that amuses her. A considered comparison of Pushkin to Keats and Byron, for instance, is briefly interrupted with the comment that, 'Neither Pushkin nor Keats thought that his own appearance disqualified him from demanding exceptional beauty in the woman of his choice'; and the analytical tone in her review of an anthology of new poetry is temporarily punctured when she can't help mentioning in passing that a description of a girl as 'full of sweet eyes' reminds her of potatoes.

Although – or perhaps partly because – Beer was an unusual reviewer, her pieces were widely read and people looked out for them. Elaine Feinstein has noted that Beer's prose 'had the tones of her own voice in it: a thoughtful, idiosyncratic, amused voice, with a seemingly effortless spontaneity,' adding, 'She was naturally downright – she never fudged or hedged – and her convictions rose from the attention she gave to whatever she read. Few reviewers offer so much pleasure to a casual reader.' Similarly, Glencairn Balfour-Paul remarks that, 'Her gift of being deadly serious, and in the same breath hilariously funny came through, toned down a little, in her prose works (as in her poetry). Like Cecil Torr, whose *Small Talk at Wreyland* was a favourite book, she kept noticing the oddest things and wrote vividly about them.' The writer Iain Bamforth, also from a Plymouth Brethren family, has said in relation to this book that, 'Patricia Beer had to lose her tight cradle religion and her broad Devon accent, but survived to be one of the sanest writers about... Although [she is] better known for her poetry and *Mrs Beer's House*... these finely poised, witty and urbane essays will come as a revelation. Not the hallucinatory stuff on Patmos; just the sober spectacle of someone writing well.'

Beer's editors were equally appreciative: Derwent May, for instance, comments that,

> Patricia Beer was one of my favourite reviewers when I was literary editor of the *Listener* – especially when she was writing about books she did not like. Then her reviews could be quietly devastating. Her beginnings and ends were always particularly elegant. Take the opening of her review of some memoirs by the poet Roy Fuller: 'In *Souvenirs*, Roy Fuller both claims and demonstrates that he can remember very little about the events of his earlier life, which is in a way unfortunate as they are the subject of his book.' An iron fist in an elbow-length velvet glove.
>
> Perhaps I was tempted to send her books she might disapprove of – I knew I would have fun with anything she considered nonsense. But she was always scrupulously fair, and what she loved she really loved. That included, especially, the works of Emily Brontë – which were always cropping up in her reviews as a touchstone by which to judge the books of other writers.

This book, which collects Patricia Beer's essays for the first time, is organised by theme. Sources and dates are printed in footnotes on the first page of each piece.

Sarah Rigby, 2001

A Note on the Essays

Patricia Beer had intended to put this book together herself, and though as far as we can tell she had settled on only one piece for definite inclusion by the time she died, she had sorted through most of her reviews, attaching cuttings of published articles to her original typescripts, and writing on them the initials of the publications they had appeared in. She had also decided upon a title for the book: *As I Was Saying Yesterday*, which she felt captured the spoken quality of the essays.

This book retains the essays in their original form except in those cases where manuscripts are no longer available. The differences between the articles as they were submitted to magazines and as they were finally published are rarely great, but where articles were cut the original text has been restored. Spelling, capitalisation and italicisation have been standardised throughout the book, to match Carcanet house style.

Acknowledgements

I would like to thank Damien Parsons, Georgina Hammick and Michael Schmidt for helping me to sort through the manuscripts of Patricia Beer, and for their help with the preparation of this volume.

Thanks also to Mary-Kay Wilmers, Derwent May, Elaine Feinstein, Glencairn Balfour-Paul and Iain Bamforth, and to the editors of the publications in which these essays were originally published.

SR

On New Fiction

Little Girl*

Esther Freud's *Hideous Kinky* started its career with two disadvantages. One was the title: it suggests whimsy, from which the book is in fact bracingly free. The phrase is explained and has real validity within the story itself, but should have been kept in its place. The second was the nature of the advance publicity, which seemed to have the bossy intention of providing the *clef* to the *roman*. There have been photographs of the Freud sisters at the launch party; they are the child heroines of the novel, we are told. Their mother is also present and her deportment described; apparently she is in the book too. It has been widely labelled as a semi-autobiographical novel, though in fact there is no such thing. And one reviewer comments approvingly that Esther Freud writes about what she knows; well, let us hope we all do that.

Over these disadvantages *Hideous Kinky* quickly triumphed. It is an impressive performance and not only as a first novel. As a novel, of course, it must be assessed, no matter what adjectives it may have picked up from the papers. It tells the story, then, of two English girls, aged seven and five, whose mother took them on the hippy trail to Morocco in the Sixties. The woman – 'Mum', as she is called with inaccurate cosiness – is calmly presented to the reader as a typical middle-class hippy of those years: irresponsible, self-indulgent, dishonest and not very bright; yet at the same time we are not openly invited to shake our fists or hiss.

Compare Dickens's treatment of Mrs Jellyby in *Bleak House*. As high-minded neglecters of their own children the two women resemble each other strongly. Mrs Jellyby's project for Borrioboola-Gha is Mum's pilgrimage to Marrakesh. One can hear Mrs Jellyby saying: 'Forget London, man. Borrioboola-Gha, that's where it's at.' Yet whereas Dickens, his co-narrator, most of his characters, and probably all his readers, thought she was dreadful, readers of *Hideous Kinky* who cannot help feeling that Mum is absurd and potentially dangerous may well be worrying that they could be small-minded, elderly and overly maternal. That is clever. That is how the Sixties used to make you feel.

We must not allow ourselves to be bullied, however. Somebody is

* From the *London Review of Books*, 12 March 1992. Review of *Hideous Kinky* by Esther Freud, *Eve's Tattoo* by Emily Prager and *A Dubious Legacy* by Mary Wesley.

trying to tell us – and fervently wishes us to know – that Mum (it may be part of the irony that as this is the only name we know her by we have to go on using it however unsuitably) is appalling. Here is one sequence that chills the blood. Leaving her seven-year-old daughter Bea with some people she has only just met, she goes off with her younger daughter to the Azouia to become a Sufi. Week after week she stays away, not making the slightest attempt to communicate with Bea nor enquire after her. The anxiety of the situation makes the narrator wet her bed every night. Mum, good-humouredly washing the sheets each morning, seems quite incapable of making any connection. When at last they get back to Marrakesh the slight acquaintances have long since left the town and Bea has disappeared: Mum is surprised and quite upset. Bea is soon found, however.

The tone of the book is set to be resolutely tolerant. Freud has protected the character of Mum from anything judgemental in several ways: one is by pushing the children in front of her like hostages. They are sweet, especially the younger one. Bea is shadowed by her understanding of their circumstances. And they are shown as being attached to their mother in spite of her embarrassing antics with prayer mats and lovers. She does not represent much in the way of security; even when they are all three on the journey home they cannot relax in case, in her unfettered way, she should jump off at the next station. But she is all the security they will experience for some time. They are disarming. It is like what happens when some crazed evangelist knocks at one's door: if he is accompanied by two small daughters who look up at him uncritically one goes off to fetch the Appletise rather than the Alsatian.

This is artful enough, but the handling of the narration is a tour de force of artfulness. The point of view is that of the five-year-old girl. She is an unusually intelligent child, with a mental age already far in advance of, say, Adrian Mole's and Holden Caulfield's (perhaps a hippy upbringing does work), but the actual narrative clearly had to be entrusted to her older self. This would hardly need to be said if the author had not created a disconcertingly strong illusion that the child really is the writer.

This is achieved partly by the quality of the observation. When a van in which the family, along with friends of the moment, is travelling, draws up at the Spanish port of embarkation, 'there was a tapping on the glass. We sat very still and John rolled down the window, letting in a blast of cold and salty air and a whiskery face with bright blue eyes.' This sounds like the authentic memory of a child, and it could have happened anywhere. The adult narrator probably put the salt into the air. Esther Freud's sensitive grasp of what a child would or would not notice and remember spares us from any kind of description for description's sake. Apart from the occasional sunset there is no fine writing. Everything is geared to the story, however vestigial it may be. 'Almost before we lost sight of Spain, Morocco began to appear at the other end of the boat. A long flat shadow across the water.' Morocco is not the subject of a word-picture. It is where they are going. Yet I have seldom been left at the end of a book with such a complete vision of a foreign country.

In the ramshackle months that follow, mostly in Marrakesh, with their poverty, unorthodoxy, perpetual restlessness and sudden strange pleasures, the child's viewpoint continues to dominate. When two Arabs burst into their room one night, each 'making a circle with his thumb and index finger and pointing through it with his other hand', she registers the gesture with the calm precision I have just quoted. Her mother is outraged – rather inconsistently given her free and easy lifestyle, if that is not too concrete a word – and Bea giggles knowingly. Beside them the younger child's inexperience has a sort of authority. Her conscious presence is certainly necessary to the story. When she goes to sleep on her mother's lap the action stops till she wakes up again.

The language of the narrative is that of a fluent, unaffected adult. The youth of the child is established by another technique: the suspension of the normal rules of composition. Characters introduced quite grippingly are never seen again. Others appear without any context and do not affect such plot as there is in the least. Dave, the man who poked his head into the van, did have some influence on the action: he made the van turn back. But the next day he was not there and the van was allowed to go forward again. The adults exchanged looks but the child did not understand, and as a matter of fact neither did I. In Morocco, after the mother's affair with an obviously phoney Italian prince, she and the children cannot find him anywhere. This is not too surprising, but they cannot find his house either, which is very unnerving indeed – and never explained.

There is one character above all the rest who endorses the tone of mellowness and charity which in spite of everything pervades the book, and that is Bilal, a travelling acrobat who is picked up by Mum in the square, soon after the prince and his house have taken themselves off. He is a very attractive invention; not that he is anybody's fantasy, but there is something magical about him from the start. Instead of going away and returning, which he frequently does, he seems to fade away and materialise again. He moves in with the family and they all love him, especially the five-year-old who is actively and consciously in search of a father.

'Bee-lal,' I said, drawing out the sound of his name. We were walking home hand in hand.
   'Yes.'
   'Am I your little girl?'

There was a long pause.

'Yes,' he said finally and he squeezed my hand very tight.

There is a sad scene when the family at last leaves for England. Bilal comes to the railway station and the little girl hopes to the last that he will travel with them, though she half-knows that he is the *genius loci* and could not materialise in London. But the revels are ended and as the train moves out he vanishes into thin air.

The title of Emily Prager's novel, *Eve's Tattoo,* brings to mind – the middle-aged mind, that is – the goody-goody Edwardian stories which prevailed in many homes well into the century: *Teddy's Button, Christie's Old Organ, Little Meg's Children.* Since those days I have always distrusted a possessive title, feeling sure that the book was going to be edifying. In this case I was right. Prager's subject is the Holocaust, and we *are* in for a sermon. I understand that she has been accused of exploiting the Holocaust, but that is not true. She seems, on the contrary, to be rebuking those who do exploit it.

At any rate Eve shows up in a very poor light. She and most of her friends were born after the Second World War and the Holocaust means nothing to most of them: 'You know, I couldn't care less about the Nazis. It's ancient history. I couldn't give a fuck.' This point of view goads Eve on her fortieth birthday to be tattooed on the arm with the camp number of an Auschwitz victim whose photograph she had come across and kept, and whom she calls Eva. This hysterical reaction, accurately described by her friends as 'some midlife crisis' and 'a bizarre over-identification', she backs up by a series of stories, which are fitted into the narrative with oddly Pickwickian effect. Each story is aimed at a different audience and each gives a different background and surname to Eva. They are simplistic stories, drawn from some foul kitty of Nazi atrocities and it is a wonder that anybody is influenced by them, but a great many people are. An aggressive roomful of Smokers Anonymous announces that next to that story their own problem 'seems like bullshit'. A literary gathering responds with cries of 'Jesus' and 'How about a book?' Poor Uncle Jim, who has Aids and gets the worst story of all, just sits in silence and nods.

The last story but one Eve tells in hospital to two nuns who are preparing her for the operating theatre after she has been run over. It is impossible to suspend disbelief about this one, not so much because of its content (though it is suspicious that the goodies have suddenly become Catholics) but because of the circumstances of its telling. The nuns listen spellbound, neglecting their job, and a doctor has to come from the theatre to hurry them up. The final story – something like the truth at last – reveals who Eva actually was, and a queasy realism sets in.

These stories provide a strong, though too obtrusive, structure for the book, but in between the supporting columns there is infill that contains much goo and rubble. The love story is contrived and unconvincing. The writing can sag alarmingly: when Eve says 'Oh hi, Dad' on the telephone there is really no need for the author to add: 'It was her father.' Some sequences are clearly meant to bring the whole question of anti-semitism to a conclusion – for example, Eve's long conversation with the old Jewish transvestite who appears especially for the purpose. But they are incoherent, and so is the moral when it finally arrives.

It is almost as if Prager was trying not to sound heartless. Anyone who has read her story 'The Lincoln-Pruitt Anti-Rape Device' will know what a very cool eye she can cast on life and death. But when people try to sound caring they usually sound soulful, and so too often in *Eve's Tattoo* does she. This is a pity – we have several reminders of how wonderfully uncaring she can be. The description of the literary party is brilliant, and fortunately there is a whole chapter of it. I particularly liked the 'clump of treelike editors', all three of whom had cheated on their wives while they were pregnant, but had then garrulously found themselves when the babies were born.

It is to these three men and anyone else within earshot that Eve tells the story about the particular Eva who was an obstetrician: she worked in situations of great danger to help women in defiance of the Nazi laws about child-bearing, and paid the price for it in the gas chambers of Auschwitz. The men really perked up when they heard the word 'obstetrician'. 'They all knew obstetricians and had worked with them in delivery rooms.'

Before I read anything by Mary Wesley I assumed she was a latterday Angela Thirkell, clanking with snobbery and gentility, and creating middle-class characters of Victorian morals and feudal manners, who lived in large country houses and were attended by threateningly common peasants. What misled me was the sheepish look on the faces of intellectuals as they admitted they enjoyed Wesley's work: so exactly what happened in Thirkell's day. The defence in both cases was that she wrote such engrossing stories.

In this respect *Dubious Legacy*, Mary Wesley's latest novel, is well up to what I now know is her usual standard. It is not wholesome enough to be called a good yarn, I am glad to say, but it is absorbingly readable. The story covers roughly the last fifty years. It is not a very long book, so time has to go by at a good pace, though it slows up reverently as it nears the deathbed. Three generations appear with a speed which can cause confusion, but this is not a serious criticism.

Whatever misled me about Wesley, I was not wholly wrong about one thing: the presence of class-consciousness in the books. The hero of *A*

Dubious Legacy, Henry Tillotson, does live in a large country house, Cotteshaw, just as I had imagined. At the start of the story it is being run with the utmost competence and poise by Pilar, a Spaniard whose husband died fighting Franco and whose chief ambition, which she eventually achieves, is to go back home and spit on Franco's grave. She is short, dark and triangular in shape: a peasant and content to be so. I cannot help feeling that there is some condescension towards her; it is certainly allowed to seem odd that a woman like her should hold such a position. As to the moral, there is none, unless it is the old saw: 'It's a wise child that knows its own father.' Four of the characters, at least, in quite a small cast, do not know theirs. *We* know that Henry is the father of two of them, their mothers being Barbara and Antonia, boringly conventional friends of his, as are their husbands. But he is not blamed. The women are warmly inviting, and in the case of Barbara, whose husband's pollen count, as she puts it, is low, his intervention is a godsend.

The most arresting character is Margaret, wife of Henry. She is not mad, just insanely self-centred, and she is no purple-faced Mrs Rochester: she is beautiful. At the time of her arrival at Cotteshaw she took to her bed and from then on left it only occasionally, though the occasions were memorable. Henry's unbelievable patience with her would be admirable if it were not balanced by his unbelievable irresponsibility, disguised as filial obedience, in marrying her in the first place. Perhaps her finest moment is when Antonia and Barbara have simultaneously gone into labour in the front hall, as a result of seeing Margaret, in one of her rare sallies, throw Antonia's older child into the lake. As they lie groaning, with everybody dashing about trying to cope, Margaret stands statuesquely on the stairs, demanding that her tea be brought up to her. Some years later she is drowned. The lake at Cotteshaw is not underused.

Beside the Wawanash*

This highly enjoyable novel, first published in 1971 and now issued in paperback over here by the Women's Press is, Alice Munro states, not autobiographical except in form. In fact, in form it more closely resembles a series of short stories, and it is no surprise to see that the author won a Canadian award in this genre. Each chapter of *Lives of Girls and Women* is virtually self-contained; characters who appear in more than one are nearly always re-introduced, however well we might reasonably be supposed to remember them. Yet each protagonist is closely connected with the central family; Del Jordan, the daughter, is the narrator throughout and though she is not the heroine of every episode it is very much her story. The first chapter, it is true, is set at a decided angle to the main narrative line; its hero, Uncle Benny, appears only peripherally in the later chapters – and his vicious mail-order bride never – but the effect is intriguing rather than confusing.

The title is accurate, for the book presents not only the growing-up of a girl, her relationships with her family and her approaches and eventual introduction to sexual experience but also the histories of her female contemporaries and older relatives, especially her mother. In other words, we are in *Kinflicks* country, but whereas *Kinflicks* tries, too hard for its artistic good, to be a, or even the, Great American novel, *Lives of Girls and Women* obeys its own natural range and scope and is consequently much more successful. Neither does it fall flat into the best-selling long lush grass of so many British autobiographies and novels about country adolescence. It is an honest book.

The story is set in a rural district of Ontario, mostly in the years of the Second World War, and the style often suggests the period. The beginnings and endings of some of the chapters weirdly recall, if not the exact voice of Penguin New Writing, a good parody of it: 'We spent days along the Wawanash River, helping Uncle Benny fish.' (The porridge-like quality of the paper likewise recalls war-time, but is probably the result of economy, rather than a desire for verisimilitude.)

The best of the sexual scenes are completely explicit; their straightfor-

---

* From the *Listener*, 17 March 1978. Review of *Lives of Girls and Women* by Alice Munro.

wardness is necessary and the reverse of bawdy, as in the description of Mr Chamberlain (newsreader on the local radio and unsystematic lover of Fern Dogherty) masturbating in front of young Del down by the creek. Munro knows when not to be explicit; the often puzzled loves of the young are more reticently portrayed.

The book draws a clear distinction between youthful and adult emotional attitudes even when exactly the same things are happening. 'Del is a bad girl' states Mr Chamberlain – he would – but in fact she is simply ready for anything and is vanquished, temporarily, by the one thing she is not ready for: that is, seeing in the character of the person she loves something she cannot bear. Del, looking back, comments that this happens to adults all the time but they can nevertheless go on loving; a generalisation, but in context worth making.

One of the most poignant sequences has nothing overtly to do with sex. On the death of Del's Uncle Craig she is presented with the typescript of the local history he has spent much of his life writing, the idea being that she shall complete and publish it. It is the Casaubon/Dorothea situation but Munro goes further than George Eliot in giving us a horribly convincing paragraph from the work in question, illustrating the scrupulous recording without interpretation of material that is worth neither. Like Dorothea, Del knows she cannot do it. 'I felt remorse, that kind of tender remorse which has on its other side a brutal unblemished satisfaction.'

One of the few criticisms that can be made of the book is that it often explains too much. The writing is in fact good enough to rely much more on implication than it allows itself to do. 'Marion had walked into the Wawanash River. People always said she walked into it, though in the case of Miss Farris they said she threw herself into it. Since nobody had seen either of them do it, the difference must have come from the difference in the women themselves, Miss Farris being impulsive and dramatic in all she did, and Marion Sherriff deliberate and take-your-time.' Half the last sentence, perhaps the whole of it, is unnecessary.

Fictions and Fancies of the Janeites*

There should be a clinical word for those who cannot leave Jane Austen alone. (The Brontës have been similarly molested but not on such a scale.) The condition is increasingly common. In recent years two books which Jane Austen did not finish – *Sanditon* and *The Watsons* – have been completed, thoughtfully but without distinction by 'other ladies'. Now we have Joan Aiken's *Mansfield Revisited*, a sequel to *Mansfield Park* and Barbara Ker Wilson's *Antipodes Jane*, an account of a journey to Australia which Jane Austen might just conceivably have taken but almost certainly did not.

Mansfield Revisited is agreeably written and at times decidedly ingenious. It is a nice touch, for example, to give Fanny Bertram, née Price, a good head for business. She never showed signs of any such talent in *Mansfield Park*, yet the idea is quite plausible. It is fashionable, too; feminist writers have been maintaining for some time, though without much evidence, that the languishing belles of nineteenth-century fiction would have made splendid businesswomen.

But though *Mansfield Revisited* is a very readable historical romance in itself, there is something puzzling about Joan Aiken's motivation when it comes to the Jane Austen connection. She claims that the book is inspired by love and admiration, yet it so absolutely flouts Jane Austen's deeply-held beliefs that it suggests something between a bold act of iconoclasm and a mildly naughty joke.

In particular it is Jane Austen's moral stance that is flouted. In *Mansfield Park* Maria Rushworth, née Bertram, after her elopement with Henry Crawford is relegated to 'a retirement and reproach which could allow no second spring of hope or character'. In the sequel Maria escapes from retirement if not from reproach, marries a profligate nobleman, receives a warm welcome from his fellow libertines and their mistresses, and has a marvellous time. This is probably what would have happened in real life, and very nice too. But Jane Austen was concerned to offer us a morality play, not a slice of life.

The reappearance of the Crawfords at Mansfield is another example.

---

* From the *New York Times Book Review*, 21 July 1985. Review of *Mansfield Revisited* by Joan Aiken and *Antipodes Jane* by Barbara Ker Wilson.

Socially, of course, neither of them could have been as gauche as that, but more importantly, the morality of their creator would not have permitted it, nor the events which followed. She did not intend that any dreadful punishment should overtake the one nor that the other should be vindicated. She just meant them to vanish into the world whose ways they knew so well.

In *Antipodes Jane* Barbara Ker Wilson describes how in 1803 Jane Austen accompanied her uncle and aunt, the Leigh Perrots, on a visit to Australia which lasted nearly a year. In its interplay of fact and fiction this book too is ingenious. Mrs Leigh Perrot's trial for shop-lifting in Bath really happened, and many of the characters they meet in Australia really existed: D'Arcy Wentworth, Elizabeth McArthur (note the names) and Philip King, Governor of New South Wales. But the story of Jane Austen's lost love is simply a version of the pious fancy that seems to be binding on all her admirers, and any conviction it might have carried is destroyed by the preposterous sequel in Australia.

Antipodes Jane is vastly, overwhelmingly informative. We are told everything we might conceivably want to know, and much, much more, about conditions aboard a convict ship and everyday life in the Colony, down to such details as the most genteel way to kill a snake when ladies are present. The characters helpfully discuss current topics like slavery and vaccination against smallpox. Jane Austen herself weighs in with educational musings: 'The noble savage – what a conversational cliché that phrase had become, Jane reflected, since Rousseau had coined it half a century before.'

The treatment of the story might be called picaresque. There is no attempt at a plot. Many of the characters launch into tales about what brought them there in the first place but this technique seems fairly natural in an account of a society where everybody was on the defensive. Apart from being a confidante Jane Austen contributes little to what action there is.

As far as narrative and author's comment are concerned Barbara Ker Wilson uses what I take to be her own style, though with occasional disconcerting leaps from expressions which Jane Austen would have employed ('a putrid fever') to those she certainly would not ('the moans, grunts and squeals of fornication'). Joan Aiken, on the other hand, attempts a mock-up of Regency prose throughout. It is shored up, and at times entirely composed of, borrowings, great and small, from Jane Austen herself. I find it difficult to imagine what it would sound like to those who had never read Jane Austen; the later Georgette Heyer, perhaps.

The dialogue in both books is the most scrupulous pastiche; every speech is a mosaic of quotation and allusion:

'Oh, I scrambled into a little education, without any danger of becoming a prodigy, I do assure you.' (*Antipodes Jane*)

'When I wear this necklace I shall always think of you and feel how kind you were.' (*Antipodes Jane*)

'Should I send Chapman to help Fanny pack for the West Indies? She could go over when she has dressed me.' (*Mansfield Revisited*)

Everything is there, all the way through, except Jane Austen's inimitable sense of rhythm, and that nobody can touch.

Popish Plot*

Muriel Spark's first novel *The Comforters* was published in 1957. *Territorial Rights* is her fifteenth novel. It is as brilliant as the best of its predecessors, which is saying a great deal. It is also different from them in several interesting ways.

In *Territorial Rights*, as in Mrs Spark's previous novel, *The Takeover* (1976), we are given a respite from the Catholic question, as a question that is. In her earlier work, like most English-speaking, novel-writing converts to Catholicism, she frequently depicts the Faith as a nuisance: something that, for example, stops people going to bed with those they love. And like most nuisances, it is inescapable: 'Ernest always agreed with Carolina that the True Church was awful, though unfortunately, one couldn't deny, true.' (*The Comforters*)

Conversion in fact is a mixed blessing. Nicholas in *The Girls of Slender Means* (1963) 'could never make up his mind between suicide and an equally drastic course of action known as Father D'Arcy.' Sometimes Mrs Spark presents it in psychological terms as a way of earthly salvation. The

* From the *Times Literary Supplement*, 7 December 1979. Review of *Territorial Rights* by Muriel Spark.

heroine of *The Prime of Miss Jean Brodie* (1961) 'was by temperament suited only to the Roman Catholic Church; possibly it could have embraced, even while it disciplined, her soaring and diving spirit; it might even have normalised her.'

Territorial Rights and *The Takeover* are both set in Italy where the Faith is much less strenuously self-conscious, so it is appropriate that we should have this break from the Catholic theme. In *Territorial Rights* the Church as arbiter of private behaviour is put in its place by Grace Gregory, whose justifiable boast it is that her years as a school Matron have taught her a thing or two: 'I don't know why the RC church doesn't stick to politics and keep its nose out of morals.' In more elegant terms Muriel Spark seems now to be doing what Grace recommends for the Catholic Church.

Instead of private sins we now have public violence, and instead of closet remorse a brazen peace of mind. Grace Gregory draws another useful distinction here: 'The unhappy ones are only the guilty amateurs and the neurotics. The pros are in their element.' Kidnapping and the professional theft of jewels and paintings shape some of the key scenes in *The Takeover*. In *Territorial Rights* similar deeds make up the entire book. Enter Grace Gregory, with newspaper:

> Such things are going on in Italy. It's worse than London. Look at this. Young boy and girl rob jeweller in Verona. Jeweller seriously wounded. And that's the identikit that the witnesses put together. Both got away. Stolen car.

There is private violence in plenty in the early novels though sometimes, through no fault of the evildoer, it remains in the planning stage. There is sensitive recognition of what is truly wicked too; Nicholas is finally converted, without the aid of Father D'Arcy, by 'a vision of evil': the sight of one of the girls of slender means going back into the burning Club to steal a Schiaparelli dress.

The vision of evil projected by *Territorial Rights* stretches from past to future, and it is public evil to which anyone, however morally insensitive, would accord the name. It takes the form not only of the items on Mrs Gregory's list but of treason as well. Personal betrayal is a subject Mrs Spark has already explored, in *The Prime of Miss Jean Brodie*. She is now concerned with the betrayal of one's country: Curran, the American, is accused of having been a German agent in the Second World War; Lina Pancev, the Bulgarian, is loyal neither to her own country nor the one to which she defects. Whether or not their actions seem more important than the betrayal of a schoolteacher by a favourite pupil depends on one's response to such suggestions as E.M. Forster's that it is worse to betray a friend than a country. But whatever the viewpoint, treason is a matter of public concern.

Territorial Rights has a vigorous plot; it is a spy thriller without the apparatus. The clues are planted as deftly and wittily as those in *The Hothouse by the East River* (1973). The clichés of ordinary narrative have literal meaning: 'There was Curran chatting away as if he had known the women all his life.'

'They need not be plausible, only hypnotic, like all good art.' The swinging Abbess of Crewe is speaking of the scenarios that her nuns are composing. She might have been speaking of Muriel Spark's novels. Authenticity, in the usual sense of the word, is not one of her aids to credibility; certainly not authenticity of the kind she parodies with such grisly effect in *Territorial Rights* when giving us extracts from the novel Anthea is reading: 'The rain poured outside. Mamie's knickers and two of John's pullovers were drying in the kitchen.' Those who come under the spell of *Territorial Rights* must recite a kind of credo: I believe that a man was cut in half and buried in two rose beds; I believe that a girl could be induced to dance on her father's grave, or rather graves.

The real authenticity for Muriel Spark exists elsewhere, though it is not inaccessible. *The Ballad of Peckham Rye* (1960) ends:

It was a sunny day for November, and, as he drove swiftly past the Rye, he saw the children playing there and the women coming home from work with their shopping-bags, the Rye for an instant looking like a cloud of green and gold, the people seeming to ride upon it, as you might say there was another world than this.

And after the violence of *Territorial Rights* has gone away into the distance we are left with a vision not so much of goodness as of eternity:

The canals lapped on the sides of the banks, the palaces of Venice rode in great state and the mosaics stood with the same patience that had gone into their formation, piece by small piece.

A Tale in Two Versions*

"'I'm just going to spend a penny," Lionel told them frankly.' 'Frankly' is an inspired adverb in the context, not only because it follows a dated euphemism, but because it points precisely to what Lionel — nostalgic ex-soldier, failed businessman, hopeless husband — is not, in the sense that he is neither honest nor open.

The quotation could also stand for the book as a whole. Beryl Bainbridge's *Another Part of the Wood* is a scorchingly brilliant study of a situation where the characters — coralled on a camping holiday in a Welsh wood — state and blurt out much, and experience in their inner misgivings much that is accurate and truthful, but seldom bring frankness to bear on their several circumstances in any way which would help themselves or anyone else.

Joseph, stimulating, warm-hearted rebel in his own story, searches his boring dreams for clues to his own behaviour, but they apparently fail to reveal that its pattern is to offer help to the self-doubting, the feeble-minded and the very young (Dotty, Kidney, Roland) in order to withdraw it at the moment of their greatest dependence. Lionel, up to the extremely bitter end, lives in the delusion that his wife May is blissfully satisfied with their style of lovemaking, which consists of a series of soft porn stories ('slowly the lovely Lalla Rookh thrust her abdomen at the mouth of the mighty Abdalla') which he relates to her in bed and which never, it seems, lead to actual intercourse.

The original version of *Another Part of the Wood* was published by Hutchinson in 1968. Beryl Bainbridge now returns to the story, which has not dated, though the trappings of some of the characters, particularly Joseph, have. The theme in general she has, of course, been faithfully attending to all the time. By the very act of rewriting the book she consolidates what could well be becoming a trend. Rewriting a novel after some years and considerable experience in the art is like moving house: the same people and the same effects, but a lot has been thrown out. Is it a desirable trend? In the case of Beryl Bainbridge, for the professionally-minded reader it certainly is: a priceless opportunity to study technique, better than a

---

* From the *Times Literary Supplement*, 29 February 1980. Review of *Another Part of the Wood*, by Beryl Bainbridge.

dozen creative writing courses. For Bainbridge herself, it must have been agony to omit so many good passages. As to the reviewer, it puts temptation in her way like leaving money around: specifically, the temptation to make variorum comments of a sophomoric nature on the two versions.

Version B is less than two-thirds the length of Version A. The plot structure is virtually identical, as can very clearly be seen by studying the presentation of events on the last day of the holiday camp, starting with the taking of a group photograph on a fine morning and ending with a lonely death that night. The two accounts are bound to be much the same plotwise, for they include no accidents or tricks of fate: everything leads automatically from something that somebody says when speaking entirely in character. For example: Joseph taunts his little boy Roland (he would) with being thin. As Joseph, again being thoroughly himself, has recently taunted the retarded teenager, Kidney, with being fat and has at the same time (in Kidney's best interests, of course) denied him the sedative pills he has been prescribed, Roland, with the logic of the intelligent child that he is, assumes that the pills make you grow and acts accordingly.

The difference between the two versions is that one is more explicit than the other, and which it is depends on what you mean by explicit. Version A is the more expansive, informative and explanatory; Version B, with its pruning and paring and suppression of apparently vital material, is perhaps the more truly outspoken.

The pruning starts in the first line: 'Balfour, unbearably shy, class-consciously shy, was waiting for them,' runs Version A. The class-consciousness of Balfour, the factory worker befriended by the owners of the holiday camp, is a fact as obvious as his acne, and somehow equated with it, but it can easily be left till later, as it is in Version B. The next example of pruning I am more dubious about. As the car that Balfour is awaiting comes fast over the bridge, containing Joseph, his girlfriend Dotty, Roland and Kidney, Version A adds: 'roses in the garden of the cottage nearby trembled at their passing.' I rather regret the omission of this hint of doom: the car *is* bearing death, as a train of events, as well as victim and killer in person, or killers if we count both Joseph with his taunts and Kidney with his pills.

I regret the passing of some snatches of dialogue too. The two versions of May's attack on Lionel when he is explaining to the company how many pieces of lavatory paper are needed by 'a man who functions normally and performs once a day for seven days' are very similar, but A includes a kind of epilogue in which May begins to speak calmly again and with her everyday fatuity.

'My mother said men would love me for my skin alone'…

'Skin alone, eh,' said Joseph… 'You'd have gone down well with the Germans, my love.'

'The Germans? Why the Germans? Why, Joseph, why?'

'Don't you know about their do–it–yourself lampshade-kits?'

This exchange marks the apotheosis of Joseph as sadistic phoney, the only thing he genuinely is. Apart from his heartlessness, to May and to humanity, he speaks in full knowledge of the painfully obsessive preoccupation of his host, George, with the sufferings of the Jews at the hands of the Germans. However, in the more reticent Version B we are left with no illusions about Joseph, even without such flamboyant proof.

In portraying her characters Bainbridge often looks back in horror, but not at what has made them what they are. They themselves are the amateur psychologists: Joseph for example, with his pretentious dreams and his immorally facile diagnoses: 'Kidney isn't simple. He's just mentally blocked. He's perfectly intelligent and normal, but he can't communicate.' When the author evokes their past it is at a point when wounds have already become scars. In the flashback which shows Dotty's brief affair with the young doctor who returned to his wife leaving her with 'a record of Scheherazade, a black jumper he bought her at Marks and Spencers, and a sketchy knowledge of the diabetic condition', she had long since lost confidence and was heading fast to her later rejection by Joseph. Version B suppresses this flashback altogether, and abbreviates others, though without detriment: Kidney's recall of his experiences in the mental hospital loses nothing of its Pinteresque menace by the compression.

In the world that Beryl Bainbridge portrays, the trouble is not that there are no answers but that there are no questions. There *is* another world, quite near, a frank world, where both questions and answers exist, as Roland discovers when he visits the nearby farm (Version A) but not in the part of the wood she is concerned with. Even May realises this; she stops short when about to ask Dotty a perfectly meaningful question about Kidney. 'She could ask herself the same question and receive an equally unsatisfying reply.' In the portrayal of such a world suggestion is probably not only as good as expatiation but far better.

The History Man*

As a title *The Anchor Tree* does not do justice to Emyr Humphreys's new novel. It belies the freshness of the book; there have been too many symbol-bearing trees among the titles of songs and stories throughout the ages. In any case, though the story is admirably clear, the title is opaque; it is introduced and explained on page 65 and there are recapitulatory allusions to it at various points in the plot, but it remains mysterious in the wrong way.

Emyr Humphreys's sentence construction does not always do him justice either. He *can* write masterly sentences; the book is full of them. But all too frequently we get such sequences as:

'I seemed to be listening to the profound solidity of the house. Built from local materials. Rebuilt rather. Under their close supervision. Inspired by Frank Lloyd Wright.'

Apart from the architectural allusion it could be Mr Jingle speaking and the narrator, Morgan Reece Dale, is no Mr Jingle, so it cannot be justified as a stroke of characterisation.

Dislocation is clearly necessary to the recording of modern conversation, yet it still seems inappropriate to narration, even first person narration. I can think of no reason why the following statement should be fragmented as it is: 'Maybe I was a soft and pampered academic. Absorbed in his private puddle of misery. Like a pig in a spiritual factory farm. Nothing but wet slates to stand on and no room to move.' If the pauses are intended to be pregnant, the pregnancy is hysterical.

But these are mere irritations. Mr Humphreys is a persuasive storyteller, and he has cleverly solved the problem of how to be realistic without being banal when representing the banal realities of twentieth-century life.

In the first place, Idrisburg, the small town where the main events happen, is American not English, which makes a great difference. It is charming, clean and well-planned and the object of civic taste and pride, with the blue hills in the distance and the tree-lined streets proclaiming the beauties of well-ordered existence. Significantly, one of the characters likens it to 'an amalgam of a Tuscan town in the top right-hand corner of

---

* From the *Times Literary Supplement*, 1 August 1980. Review of *The Anchor Tree* by Emyr Humphreys.

a quattrocento painting and an illustration from an old-fashioned children's book'. It is out of this world in fact. In the second place *The Anchor Tree* is by way of being an historical novel, set in the present.

Morgan Reece Dale, hero as well as narrator, is an historian by profession. The novel opens with his wife Eunice, already estranged, asking him what kind of an historian he is, and the emotions of their final quarrel close in on this point.

Dale sees himself as a historian to the extent that as such, and not only as a citizen, he takes responsibility for the state of the world as it has been inherited by the younger generation, especially Judith, the teenager with whom he becomes infatuated on his arrival in Idrisburg. He assesses both his moral and his social standing in terms of his abilities as an historian. When finally Judith tells him: 'You don't know your history, Morgan,' it is the ultimate condemnation.

In its presentation of history *The Anchor Tree* goes back in two stages: firstly to the Second World War, which has formed or modified the fortunes and dispositions of most of the characters. As a baby, daughter of a refugee, Judith was rescued from the roadside near Dachau by Arnold Norrcop, then an Army officer, now virtual headman of Idrisburg; he and his wife Rose adopted and brought her up. Two of the characters are in the end judged by what they did in the War. Countess Cornelia von Kalwitz, friend of the Nazis, who on their defeat made her home in America, is shown in spite of her penitence and amiability as increasingly under the shadow of her early allegiance, whereas Heber S. Hayes, vicious opponent of Dale's dearest plans is seen in progressively softer colours because after all he had fought, and been twice wounded, in North Africa.

The second and much longer leap takes us back to an earlier conflict between Robert Morgan Reece (Dale's ancestor), and Oliver Lloyd, brothers in Christ who left Wales in the eighteenth century to found a community of love and peace in the forests of Pennsylvania. Reece being considerably more idealistic than Lloyd, they eventually disagreed. Reece founded Cambria Nova; Lloyd went on to establish the nearby settlement of Idrisburg. While Idrisburg, as we have seen, flourished, Cambria Nova collapsed into overgrown rubble.

Humphreys shows us enough of the two founders to capture our imagination, as they plod westward in Christian harmony, deep into Indian territory, pointing out to each other the turkeys, the creeks, the great Ohio river, the elk and buffalo and the marvellous fertility of the land. It is not surprising that Dale, reading the records left, should decide to excavate the ruins of Cambria Nova and perhaps restore the community to life, and that so many citizens of Idrisburg should be inspired to join him.

The enterprise not only forms the framework of the plot but energises the characters into something like total self-display. The notorious self-repetition of history takes the form of a latterday struggle between idealism and pragmatism. It is all very convincingly done.

Magwitch Land*

The first chapter of Patrick White's *A Fringe of Leaves* employs the time-honoured theatrical device of having bystanders discussing the main characters before they actually appear ('Look where they come'). In this case it works extremely well, for the couple who have been allotted this usually thankless role, Mr and Mrs Stafford Merivale of Sydney, are interesting and almost a short story in themselves. Furthermore, they talk in their author's favourite and most effective manner, seeing through themselves and each other without the slightest intention of modifying whatever it is they see. They have just been to say goodbye to Mr and Mrs Austin Roxburgh who are about to sail back to England on the brig *Bristol Maid* and are complacent at the performance of a duty. 'No one can accuse me of neglecting duty' says Mrs Merivale, quite undeterred by 'the suspicion that those acquainted with her must know that her claim was not strictly true'. The Merivales are accompanied by Miss Scrimshaw, famous at this point chiefly for her Exalted Connection.

It is extraordinary how much useful information these three pack into their conversation, and without a hint of 'this too you know'. We hear how Garnet Roxburgh, Austin's brother, has emigrated to Van Diemen's – we are in the 1830s – and there is a subtle suggestion of bad behaviour on his part. 'I was always a plodder' says Mr Roxburgh, contrasting himself with Garnet, and, as we know, those who do not plod always do something much worse; according to the plodders that is. We learn almost as much about Austin Roxburgh as we ever do get to know: his bookishness, invalidism, gentle birth and the latent quixoticism that brought him so far to visit his brother. About Ellen Roxburgh, née Gluyas, we are told not only that she is beautiful and much younger than her husband, but that she is probably not a lady – she might even have come from *Cornwall* –

---

* From the *Listener*, 30 September 1976. Review of *A Fringe of Leaves* by Patrick White.

and that something is wrong between herself and her brother-in-law.

This vital chapter ends: 'The occupants of the carriage were rolled on into the deepening afternoon, and finally, like minor actors who have spoken a prologue, took themselves off into the wings.' The Merivales stay in the wings but Miss Scrimshaw emerges at the end of the book to play yet another Shakespearean role: that of Hymen.

As the afternoon darkens so does the story. The Roxburghs sail away to shipwreck, terror, mortal danger and hardships of every kind. Black cannibals kill Austin and reduce Ellen to servitude, humiliation and naked- ness, except for the fringe of leaves which she constantly renews. At last she escapes with the help of a convict Jack Chance, a murderer, who has himself escaped from a penal settlement. It is an epic story which does not need the help of symbolism, though it sometimes gets it. The events are those of history, significantly altered: in real life, for example, the heroine's husband was captain of the brig, a man of action, and in real life she herself turned against her convict rescuer.

The story is of course superbly told, and the epic quality is not at all impaired by the fact that the narrative is strangely quiet and tidy. Dreadful events are described almost casually and without distress; contrast this ship- wreck, for example, with the one in *Kidnapped*. But this is no criticism; 'It can't be happening to me' is no doubt an element in most dreadful events.

One of the most vivid parts of the book is the description of life at Moreton Bay where Ellen finds bodily safety when her physical adventures are at an end: the passing of the chain-gangs amid 'torrents of abuse, warn- ings, simulated farts, and above all, the sound of blows', the unearthly cries of men being flogged, the atmosphere of hatred and despair that pervades the settlement. This is indeed the opposite side of the globe from polite nineteenth-century England, though it was evoked if not depicted by the greatest contemporary novelists. Dickens sent Magwitch here and brought him home again surrounded by a smell of violence and degradation which even the inexperienced and insensitive Pip knew for what it was.

The novel has four epigraphs and the first of these is Wordsworth's couplet about 'perfect Woman, nobly planned'. Ellen is indeed a wonderful creation. It is not easy at first to say exactly where her perfection lies, as it seems to consist of docility; all her life she has sweet-temperedly done what others expect of her and will probably go on doing so. But it is really not so much docility as wise acceptance and this is what gives her such dignity and charm. If she had ever mentioned to Carlyle that she accepted the Universe his answer would perhaps not have been a snappy 'Madam, you'd better' but an affectionate 'Madam, you certainly do.'

On New Poetry

A Grace of Accuracy*

Day by Day, a collection of sixty-three of Robert Lowell's latest poems, with an appendix of three translations, is now published in England six months after his death. It calls for none of the decorum that made most reviewers of Auden's *Thank you, Fog* concentrate on what was genuinely good and turn their eyes away from the rest. These poems need no more leniency than do *The Tempest* or *Persuasion*. They are great by any standards and in any context.

Like *The Tempest* and *Persuasion*, this book may be called autumnal and not only with the intonation of those who, witnessing a beautiful autumn, regret a fine summer all the more. Lowell here explicitly portrays the fall as the season of quick and painless death:

> this is mid-autumn
> the moment when insects die
> instantly as one would ask of a friend.
> > 'Ulysses and Circe'

Throughout the book he speaks about the end of life. In the poem he wrote for John Berryman after reading his last 'Dream Song', he sounds very close to the fellow-poet who has died, not only in sympathy but in fact:

> To my surprise, John,
> I pray *to* not for you,
> think of you not myself,
> smile and fall asleep.

In his memorial address Seamus Heaney said that some of Lowell's last poems were like prayers. They are; and like hymns too, not just because they give 'darkness some control' but because they suggest, with the assurance of hymns, the diurnal feeling of being a day's march nearer home.

The violence that has always been a part of Lowell's poetry is still present. Violence is taken for granted as something that on the whole you

---

* From the *Listener*, 9 March 1978. Review of *Day by Day* by Robert Lowell.

expect and on the whole you get, like air. Boston is 'a city of murder, an American city'. Social drinking is 'the surge of wine before the quarrel'. History is the savage killing of Harold at Hastings followed by the savage depredations of the Conqueror:

> ox, cow, swine,
> the villages and hundreds
> his French clerks tore to shreds
> and fed
> to berserk hawk and baron.
> 'Domesday Book'

One outburst always leads to another, as in the case of the swans on the Liffey:

> This spring a Persian exile
> killed one cruelly, and its mate
> refused to be fed –
> It roused an explosion of xenophobia
> when it died.
> 'Last Walk'

Sometimes it is a question not of cause and effect but simply the passage of time. The protagonist of 'Death of a Critic' whose reviews were 'once the verbal equivalent of murder' and who was proud to feature in Little Magazines with his victims, 'the barracuda and his prey', has no wish to be done by as he did, but he will be, for 'time, the healer, made me theirs'.

Yet there is gentleness where there might well have been violence. 'Last Walk?' describes with distressing poignancy the almost certain end of a relationship, but though the incidental imagery is harsh ('the Liffey, torren-tial, wild/accelerated to murder… /black, rock-kneed, crashing on crags'), the symbol of parting is no more violent than melting snow. In 'Visitors' when the ambulance men come to take the patient away, though he thinks he hears 'a handcuff rattling in a pocket', he follows his 'own removal/stiffly, gratefully even, but without feeling'. His visitors are seen not as pumas or anacondas but cows. It is a terrifying poem but the fear is in the non-violence.

'I don't think that a personal history can go on for ever, unless you're Walt Whitman and have a way with you. I feel I've done enough personal poetry' said Lowell after *Life Studies*, but added that he might come back to it, and of course he did, and now has again. The subject matter of *Day by Day* is largely autobiographical. It is not limited to the experiences of recent years but goes back: in 'To Frank Parker' to a school friendship, in 'Joan Stafford, a Letter' to his first marriage. About his autobiographical poems, Lowell gave us fair warning over a decade ago: 'There's a good deal of tinkering with fact. You leave out a lot, and emphasise this and not that. So there's a lot of artistry, I hope, in the poems.' There is.

Lowell's habit of reworking his poems is well known and its fruits have been much discussed since the days of *The Land of Unlikeness*. The revisions in these poems are not as extensive as some, but are significant. We know about them principally because the original versions of such poems as 'Fetus' and 'Since 1939' (under different titles) and 'Ear of Corn' first appeared in the *New York Review of Books*. Often the alteration introduces an ambiguity which is almost a pun. In 'Fetus', 'The court cannot relive the misstep' becomes 'The court cannot reform...'. 'Since 1939' introduces more considerable changes: the boy reading Auden on the train becomes a girl, the poet's bride, which gives much more point to the poem as a whole.

In form, what Lowell claimed for *Life Studies* applies to these poems too: 'they can be gotten on the first reading'. They are not 'highly-wrought' – his word for his early poems – but move with apparent spontaneity and assume what seems to be the shape natural to their content. In the last poem of the collection, 'Epilogue', Lowell at first regrets his inability to use more formal techniques:

> Those blessed structures, plot and rhyme –
> why are they no help to me now
> I want to make
> something imagined, not recalled?

But he concludes the poem by defining, admirably, what he has already put into practice:

> Yet why not say what happened?
> Pray for the grace of accuracy
> Vermeer gave to the sun's illumination
> stealing like the tide across a map
> to his girl solid with yearning.
> We are poor passing facts,
> warned by that to give
> each figure in the photograph
> his living name.

The Old, the New*

Until quite recently the work of Norman MacCaig has, as often as not, been mentioned in the same breath as that of Hugh MacDiarmid. Apart from the fact of their being close friends and flyting companions, and both poets and Scots, I see no reason why this should be so. It must be something to do with politics, for the critics concerned usually try to demonstrate either that MacCaig was not a political poet by comparing him with MacDiarmid who was, or the other way round. Both seem aimless proceedings.

I originally heard MacCaig called apolitical at a moment when I had just read MacDiarmid's 'First Hymn to Lenin' and so could not help feeling the adjective to be quite an accolade. As time went by I realised it was used pejoratively but, I noticed, only by those who, while asking rhetorical questions like 'What political ideas could a poet possibly bequeath to the human race?', nevertheless, perversely, felt there was something missing in a poet who did not attempt to. So it was nothing to take seriously.

In fact, MacCaig *behaved* politically enough, and with admirable resolution. In the Second World War he declared himself to be a conscientious objector and was imprisoned in Wormwood Scrubs, though he had expressed readiness to serve in the army medical corps. But neither that experience nor any other made him a political poet. Some critics have tried to build up such a role for him by pointing to poems like 'A Man in Assynt' which are social rather than political. MacCaig comes into the category of people admired by Proust who believe that art has no use for proclamations but works in silence. Or, in his own words (part of a radio broadcast last year), if his readers required anything in the way of a message, political or otherwise, they had better try Tesco's.

In MacCaig's poems about MacDiarmid, scattered, though thinly, over the whole of his own career, he did once allude to the 'ramshackle ideas' which MacDiarmid tended to blow up, but, significantly, he presents his friend chiefly as pure poet. In 'Two thoughts of MacDiarmid in a quiet place' he speaks of him as the craftsman who understood, and helped others to understand, the techniques of prosody. Here he turns to a metaphor of fish:

---

* From *PN Review*, September/October 1991. Review of *Collected Poems* by Norman MacCaig.

the swimming of words – slippery adjectives
with their pilot fish nouns, muscular verbs
glinting in the shadows –
or swordfishing through a blue wave

MacCaig, the lifelong dedicated angler, could not say fairer than that.

Whatever the situation may have been in the past, in this new *Collected Poems* MacCaig stands alone. People will no doubt go on fossicking about for things in it which are deliberately not there, but I expect they will fossick with diminishing confidence; for it is an impressive volume. Published to celebrate MacCaig's eightieth birthday, it consists of nearly 700 poems. He has done some judicious adding and subtracting, which is his privilege, and has continued to suppress the earliest examples of his work, which again he has every right to do, especially as they were sent to the publisher without his knowledge.

The development of MacCaig's work can be seen with uncommon clarity in this *Collected*. The first four books, starting with *Riding Lights* (1955), show his early use, and mastery, of traditional techniques: full rhyme (increasingly infiltrated by half-rhyme), predominantly iambic metre, formal stanzas, and time-honoured poetic devices. Then in *Surroundings* (1966) comes a dramatic change.

MacCaig has told us all about it, in the broadcast mentioned earlier. It seems he took up pen and paper one day and without making a conscious choice and without any immediate realisation of what he was doing wrote a poem in free verse. It was as sudden as the conversion of St Paul, and as well-documented and, relatively to the circumstances, as far-reaching in its effects. There have been other startling metamorphoses, of course, among the poets of our time: Yeats, for example. But whereas nobody, I imagine, would deny that 'The Circus Animals' Desertion' is a better poem than 'The Lake Isle of Innisfree', there could be widespread debate as to whether MacCaig was better or worse for his conversion. And indeed the same thing might be said of St Paul.

It is more helpful to compare MacCaig's progress with that of Robert Lowell slightly earlier in the century. He too moved from traditional to free verse, but if readers prefer, say, 'The Quaker Graveyard in Nantucket' to 'Skunk Hour', it is a question of personal taste rather than a critical judgement, and so it would be if they found 'Skunk Hour' the more enjoyable of the two.

In a sense MacCaig did not need free verse, the main two reasons for turning to which are a quest for a more bewitching rhythm and a desire for greater spontaneity. He had these gifts already. In *A Common Grace*

(1960), the poems are in no way constricted or deprived of music by their form; here is a verse from 'Two ways of it'.

> You are no Helen, walking parapets
> And dazing wisdom with another beauty
> That made hard men talk of soft goddesses
> And feel death blooming in their violent wits
> With such seduction that they asked no pity –
> Till death came whistling in and loosed their knees.

No less and no more musical and footloose is the poetry of his new style. He is still using it in *Voice-over* (1988), as in 'Compare and contrast'.

> The great thinker died
> after forty years of poking about
> with his little torch
> in the dark forest of ideas,
> in the bright glare of perception,
> leaving a legacy of fourteen books
> to the world
> where a hen disappeared
> into six acres of tall oats
> and sauntered unerringly
> to the nest with five eggs in it.

When, in 1917, T.S. Eliot, no doubt startled to find himself and his fellow modernist poets so vulgarly abused, spoke wistfully of an ideal state of society in which 'one might imagine the good New growing out of the good Old, without the need for polemic and theory; ... a society with a living tradition', he was envisaging a land of various poetic groups, schools and movements all co-existing amiably and fruitfully, a concept which to this day is still no more than a pleasing fantasy. But there was another solution to the discord: the rise of individual poets in whose persons the good Old and the good New were creatively reconciled, and this Eliot lived to see. Such a poet Norman MacCaig certainly is. Throughout the vagaries of twentieth-century poetry he has been one of those who have made the weather.

Nine More for the Muse*

I have come to look forward to the Faber *Poetry Introductions*. There is always something lively going on in them. Number 3 is by no means a disappointment. The nine poets here collected have (personally) much more in common. Those who give their age are young, sometimes surprisingly so: Andrew Motion was born in 1952. They have all experienced higher education, mostly at university. Poetically, they are all observant of tradition without getting caught in it. Of course we find a few modish and derivative concepts: the almost statutory going for a piss in the night (which resulted recently in so many valid poetic experiences) and an above-average number of elderly relatives with their hands picking at the bedclothes. But on the whole the poetry is fresh and vigorous and I finished the book hearing nine separate voices.

It is only when the poets speak of nature and the countryside that the poems sag, sometimes to the point of collapse. 'Pommy bastard nature poetry', as an Australian once described it to D.J. Enright, can be left safely only to the masters. Nature is a death-trap to those who are still feeling their way. It is not that the experiences themselves sound affected or feigned. I am convinced that John Cassidy has clambered up the Pennines, that Gillian Clarke has seen a dead fox in a tree, and that Valerie Gillies has watched a salmon leaping, just exactly as they say they have. Their descriptions are open-eyed and watchful. Any failing must be something to do with the rhythm. Take poems about the Pennines: John Cassidy describes his own movements vis-à-vis the mountains ('pulled thighs', 'driving your legs') and the rhythm is, appropriately for once, pedestrian. But in the best Pennines poem I know, Ted Hughes's 'Pennines in April', the poet represents by means of his rhythm the movement not of himself but of the mountains, a much more exciting thing. (This indicates perhaps the chief technical difference between Ted and the School of Ted.)

Occasionally the poets use poetic devices without seeming to know

---

* From the *Times Literary Supplement*, 7 April 1975. Review of *Poetry Introduction 3* (various).

why; that is, the reason is not apparent to the reader. What, for example, is the purpose of the reiterated vowel sound in Gillian Clarke's 'Railway Tracks':

> ... leaping from sleeper
> To sleeper, along these lines that lead deep

or the sibilance of John Cassidy's 'Slowness is essence of quince'? Occasionally an imaginative trope gets out of hand: Ian McDonald, in an otherwise successful poem, 'Rumshop Girl', describes the girl as 'full of sweet eyes'; well, anybody would think of a potato. Sometimes – and this could be the reader's perverseness – ordinary human anxieties are aroused, on non-essential points, in a way which interferes with concentration. Gillian Clarke's description of her young son Owain, in 'The Sundial' as being out of doors all day though in a state of high fever filled me with Mr Woodhouse-type worries that distracted me from a worthwhile poem. Many of the poets have rejected the mellifluous or clinching pay-off line almost too thoroughly: Valerie Gillies's interesting poem 'Tracer' ends in limp cacophony: 'He stands as an initial leading in to genealogy.' Oh God, we asked to be delivered from the purple pay-off line but this is ridiculous.

The poets make good use of the experiences they have had in more colourful countries than our own. John Cassidy draws on his years of National Service in East Africa: 'Leopard' shows him leaving the 'gin-bright wives' of the mess dance behind him and stepping out into the night where

> There were fires glimmering on a far ridge
> And, distantly, the drums of another dance.

He meets a creature he takes to be a dog till he sees 'eyes like lamps'. They watch each other.

> Then the eyes went out and he wasn't there.
> The grass shivered after him.

Valerie Gillies draws on her knowledge of South India, in, for example, 'Blossom'. But the foreign experiences of both these poets have been incidental, and the colours, though well-applied, are decorative rather than organic. Ian McDonald, born and brought up in Trinidad, is in a stronger position. He dazzles us quite relaxedly with reds and golds, with jewel-bright frogs, bees blazing with fury in the sun, railways shining like swords, flailing mackerel beating up silver rainbows. People smell of cedar, bay rum, khus-khus and cane-field sweat. The rhythms are Caribbean. Everything is exotic to us, natural to him: most enjoyable poems.

The other poets, Paul Groves, Andrew Motion and Tom Paulin, all present interesting and competent work. So does Jeffrey Wainwright; his two sequences, '1815' and 'Three Poems on the Battle of Jutland 1816' are impressive. But the poems I liked best of all were Kit Wright's. There are only seven in this anthology – his in fact is the smallest section – but they tell. (More of his work can be found in *Treble Poets I*, recently published by Chatto.) He stands out from the rest; as a poet he simply has more bounce per ounce.

Kit Wright's poems are urban: no sunlit rocks, no storms in the hills, not a dead seagull in sight; he speaks in terms of newsagents *cum* tobacconists, cars in a wet street, salesmen in a bar. He can make a serious point without solemnity, as in 'Every Day in Every Way'. Some of his puns are worthy of Thomas Hood:

> Within, to Staten Island
>   my love and I did ride:
> despairing of the port we kissed
>   upon the starboard side.

His wit has the friskiness of Auden in his prime, and the melancholy too:

> But is it right, the other said
>   that time should use us so?
> That I, a lovebound hairy man
>   long, so long ago
>
> should hawk my bones from door to door?
> I do not ask for much, just more.

The ingenuity of his rhymes, e.g. china/vagina would startle even Gerard Manley Hopkins; on reflection, particularly Gerard Manley Hopkins.

Songs of Women*

Damn them – oh, damn them. They grumble because they say women *will* try to write like men and can't – then if a woman tries to invent a female poetry, and uses every feminine characteristic for the making of it, she is called trivial.

> Critics: in your sight
> no woman can win;
> keep you out, and she's too tight;
> she's too loose if you get in.

The first comment is by Dame Edith Sitwell and the second by Sor Juana Ines de la Cruz, a seventeenth-century nun. Whether it is a question of poetry or sexual behaviour, this complaint that according to male critics women simply can't get it right has echoed down the years, and unfortunately it can be according to female critics too. I am a feminist and yet I believe that in compiling *The Penguin Book of Women Poets* the three women editors – Carol Cosman, Joan Keefe and Kathleen Weaver – have in no way advanced the cause; and their preface suggests that they meant to.

Quite apart from the inadvisability (which is too obvious to dwell on) of isolating women as though they were freaks, any anthology of all-female poetry is a gratuitous demonstration of the fact that there never have been, and that there are not at present (the near future will, I think, be different in this respect) as many first-rate women poets as men poets. Whatever the reason for this, the only way forward is to define the reason and do something about it. Male chivalry, like that of Sir Arthur Quiller Couch who included nineteen more women in his *Oxford Book of English Verse* than Dame Helen Gardner later did in hers, is not the answer. Neither is the female solidarity that persuaded itself that anything written by a woman is intrinsically significant. Some of the inclusions in *Women Poets* are weak by any standards; similar work would not be considered for a 'Book of Men Poets' if it existed which of course it does not. We find a particularly slack passage from 'Aurora Leigh', a poem by Edith Sitwell, 'Trio for Two

---

* From *Books and Bookmen*, February 1979. Review of *The Penguin Book of Women Poets*, edited by Carol Cosman, Joan Keefe and Kathleen Weaver.

Cats and a Trombone', which anybody, not just malicious male critics, would consider silly, and some of the more fatuous self-indulgences of Gertrude Stein.

The editors have had to recruit very widely indeed. Abbesses are dragged out of their cloisters, courtesans out of their beds and princesses away from their embroidery. The collection spans thirty-five centuries and approximately forty literatures. 'It is fortunate,' say the editors, 'that this book is appearing at a time of growing interest in foreign literatures.' It is certainly just as well. But it is a great disadvantage that, except for those whose Sanskrit, Yiddish, Tamil, Ladino and Maori are in good enough working order for them to refer to the originals, readers are very much at the mercy of translators. Many of these particular translators are skilful in general and here at their best: Michael Hamburger and Elaine Feinstein, for example. It is only every so often that a piece of outdated slang breaks up the mood: 'Drat my hateful birthday' (John Dillon translating from Latin) and 'pint-sized' (Patrick Diehl translating from Byzantine Greek). But if anything was needed to demonstrate the maxim that in the translation of poetry what disappears is the poetry this anthology would do it; which is an awkward fact indeed for with a subject like 'women's poetry' we need far more than paraphrase if we are to learn anything at all.

The subject matter is surprisingly varied. Writing in the *Times Literary Supplement* in 1974 Dame Rebecca West said that 'after a course of study in Contemporary Women Novelists it is as if one heard a massed female choir singing "Oh don't deceive me, oh never leave me, how could you use a poor maiden so?"' Women poets, it seems, are not to be similarly heard perpetually lamenting in the valley below. Occasionally they do, of course, though no oftener than men. The twelfth-century Comtesse de Die, though the biographical notes say that her poem is answering back an indifferent troubadour with a 'mixture of scepticism and self-respect', is obviously expressing the statutory moan:

> I love him more than all the world
> Yet he cares not for me:
> Not for my pity or gentility
> My worth, intellect or beauty.
> I am deceived and betrayed
> As I should be if I were ugly.

But in this anthology the moan dies away as the years go by. In the twentieth-century section there is almost none of it; if a woman is suffering from the absence of a man, it could well be, as in Amy Lowell's 'The Taxi', that she is the leaver rather than the left.

But the subject matter, though varied, is unequivocally female. Daughters write about their father-fixations, mothers about the loss of their daughters' virginity and their death in childbed. Courtesans write about women's sexual responses, and not only courtesans: Huang O, a respectable married woman, daughter of the President of the Board of Works of the Ming Court, is remarkably forthright:

> You've made me all wet and slippery,
> But no matter how hard you try
> Nothing happens. So stop,
> Go and make somebody else
> Unsatisfied.

The limitations imposed on women by society are frequently mentioned, but in translation it is often difficult to catch the tone of the comment. How would Catharina von Greiffenberg, writing in German in the seventeenth century, have spoken the original of the following lines?

> Not he who holds the sceptre high atop the eagle's throne
> Nor students of the stars, nor brawny heroes bold,
> Were first to whom the Resurrection was made known.
> To weak women you appeared, O mighty Christ.

There is no doubt, however, about the tone of Rahel Morpurgo, when, writing in Hebrew in the early nineteenth century, she concludes a scathing poem: 'The wisdom of women to the distaff is bound.'

The editors display considerable naivety in their belief that if the writer speaks as a woman, then in sober actuality the writer *is* a woman. Have they never heard of dramatisation, or of homosexuality for that matter? When an anonymous poet declares:

> I see you creeping on tiptoe
> To kiss me from behind
> My hair heavy with perfume,

the writer must be a woman and into the anthology she goes. I am particularly dubious about the inclusion of 'The Song of Deborah', taken from the Old Testament. Heaven knows that women have always been allowed to prophesy, the sensitive other-worldly creatures, but I am willing to bet that the writer of the 'Song' was a man, and possibly inspired by the traditionally masculine Holy Ghost for good measure.

One especially annoying feature of the anthology is the passivity of the value judgements embodied in the biographical notes. Almost invariably a poet is 'universally regarded as…', 'universally considered to be…', or, 'generally thought of as…', and then follows some phrase like 'the most important German poet of the nineteenth century', 'one of the great lyrical geniuses of Spanish letters' or 'the most outstanding woman writer of Hungary'. All this cagey hearsay recalls Mr Casaubon in *Middlemarch* who told his young wife that certain paintings in Rome were considered to be very fine and when she asked him whether *he* liked them seemed not to know what she meant. In this present context the approach is depressing. Have the editors no opinion? It is almost as if they were waiting for a gentleman to tell them.

Flowers of the Forest*

These five collections of poetry have many common factors: they are all by American women who, though relatively at the beginning of their careers, have already published work – much of it clanking with awards – which has established their names; and all the volumes are interesting and enjoyable.

The subject matter is almost a common factor, too. Lisel Mueller uses as epigraph to 'On Reading an Anthology of Postwar German Poetry' (*The Private Life*) the words of Brecht:

> What times are these, when
> it is almost a crime to talk about trees
> Because that means being silent about so much evil?

and develops the theme of the individual's preservation from cosmic disasters of which he cannot help being grievously aware. The other four poets strike much the same overall note. They are far from insensible to 'the hurt and death no one wants' (Sheila Cudahy's phrase in 'Peace March': *The*

* From the *Times Literary Supplement*, 29 October 1976. Review of *The Bristle Cone Pine and other poems* by Sheila Cudahy, *The House on Marshland* by Louise Glück, *Separations* by Marilyn Hacker, *The Private Life* by Lisel Mueller, *Claiming Kin* by Ellen Bryant Voigt.

Bristle Cone Pine); they write about war, revolution, concentration camps; but they reserve the right to talk about trees too if they feel like it. Literally trees; I have never come across such a vast and variegated forest. They are real trees; nature is depicted by these poets with affection and exactitude as in, for example, Louise Glück's description of the running of the deer: 'as though their bodies did not impede them' ('Messengers': *The House on Marshland*); but it is not depicted for its own sake. Sheila Cudahy's bristle cone pine conveys an overt message: in order to survive, it

> hoards its life within a single line
> of tissue and allows the rest to die;

analogously, in times of stress humans do this too and find 'they have allowed too much to die'. Louise Glück's shad-blow, japonica, apple and flowering plum, evoked with great charm, are all accompanied by human figures whose wishes and actions they symbolise.

Many of the figures in these poets' landscapes are, naturally, women, and the female situation receives a fair but not undue share of attention. Marilyn Hacker, in the impressive sequence 'Geographer' (*Separations*), makes a resonant Lib statement;

> Last century, I would have died in child–
> birth, proving nothing at all in my death
> except that women were duped, even to death.

Ellen Bryant Voigt, in 'The Marriage' (*Claiming Kin*), is both caustic and compassionate in her presentation of the wife's point of view:

> She knew there were other women –
> his baroque excuses for silence –
> but knew in the weaker hemisphere
> of her heart, that stringent
> muscle pumping in, valved open;

and so does Lisel Mueller in 'Divorce'. But nobody is fixated on the subject. Indeed when Sheila Cudahy discusses essentially masculine reactions, as in 'Soldiers', the verse is more energetic than in 'Women's Ward', a poem which purports to deal with feminine experiences, though in fact the smells and injections could happen to anyone, and the tubes are not Fallopian.

The poets are fully aware of what they are doing in their poetry. Marilyn Hacker, again in 'Geographer', is as chatty and self-conscious about her own methods as Eliot in the *Quartets*: 'I have written a lot of lines that end with *death*.' Louise Glück in 'To Autumn' sees a poetic career stretching out ahead:

> I am no longer young. What
> of it? Summer approaches and the long
> decaying days of autumn when I shall begin
> the great poems of my middle period.

Lisel Mueller concludes the poem 'Hope':

> It is the serum which makes us swear
> not to betray one another;
> it is in this poem, trying to speak.

When it comes to technique the poets fan out. The most exhilarating from this point of view is Marilyn Hacker. For one thing her book is more substantial than the others and permits greater variety, though I think she would display surprising versatility even in a slim volume. As well as experimenting with techniques of her own she employs traditional forms including the more difficult ones: the regular sonnet and the villanelle. Her rhymes – abundant – are cogent, and her parentheses – again, abundant – are adroit. Stylistically, her simplicities range from the Wordsworthian near-banality of:

> I walked across the city in the rain,
> river to river, then walked back again,

to the blurting-out of such (impeccable) sentiments as:

> oh how I wish there were more
> boozy women poets, aged sixty-seven.

Her heightened manner is seen in, for example, the dark hallucinatory drama 'The Callers'. Altogether *Separations* is a most inventive collection.

The other four poets are less versatile; but each has a distinctive voice. Sheila Cudahy speaks forcefully and unequivocally. She is at her best when her statements are less rigid than in the didactic title poem of *The Bristle Cone Pine*. 'The Last Late Show' for example, which describes the consolation that the mother of a stillborn child finds in the 'Bette Ali Joan thoughts' inspired by the soap operas she has watched on TV is a fluid and persuasive communication.

> Then Bette Davis Joan Crawford Ali McGraw smiled
> and rising far above me said,
> 'You are the mother of
> the most beautiful dead child
> in the world'
> and that was true.

Louise Glück can be forthright, too. 'Love Poems' ends:

> No wonder you are the way you are,
> afraid of blood, your women
> like one brick wall after another.

But the prevailing tone of *The House on Marshland* is one of subtle and occasionally sinister allusiveness, as when in 'Departure' a traveller is less moved by saying goodbye than the tearful father

> And already in its deep groove
> the train is waiting with its breath of ashes.

'Jeanne d'Arc' is a fine poem and, incidentally, shows Glück's assured use of the long sentence.

Lisel Mueller is over-fond of the word 'small' – small poem, small mistake, small laugh, small hands; one gets to wait for it. And sometimes the accumulations of instance and example by which she conveys her ideas are not quite pointed enough, as in 'Alive Together' and 'Spell for a Traveller'. But many of the poems in *The Private Life* are as precise and energetic as could be desired. I particularly liked 'Life of a Queen' and the resourceful 'Palindrome'.

Ellen Bryant Voigt's vigorous imagination hardly ever fails her. 'Farm Wife' is a good example of her method: after the scene has been set – the farm buildings and the farmer ploughing with the birds wheeling round him – we get a sharply realistic glimpse of the wife who has been baking as 'she stands in the door in her long white/gloves of flour', after which she glides out surrealistically into the landscape.

> Let her float
> like a fat gull that swoops and circles...
> before the pulley cranks her down
> the dark shaft, and the church blesses
> her stone bed, and the earth seals
> its black mouth like a scar.

Love Among the Haystacks*

The Faber Book of Blue Verse is quite a stylish title in itself. Unfortunately it is not accurate. The only definition the *OED* gives of 'blue', except of course when talking about the colour, is 'obscene' and I doubt if even Mrs Whitehouse would so describe many of the poems in this anthology. 'About Coupling' (Fleur Adcock) is simply an elegant poem about masturbation, as agreeably far from lewdness as it is from gentility. 'Arsehole' (Craig Raine) is a poem which belongs − to adapt Leavis − more to the history of publicity than of pornography. The editor, John Whitworth, seems to have been blessed with the same sort of mind as the Bowdler family, who made their fortune by seeing smut everywhere.

The book had much better have been called The Book of Naughty Verse; it appears to be intended for moments of innocent devilry. And many of the devils appear to be schoolpersons. One of the techniques employed here used to be very popular behind the bicycle sheds of my youth. You start a poem with two rhymed lines, the rhymes being, say, 'luck' and 'stuck'; you then move on to the clinching line and just when everybody is expecting a Worse Word you dodge it and everybody falls about.

Then there are the acrostics. Oliver St John Gogarty's poem about coming back from the wars, 'The Gallant Irish Yeoman', included in this anthology, is demureness itself until somebody points out that the first letters of the lines say THE WHORES WILL BE BUSY ('Good gracious') and everybody laughs at you for not seeing it. As a matter of fact in spite of my bicycle shed experiences I might not have seen it myself but for a helpful editorial note anxious that I should miss nothing.

Some of the poems lose their impact from too much advance publicity. For a long time now there has been a certain type of man who claims to know all the verses of 'Eskimo Nell' off by heart, though without actually airing this accomplishment. When I finally came across the words it was like reading a Victorian novel the plot of which hinges on a Secret. When at last the Secret is revealed, even if it consists of murder, imposture, forgery and arson, one's reaction is 'Oh, is that all?'

---

* From *PN Review*, January/February 1991. Review of *The Faber Book of Blue Verse*, edited by John Whitworth, *The Chatto Book of Love Poetry*, edited by John Fuller, *Whatever You Desire*, edited by Mary Jo Bang and *Take Any Train*, edited by Peter Daniels.

Gavin Ewart is almost laureate of the anthology, with eight contributions. Alistair Elliot just beats him with ten, but he tries harder for he is translating and has a responsibility to his authors. Intrinsically Ewart is the better man. He writes with his usual dexterity. He uses all the right words straightforwardly when appropriate, as in 'Circe', but his best skills are to be seen in the entertaining 'Semantic Limericks', where from dictionary definitions emerges a well-known limerick in which an adult male person who has lived a relatively short time is deterred from his designs on certain large web-footed swimming birds of the genus Cygnus by a person employed to carry burdens who, with an alternative suggestion, informs him that they are kept in store for the gentlemen with Spanish titles. I am sorry about the abridgement; please read the full versions.

I get the impression that Gavin Ewart knows exactly what he is doing, unlike some. One of his inclusions is entitled 'A Very Shocking Poem Found among the Papers of an Eminent Victorian Divine'. It is not very shocking and he knows it. It is both witty and at the same time no laughing matter.

My own reservations should be offset by my expectation that the book will give enjoyment to many people: to groups, such as medical students (whom I have several times heard singing:

> Life presents a dismal picture
> All around is toil and gloom.
> Father has an anal stricture
> Mother has a fallen womb);

and perhaps some qualified doctors too; and to individuals who like to shock, the sort who would send the book to a favourite nun. (There is a fair bit of anti-Catholicism in it, for good measure.)

The one thing that really worries me is the inclusion of fine poems which are not being blue: Rochester's 'A Song of a Young Lady to her Ancient Lover', for example, and, an even more Bowdlerian choice, Thomas Hardy's 'The Ruined Maid'. Does the editor think of *Tess of the d'Urbervilles* as a blue novel? Yes, I expect so.

I have to guess about John Whitworth's intentions; he makes no attempt to explain them to us. John Fuller, in editing *The Chatto Book of Love Poetry*, does. His introduction is a lively guide to the anthology, the more so as the reader is bound to disagree with some of the critical points he makes. It would be a captious person who would dislike the actual inclusions – it is an enjoyable book – and to lament what any anthologist has excluded is always an unprofitable exercise.

The laureate of this collection is undoubtedly Browning, both numerically and critically. The editor considers him to be 'the real starting point of modern analytic love poetry' and is prepared to single out 'Love in a Life' as the first example of such poetry. The selection from Browning's work is extensive enough for readers to make up their own minds about such pronouncements.

As it happens, 'Love in a Life' exemplifies an essential feature of the anthology itself. The poem starts:

> Room after room,
> I hunt the house through
> We inhabit together.
> Heart, fear nothing, for, heart thou shalt find her –
>
> Next time, herself! – not the trouble behind her
> Left in the curtain, the couch's perfume!
> As she brushed it, the cornice-wreath blossomed anew:
> Yon looking-glass gleamed at the wave of her feather.

It is immediately preceded by two poems which also speak of a woman moving about a house and a man sharply conscious of her: Hugo Williams's 'Sure' and Christopher Reid's 'At the Wrong Door'.

This ordering of the collection by way of theme and therefore, necessarily, of imagery is Fuller's principal means – there are others which he states – of avoiding an arrangement by date either of birth or publication. He is adamant that that method can do no good, or at least not the sort of good he wishes to do. I think most readers will agree with him. I certainly do. The putting together of Philip Larkin's 'Broadcast' and Richard Lovelace's 'Elinda's Glove' would demonstrate, even if it stood alone, how well Fuller's method can work. Concentrating on the bare hands in 'Broadcast' I had not noticed the glove before. It makes all the difference.

Deliberately, there is no attempt to give each century or poetic epoch a fair share of the cake. The editor is firm about that too. There is to be no translation, therefore no Anglo-Saxon poetry and, these days, when Middle English is deemed incomprehensible, nothing much of that either. The eighteenth century has only a few crumbs and so has the early Romantic period. John Fuller gives most weight to the late sixteenth and seventeenth centuries and to the last 150 years. He confidently explains why.

The only point where he seems to be on the defensive is when he justifies his plan of omitting the authors' names from the main body of the text. He need not. To take the matter lightly: for adding to the general entertainment by letting us guess he will easily be forgiven. To take it seriously: for anything which frees a poem from the extraneous facts on which too many people rely he should be awarded a medal.

A few years ago women frequently sent letters to the papers (on a whole range of subjects) that began 'Writing as a lesbian ...' and I used to wonder how that would be. *Whatever You Desire,* an anthology of lesbian poetry edited by Mary Jo Bang, does not, I hope, give the answer. Recognising only two names in the longish list of contributors and having been severely depressed by the poems themselves, I turned to the biographical notes and was startled by the sheer silliness displayed by all but a few honourable exceptions. The majority of those taking part are not only gay but coy, fey and twee as well. One who is 'resisting the temptation to have a kitten' also 'dedicates her poems to her bicycle, Edge, stolen 25.9.89'. Another offers to 'provide us with a heartfelt understanding of the menopause' (but refrains). They are very vain. They testify to innumerable talents some of which would not be easy to combine, like weaving, playing the saxophone and taking part in a women's revolution. They sprinkle great drops of ego all over us like somebody preparing a lettuce.

As to the poems: the two professionals, Maureen Duffy and U.A. Fanthorpe, who supplied seemly biographical notes, write as always with professional competence. The rest write as amateurs. I am not afraid to say this, as some of their comments, about deadly academic literary critics, for example, suggest that they would take this as a compliment.

Take Any Train is a companion book of gay men's poetry, edited by Peter Daniels. The verse is on the whole equally undistinguished. A fine poet like Edwin Morgan would stand out anywhere; never more so than here. Driven once again by melancholy to the biographical notes, I found that the men are not quite as silly as the women, though we sometimes get the same conceit and folly: 'His primary impulse, as far as poetry is concerned, is to tell it like it is. Major passions are honesty, variety, and an absolute sweetie called Bart.' (I rather like the sound of Bart but that is not the point.) We also get the whimsy: the hovel, the hamster and the swiss-cheese plant, the birthplace shared with Diana Dors.

Both the men and the women are, very properly, happy to proclaim themselves homosexual. It is sad that they feel the need for so many other labels as well, beyond the national average: 'actress, mother of four, gardener and goatherd'; 'a Quaker, a former teacher, a pub landlady and an arts administrator'; a born-again oboist; an assertiveness trainer.

The editor of *Take Any Train* feels that those of us who are not gay are at a disadvantage as readers. He mentions a poem in his anthology 'which captures an essentially homo-erotic combination of wishing-to-be and wishing-to-have'. 'I don't consider it,' he adds, 'a failure of the poem that some heterosexuals found this hard to grasp.' Well, writing as a hetero-sexual, I think I just about managed to cotton on.

Sinking to the Occasion*

It might seem a pity that the sale of the Duchess of Windsor's jewellery did not take place till after John Holloway had compiled *The Oxford Book of Local Verses*. He defines local verses as, primarily, rhymes that have been inscribed on some material object which might stand in a particular place, like a sundial, but could be movable, like a brooch. In the Beau Rivage auction rooms he would have found examples that would have fitted exactly into his definition. The Duchess was a born local versifier. On the solid gold cover of a note-book she had had engraved her thoughts about the abdication crisis, one couplet of which runs:

> Out of his crown he's torn the gems
> He's thrown his sceptre into the Thames.

In fact it is a flight of fancy to suppose that Professor Holloway would have sought out this specimen of his chosen genre and put it into his book. Its awfulness would not disqualify it; he has included others almost as awful, though, I admit, none so inappropriate in tone to its subject matter. His lack of interest in graffiti which are rampantly present is what would rule it out. It is the unknown, the forgotten, which charms him.

He seems positively to shrink from any first-hand knowledge of his material. His introduction is frank and unblushing about his failure to consult primary sources; he had neither the time nor the money, he explains. He has found his verses in other men's books. They are mentioned in the notes; their titles would make an anthology in themselves. He has relied on such travel books as E. Bogg's *A Thousand Miles of Wandering along the Roman Wall* (1898) and J.J. Hissey's *Across England on a Dogcart* (1891); on such guidebooks as the *Highways and Byways* series; on such works of specialist interest as A. Hayden's *Chats on English Earthenware* (1909) and T. Wright's *Romance of the Lace Pillow* (1919). These volumes give off a reliable whiff of old bindings but are otherwise untrustworthy. He acknowledges this.

He has seen only a very few of the objects and inscriptions he has chosen

---

* From the *Times Literary Supplement*, 17 July 1987. Review of *The Oxford Book of Local Verses*, chosen by John Holloway.

and as to most of the others he neither knows nor appears to care whether or not they are still where his authorities found them. He is not unmindful of the intimate connection between objects and words. He likes, for example, to bear in mind that as the weathercock at Olney swings around it is saying, as it has done since 1829:

> I never crow, but stand to show
> Whence winds do blow.

But he does not really appreciate the indivisibility of words and medium (so well demonstrated by the sampler in the jacket illustration). He has, after all, set himself the task of lifting the one from the other.

It may well be that he has had no real confrontation with what he calls local verses in everyday life. He quotes rhymes written on Sunderland Ware mugs and various items of Liverpool Ware but perhaps has never had an experience similar to that of most Devonians of my generation: the attempt to outstare an aggressive jug morning after morning at the breakfast table as it declares:

> Earth I am it is most true
> Disdain me not for so be you.

A secondary part of the editor's definition is that local verses can be those inscribed on local memories, which lets in charms, recipes, riddles and ballads. So we have a collection of 539 sets of verses which we have to take entirely at their face value, in the knowledge that they have probably been modified by the pious Victorian tinkerings of E. Bogg and his colleagues and have certainly been distorted by the vagaries of oral tradition.

At this point, one has to return to John Holloway's very proper insistence that if an anthology of verse is not a source of pleasure and interest the anthologist has been wasting his time. He need have no fears on that score. In spite of any reservations that may be caused by the provenance of many of the texts, the book is enjoyable and moving. But he goes on to explain that it 'has pursued pleasure and enlargement of the experience within the range of certain guiding ideas'.

It is these guiding ideas – that is, his concept of 'local' – that I find unhelpful. In the first place, I cannot see why the verses should be arranged according to regions. There is nothing regional in subject matter or spirit about any of the sections. The editor himself draws attention to the way in which the same kind of verse crops up in many parts of the country.

I carefully studied the Devon contributions in the South and South-

West section and could find no local voice. There was one epitaph, on a
Bideford tombstone, which made me think for a moment that I had.

> Here lies the body of Mary Sexton
> Who pleased many a man, but never vexed one,
> Not like the woman who lies under the next stone.

This seems to display a vengefulness exercised for its own sake, for how
could the adjoining corpse either profit or be hurt by the words? I
wondered if it was an example of that disinterested and larky bitchiness
which really is a Devonian characteristic. But I decided the notion was
fanciful.

There is no doubt that the book does have coherence and unity so
perhaps one might simply put forward another title. My suggestion would
be *Amateur Verses*. As the book contains work by several of our greatest
poets from Milton to Yeats this may seem a rash proposal. But in fact the
professionals could be eliminated in five minutes. For the most part they
are either playing about or cheating.

Milton was cheating. His sonnet 'When the assault was intended to the
city' was written in the form of an appeal for mercy to whatever 'captain
or colonel or knight at arms' might lead a raid against his house and it reads
as though he had pinned it up on his 'defenceless doors'. In reality he had
done no such thing, of course. Milton was the last person to waste a well-
turned sonnet on a small posse of soldiers of whom probably only one
could read. It was all in his mind, an excellent place to be.

Thomas Hardy's 'Inscriptions for a Peal of Eight Bells' was equally cere-
bral. No parish council would pay anyone actually to engrave rude remarks
on their bells.

> Thomas Tremble new-made me
> Eighteen hundred and fifty-three
> Why he did I fail to see.

It is good fun of the sort for which Hardy is not generally renowned,
though there is one line that could scarcely be more Hardyesque: 'So that
in tin-like tones I tongue me.'

Ben Jonson, in composing rhymes for a lintel at the Devil Tavern or
for a trencher sent to the Attorney General William Noye when he was
entertaining Charles I (respectful jokes about Noye's Ark), was writing
nothing more than jolly, social doggerel. Neither was Byron at his professional peak when he dashed off a quatrain of album verse for a visitors'
book in Athens.

In any case only five percent of the entries are the work of professionals, so we really have a chance to study amateur verse through the centuries, always bearing in mind that some of the verses presented as the unschooled outpourings of vigorous and eloquent but unliterary people may in fact be the lamplit work of E. Bogg in his mellow prime.

Some of the amateurs knew their place in the world of letters and did not object to it. Mr Ford of Silkstone, Yorkshire, who flourished in the 1860s was apparently content to be the village poet and to address himself to such limited subjects as a tree struck by lightning.

> When didst thou first behold the blush of morn?
> When wast thou once a tender sapling born?...
> Speak if thy knotted trunk has got a tongue,
> And tell us how things looked when thou wast young.

I would guess he was the village schoolmaster as well.

Not all the poets handled their scansion as correctly as Mr Ford. A Darlington sweep, ambitiously composing some lines for his professional signboard, got himself into terrible difficulties.

> Richard Bolam is my well known name
> For sweeping chimneys extoll'd by fame...
> With my machine and attendant by my side
> I'll sweep your chimneys either strait or wide.

There is a similar diversity of talent in the use of rhyme. What started out as rhymed verse on a war memorial fountain in Yorkshire collapses before our eyes.

> If you want to be healthy, wealthy and stout,
> Use plenty of cold water inside and out.
> Let animal and Man drink freely.
> A pint of cold water three times a day
> Is the surest way to keep doctor away.
> Whoso thirsteth let him come hither and drink.

It will be obvious from these quotations that the anthology contains some sorry stuff, and one does question the wisdom of publishing so many examples. But there are a few brilliant exceptions. Anybody who has ever judged a poetry competition will recognise the mix. If this anthology were a competition I should unhesitatingly award the prize to the following Lincolnshire poem, which I had not heard before, and shall now never forget.

Sad is the burying in the sunshine
But bless'd is the corpse that goeth home in rain.

The point is that it is not a competition. It is not easy to tell how egalitarian Professor Holloway is. One or two of his comments suggest that he sees no boundary between 'popular' and 'literary' poetry. If this is so, I am surprised that his own book has not enlightened him.

Whatever their degree of technical skill, however, the contributors have one thing in common: an honourable wish to rise to the occasion, whatever it may be, even though their ability to work with words may not be as sure as their feelings. These poets are not concerned with self-expression. They celebrate; they rebuke; they communicate.

The Notation of Pain*

The Cost of Seriousness is about haunting and being haunted. After years of perfecting his poetic skills Peter Porter has been overtaken, much as Thomas Hardy was, by a subject from which he cannot escape and the result is his most brilliant and moving book yet. It is, and must needs be, a deeply saddening work, for the central poems are about the death of his wife four years ago. The haunting takes place partly at the level of domestic continuities such as many of us have experienced: 'A card comes to tell you/you should report/to have your eyes tested.' ('Non piangere, Liù') but in 'The Exequy', a poem as beautiful and distressing as that of Henry King's, on which it is modelled, Porter evokes a ghost of quite uncommon poignancy:

> I owe a death to you – one day
> The time will come for me to pay
> When your slim shape from photographs
> Stands at my door and gently asks
> If I have any work to do
> Or will I come to bed with you.

---

* From the *Observer*, 9 April 1978. Review of *The Cost of Seriousness* by Peter Porter, *Frequencies* by R.S. Thomas, *Her Storms* by Sheila Wingfield and *Admissions* by Sheila Wingfield.

And in 'The Delegate' he goes even further imaginatively by describing what it is like not to be haunted but to haunt.

In 'The Exequy' Porter speaks of 'the pointlessness of poetry', and by fear of this he is haunted too. The title poem concerns the inadequacy of 'those forgettable objects words' when it comes to the notation of pain; and in 'Looking at a Melozzo da Forli' he expatiates

> From his flat–bottomed cloud, God observes
> Earthly love and sadness, saying
> After all, this is only a language of gestures.

But somehow the jovial description of the cloud makes it all seem slightly less dreadful, and indeed, whatever his pessimistic assertion about art, Peter Porter's demonstration that it is in fact far from incapable of defining pain makes the book not wholly saddening.

Farewell, a long farewell, to Prytherch country. In *Frequencies* R.S. Thomas, who has in his last two books, at least, been moving away from it as a theme, has disappeared over its horizon, and in 'Gone?' he now postulates a time when, in a literal sense, too, there will be nothing to show it was ever there. He misses those who looked on the Welsh landscape as it was 'and found no beauty/in it, but accepted it'. But the clergyman who devoted his earliest poetic attention to his parishioners, now, having exhausted them – as a subject, I mean – has thoroughly turned his imaginative concentration on the God whom presumably he was trying to present to them at the time.

His attitude is the hoping–it–might–be–so of Hardy but without the charm. The meek, mild creatures who kneel on Christmas Eve in 'The Oxen' have in Thomas's 'The Empty Church' been replaced by stone and shadow. God is glimpsed in a variety of guises, from Job's boil-inflicter to Herbert's hospitable squire. Thomas's tone when speaking of either the ways of God or the ways of man oscillates from the noble to the peevish, and from the fresh to the stale: his censure of man's materialism when celebrating the great feasts of the church is old paper-hat.

There is a deliberate grandeur in some of the lines which seem new to Thomas:

> Wordsworth turned from the great hills
> of the north to the precipice
> of his own mind.

In view of the subject matter of this collection it is remarkable how rarely the vocabulary is abstract. Sometimes indeed the concreteness of both

words and imagery is unfortunate. The passage about Wordsworth
continues

> ... and let himself
> down for the poetry stranded
> on the bare ledges.

In terms of poetic climate it is a far cry from the *noli me tangere* of R.S.
Thomas to the warm strong impersonality of Sheila Wingfield. *Her Storms*
is a selection of poems spanning five decades. It is a pleasure to have them
all together, though they are rather crowded on the page; and an advantage. Nearly all experienced poetry-readers have a favourite Wingfield
poem – for many it is 'Poisoned in Search of the Medicine of Immortality'
from *A Cloud Across the Sun*; a fine poem indeed – but they may know
surprisingly little of her complete work.

Admissions, which consists of poems written in the last four years (thirteen of them are included in *Her Storms*), shows her technique at its very
best and demonstrates her especial mastery of the short poem. Her more
sustained work is usually less exciting, in my opinion; certainly 'Beat Drum,
Beat Heart', a poem of book length, which apparently kept Sir Herbert
Read awake all night, had no such effect on me.

One feature of her work which comes into full play in this volume is
her range of often recondite allusion and reference. Occasionally her introduction of some curious fact which needs an explanatory note, like the
Hebridean black pebble in 'Dark Romney Marsh', is disruptive, and occasionally one's own ignorance makes one want to scribble irritably in the
margin some such remark as 'Pausanias, who he?' But for the most part
these allusions seem to spring naturally from the full life of someone who
notices such things.

Some of her most delightful poems equate the reactions of mankind and
those of the natural world in a truly Wordsworthian spirit. In 'Ilex' she
speaks of the noise of the leaves:

> Yours rattle dryly
>
> As if from little fears
> And doubts continually
> Moving, hidden
> In your dark centre.

Dead Fifty Times*

No myth will ever come to any good
but biting the wasp's apple; being blood.

This couplet, which concludes Terence Tiller's fine poem 'Substitutes', would make an appropriate epigraph to the present collection of the poems of Peter Redgrove, his myths having come strikingly to good and by means of the very process of unreserved involvement that Tiller's poem advocates. *Sons of my Skin* is a two-hundred-page selection of the poems Redgrove has written in the last twenty years. They are arranged chronologically and are taken from his six published books, starting with *The Collector* which appeared in 1959, and from a group of recent poems which have not yet been included in volumes. The choice has been made by Marie Peel who also provides an introduction in which she usefully describes his poetic development and outlines his principal themes. But, as she points out, 'the free seeding of my choice is in the minds and imaginations of readers'. In fact, it's up to us.

This is an immensely impressive book, and like most impressive books, is not for lotus-eaters. It is demanding and in parts difficult. The critics, talking on Radio 3 shortly after publication date, tended to dwell more on the earlier poems, which are thoroughly accessible, than on the later ones which are not, or at least not immediately. One critic even seemed to suggest that the later poems might not repay the reader's effort. In fact they do, because Redgrove's method of enacting the experience without necessarily giving the explanation means that one *can* savour the former without ferreting about for the latter. A good example of this is a very recent poem of Redgrove's – not included in this book – 'The Navy's Here', the presentation of a woman's dream in which all the images are multiple, and apparently menacing: an infestation of mice, for example, and of course the navy itself – a lot of ships with a lot of people in each one.

Power sliding off great faces of water,
Power in flat sheets rising...

---

* From the *Listener,* 20 November 1975. Review of *Sons of My Skin: Selected Poems 1954–1974* by Peter Redgrove.

> After our small hooves clattering all night
> Our pinsize toothmarks in the butter...

The poem is exciting and valid even before we realise that we are meeting Jung's concept of the animus.

A central poem, 'Dr Faust's Sea-Spiral Spirit', the title poem of the volume that appeared in 1972, can also be appreciated in two stages. Anyone may see that it is about energy that comes spiralling in from the sea.

> It fashioned Glastonbury Tor
> With helical fingermarks.
> The burglar by night bears
> Ten small tough patterns of it
> Through the polished house.

But in fact it also says something more specific than this. It is a poem that tenderly presents sexual pleasure and particularly the female orgasm.

> When men and women embrace
> They impersonate it
> They are a cone of power
> An inbuilt beehive.

As we know from his novels and his plays Peter Redgrove has strong dramatic and narrative gifts and he displays both in these poems, though with a difference. 'Sam's Call' appears to pursue an orthodox story line with an account of Sam's death and the discovery of his caul – hence the punning title – but the last verse lifts the poem right out of chronology with a description of how Sam used to be able to tell the time in his sleep. 'Mr Waterman' (*The Nature of Cold Weather*, 1961) is a springy dialogue, set out as prose, in which ordinary speech and heightened speech tug against each other. What sounds like fact – though it is fact as seen by a patient talking to his psychiatrist – flares into brilliant fantasy. It becomes a play; we can hear voices other than the patient's, realistic voices.

I dread the time (for it will come) when I shall arrive home unexpectedly early and hear a sudden scuffle-away in the waste-pipe, and find my wife ('just out of the shower, dear') with that moist look in her eyes, drying her hair: and then to hear him swaggering in from the garden drains, talking loudly about his day's excursion as if nothing at all had been going on.

Redgrove's poetry has frequently been called surrealistic but I imagine this
is a word that he himself would not welcome. He seems not to work by
means of the chance encounter, the purely associative linking together of
things. There is reason and a coherent vision behind even his most
startling juxtapositions: the ships and the mice, for example, in 'The
Navy's Here'. He is not interested in presenting the merely unlikely,
however fruitful the resulting confusion might be. Extraordinary reality is
not surrealism.

He is not one of those mid-twentieth-century poets who write as
though modernism had never been. Any critic wishing to claim him as yet
another of the true heirs of Thomas Hardy would have his work cut out.
He has rejected the metres of the last three centuries more thoroughly than
most of today's significant poets; the author of 'Sir Gawain' and perhaps
Langland seem to be his only begetters. Traditional rhyme, too, is something he rejects with unusual consistency, that is, the rhyming of words;
he makes his thoughts and images rhyme and can construct a whole poem
out of a pattern of echo and repetition. 'From the Reflections of Mr Glass'
is such a poem. Images of transparency are present some time before the
word is mentioned; once it is (Mr Glass, what do you expect/When you
plant the transparent apple-seed?) the word chimes and reverberates on to
a powerful conclusion:

> The man who arrests me becomes transparent!
> The man who shoots me becomes transparent!
> The woman who loves me becomes transparent!

Any reader wanting guidance to Redgrove's poetry would find it in
Donald Davie's *Articulate Energy*. Not that the critical book mentions him
(indeed it appeared in 1955) but it suggestively defines the very sort of
energy which characterises his poetry, a vigour springing largely from a
bold and deliberate use of syntax and grammar. To take an example: he
does not see a noun and a verb as parts of speech which exist indepen-
dently of each other and so can give the noun the function of the verb
'She ghosts that firm white cigarette in sips'. Similarly, he does not see
subject and object in their conventional places: 'A piano plays my aunt in
a lacquered room.' (Dylan Thomas sometimes did this: 'a hill touches an
angel'.)

An interview with Peter Redgrove, conducted by Jed Rasula and Mike
Erwin, appears in this autumn's *Hudson Review*. It is an exciting discussion
and I recommend it. The poet is franker about his personal life than a critic
would be qualified or have a right to be, and the autobiography genuinely
helps one's understanding of the poetry.

Redgrove's account of his recent poetic collaboration with Penelope Shuttle and 'the mingling and exchange of abilities' which this involves is very interesting in itself, and also throws light on the question of the surrealism ascribed to him. Equally suggestive is his description of the insulin shock treatment he received in youth, and his later feeling that it provided justification for writing poetry: 'I've been dead fifty times, I have something to say.'

On Religion

Happy Few*

I have not met Max Wright, but a few years ago I read two chapters of a book he was writing about the Plymouth Brethren. I thought highly of the script and looked forward to hearing how it was getting on. Now I have the finished work. *Told in Gath* is published in the streets of Askelon and the daughters of the Philistines rejoice (2 Samuel 1.20). I align myself on this occasion with the daughters of the Philistines. This seems to me a necessary book.

Far too little has been written about the Brethren. Over the years many people have had the relevant experiences but not the relevant skills, for by tradition the persuasion is by no means learned. The Brethren as I knew them long ago were eloquent in the sense that they loved the sound of their own voices, but the language they used was very odd, a mixture of pastiche and ineptitude which Max Wright can imitate with distressing accuracy when he needs to. The authors of such books would have had to be backsliders (the word 'apostate' was not used – it was thought to sound both Popish and highfalutin) and they might have preferred to forget what life was like before they slid back. These defections (another neglected word, being suggestive of the politics of this present world) tended to take place in youth; the first whiff of real education, however acquired, often did it.

The potential of the Brethren as subject-matter has of course been exploited by writers in all genres, but seldom with much credibility; the picture Peter Carey gives of them in *Oscar and Lucinda,* for example, is what might politely be called a travesty. Edmund Gosse is the nearest to an exception. In *Father and Son* he does not tell the whole truth and nothing but the truth, for though the book was not published till 1907 it was well within the hagiographical convention of the previous century, but it tells quite enough of the truth to be getting on with.

There is two-way traffic on the Damascus Road, and many Brethren have found that at the moment of apostasy the voice from heaven was the voice of Gosse. He is the patron saint of backsliders, and has stood beside them. He often materialises today. Max Wright's opening paragraph relates

* From the *London Review of Books*, 23 May 1991. Review of *Told in Gath* by Max Wright.

how he first read *Father and Son* in the course of one September afternoon when he was seventeen. 'There are not many joys,' he says, 'to compare with the discovery of the right book at the right time.' I have no such experience to recount; I came to the book later in life. But my qualifications to review *Told in Gath,* apart from the essential one of being a backslider myself, are bound up with the Gosse family.

My grandmother broke bread with Philip Henry Gosse. Not many people know that. She had come in from Dartmoor where she was born, to seek excitement as a housemaid in one of the villas that were going up all round St Marychurch and in one of which the Gosses lived. So they both worshipped in the local Hall. The moorland Brethren were very strong in those days, with nearly as many adherents as the Flat Earthers, and considered themselves to be as superior to those of the cities of the plain in holiness as they were in altitude, so she would have attended the Breaking of Bread – we were not allowed to use a more papistical expression – in a marked manner. P.H. Gosse would certainly have noticed her, but she can never have shared food with him in a secular way; there was a strict though of course unacknowledged pecking order. But perhaps he got his servants to ask her to tea in the kitchen. In due season my mother (P.H. Gosse just missed her) worshipped there too, and in childhood so did I, if you can call it worshipping. There the line ended.

It was from this background that I can testify to the complete authenticity of Max Wright's book. He is over ten years younger than I am and was born and brought up in another place, Northern Ireland, but the Brethren were not only timeless but, in spite of their neat little houses, of no fixed address, except in the sense of heaven being their home. The only thing he describes which is new to me is the practice of reading somebody out of the assembly for fornication. ('Excommunicating' would be one more forbidden word.) Whether this means that my brethren were more lethargic about committing and condemning fornication than his or just more stealthy I do not know. Everything else is precisely as I remember it. I recognise even the clichés. Over the years our brethren across the sea had apparently been declaring, in an extremity of liberalism, that we might conceivably meet Roman Catholics in heaven, not many but some, exactly as their brethren in Devon had been declaring, starting with P.H. Gosse and including my mother. They could not have meant it, given the virulence of their anti-Catholicism. It was just a form of words, a mood.

Max Wright tells us everything there is to tell, in Gath or anywhere else, about the Brethren, and as he is scrupulously accurate his book could be valuable for that alone. It is likely to be consistently interesting to those with no knowledge of the Brethren beyond their being a group of fundamentalist Christians who base all their beliefs and behaviour on those of the early Church as described in the Bible, without the help of any extraneous information, knowledge of languages or trained ministry; who have no set services yet never deviate from their procedures; who are poorly integrated with the world they live in; who are flattered that Jesus Christ called them peculiar (Titus 2.14); whose attitude to everything is negative; and who doubt if Ian Paisley is saved. Such readers might well be curious about the details.

And these Dr Wright supplies. As a teacher of philosophy he is obviously aware that he is dealing with no system of thought. One can work one's way down the long column in the *OED* which defines philosophy, from 1 to 9b, without coming across anything which sounds like any mental process engaged in by the Brethren. Their guiding notions are wild without being free, a kind of folklore. So he takes each of the observances most characteristic of the Brethren and dearest to their hearts and shows how they worked in practice.

A good example is extempore prayer. Several sects claim to pray on the spur of the moment and some really do. With the Brethren, though it was statutory that there should be no set form of prayer such as Papists go in for, no real spontaneity took its place. Their prayers were a ragbag of stale exhortations, updated with topical sideswipes, addressed to those present in the flesh; informative remarks addressed to God, who often had to be reminded that it was Sunday; and any odd bits and pieces that were good for padding. This last was important in view of the essentially competitive nature of this kind of prayer. It had to be long-winded. It also had to be loud and determined, so often were two brethren guided to rise to their feet simultaneously, when it could become a trial of strength.

One brother, contender on both counts, used to bolster up his prayer with a favourite poem, as Max Wright relates.

It was part of Brethren folklore that these verses had been written by the inmate of a lunatic asylum. Why this alleged fact was found worthy of remark may not be immediately obvious to the outsider, but I suspect that the moral of the story was that the madman, though deranged, had, through the grace of God, never lost contact with the great truth that no account of the divine love will ever be definitive. And so Mr Stevenson would never fail to slot his favourite into his prayer in a way which must have sounded odd to one hearing him for the first time without the required background knowledge. 'As the lunatic,' he would intone, 'has put it so beautifully…'

And then he quoted the poem. Few would call it beautiful but, to be fair, it was a great deal saner than the hymns in Moody and Sankey, of which, incidentally, there is a vivid account in another chapter.

The book is often anecdotal, and very funny in this deadpan way. I particularly like the story about a brother in County Armagh delivering a fervent gospel address which centred on Felix, the governor of Caesarea who appears in the Acts of the Apostles being preached to by Paul. (Not Saint, of course: we were all saints.) The humour is not in what happened to Felix, which is sad by any standards: he rejected God's plan of salvation, threw Paul into gaol and swept out, presumably to hell. Neither, obviously, is it in what happened to Paul. It is in the words of the preacher who in momentary lapses of inspiration, knowing nothing and caring less about oxymoron or indeed Latin, kept apostrophising the governor as 'Unhappy Felix'.

Edmund Gosse in his preface to *Father and Son* thinks it necessary to explain and almost apologise for his mingling of 'merriment and humour with a discussion of the most solemn subjects'. He trusts his readers, however, to understand 'that the comedy was superficial and the tragedy essential', and indeed we do. Nearly a century later we would be surprised if it were otherwise. There is darkness enough in *Told in Gath* to balance considerable merriment, and much of it is implied rather than spelled out. In the account of extempore prayer, for example, though the tone is light almost to jollity and it is with laughter that we realise the prayers were not extempore, it is with something like desolation that we see they were not prayers at all. Some miseries had to be more explicitly told: the long years of childhood panic when the boy was desperately trying to follow the Biblical instruction 'Believe on the Lord Jesus Christ and thou shalt be saved,' not knowing how it was done – who does? – and trying again and again, mortally terrified that he had not got it right; and the long months of emotional blackmail leading up to his adolescent submission to baptism by total immersion, the Brethren's most cherished observance, an obscene ceremony the way they did it.

It is clear, I hope, that I admire *Told in Gath* for many more qualities than the clarity and completeness of its information, but there is something else as well. I should explain why I have called the book necessary. After all, people can sustain relationships and earn their living without knowing that the Brethren existed. The answer is that I have long been convinced that this kind of Christian fundamentalism should be opposed by some fairly firm writing-on-the-wall, and, now, that this book could be it.

Max Wright quotes in full Edmund Gosse's terrible denunciation of the religion in which he had been brought up. The most damning sentence is this: 'It encourages a stern and ignorant spirit of condemnation; it throws altogether out of gear the healthy movement' of the conscience; it invents virtues that are sterile and cruel; it invents sins which are not sins at all, but which darken the heaven of innocent joy with futile clouds of remorse.' These judgements are perfectly true, though perhaps the language is overblown for nowadays. Gosse may still have been under the acutely painful influence of his father's death-bed, when Philip Henry Gosse shouted blasphemies at the God for whom he had sacrificed so much. Edmund Gosse, however, had grounds for comfort which have been denied to those who came after him. He was sure that the evils he had endured had passed away and would never return, and he was unselfishly glad that the dying Puritanism he had analysed would not survive to ruin anybody else. Unfortunately he was wrong. He came to his conclusion, even if he did not publish it till later, in the 1860s. Apostates of the mid-twentieth century know that nothing had changed by then and have lived on to see that it still has not.

The Brethren are convinced otherwise. One or two of us have spoken our minds but they sweep our revelations under the seats, and it is not just a case of 'Well, they would, wouldn't they?': they genuinely feel they have altered, and of course for the better. My own book about them (to which Dr Wright generously alludes) was officially put down by their spokesman as a 'vivid and humorous account of an age that is past'.

If they *have* altered, it could be for the worse, to judge from the last chapter of *Told in Gath,* which gives a devastating picture of thoroughly modern Brethren, modishly referring to Scott Fitzgerald and Pan Am jumbo jets bound for South Korea, slapping God on the back in prayer, competitively singing hymns in alternate lines (gallery v. floor, under-forties v. over-forties), and 'pretending self-indulgently that if Christ was not risen from the dead they would go home and put their heads in the gas oven'.

Their capers, as Max Wright calls them, made him feel a bit faint; and made me feel that Edmund Gosse did not know his luck. But on second thoughts we both realised, I am sure, that it was much the same. That sentiment about the gas ovens was entertained long before there were such things; God was always treated too matily, never with the reverence He deserved; and before jumbo jets and trendy novelists there had been the GWR and Mrs O.F. Walton. It was just like the Brethren to fluster us up with crossed signals and pious cosmetics.

Told in Gath is a positive book. It will help many escapees from the Brethren to be defined so carefully. When we first turned off the Damascus Road – to become atheists, Catholics, Laodiceans (Revelation 3.14–16) – many of us, I imagine, lugged our Brethren-induced oddities with us and may never be able to set them down. We are probably still a peculiar people, and semasiology prevents us from taking the adjective as the high compliment that St Paul (I refuse to continue the discourtesy of docking him of his sainthood) intended to convey to us from the Lord. But, if we are still to some extent what we like to think we are not at all any more, we can take comfort from St Paul's robust command: 'Let no man despise you.' (1 Titus 2.15). Certainly not.

Seeing the Light*

'I like the revivalist *coup de foudre* for its recognition that true revelation can instantly change a man, so that his sins simply fall away from him, to be replaced by present joy and future hope.' Philip Toynbee introduces *Part of a Journey* with a *Which*-type survey of the various concepts, and consequent terminology, of religious conversion; at one point making it sound like the best china ('"Rebirth" should be kept for very special occasions') and the next like an unpretentious hock ('I've always liked "Amendment" for its modesty and dryness.')

He does not really recommend the *coup de foudre*, however. Though he likes the idea, he perceives its attendant difficulties. 'The danger of "seeing the light", "being saved", etc is that this tremendous experience may deceive the newly-converted into believing that his spiritual journey is over.' He is perfectly right, as any cidevant member of a hellfire sect can confirm. In the testimony meetings of my youth, so much weight was put on the essential instantaneousness of conversion that it was a point of honour to be able to specify the actual date of one's salvation, and those who could not name the day and therefore had to fall back on some formula such as 'Once I was blind, now I see', did not show up at all well and were regarded as rather second-class sinners.

Philip Toynbee gives himself no airs as a sinner. He is capable of an occasional rhetorical flourish about 'the stews and gutters of Babylon' and his own early apprenticeship to drunkenness, gluttony and lust, but the rakehelly vocabulary, which suggests a story-book rather than a confession and the fact that his companions in these haunts – referred to by their Christian names but with full identification in a footnote – are part of our

---

* From the *London Review of Books*, 16 July 1981. Review of *Part of a Journey* by Philip Toynbee.

national heritage of cardboard villains, make the whole situation sound quite easy. And for the most part he regards himself, bleakly, as 'not so much a sinner as a meagre man' and prefers the comment of an old friend that he used to be a bit of a lad, which he considers to be 'a useful phrase to remember when falling into too noisy a grovel about past sins'. Certainly he trounces the early Christian saints for 'moaning that they were the worst sinners in the world. Surely they'd simply fallen over backwards into another kind of self-conceit'. The fact remains, however, that he had an unusually profound sense of sin, apparently induced and reinforced in childhood: 'This first expulsion from school must have greatly strengthened my conviction of sin, for my mother's accusation had now been endorsed by a quite separate authority.'

Philip Toynbee's quest, of which we are shown two years (1977 to 1979), with flashbacks, was nothing if not gradual. Not for him the blinding light from heaven, the fall from the horse and the long swoon leading into lasting new consciousness. Physically he may have known something like this. In the preface he describes how he underwent a course of ECT, and it does sound rather like the stages of St Paul's experience, though more prolonged. But spiritually it was quite otherwise; he was always on the road to Damascus. 'The process has been very slow, partial and recidivist; the moments of change so imperceptible that I have always doubted whether they really qualified.'

He saw himself as a pilgrim, not only metaphorically but literally; a real pilgrim moreover, not one who goes by luxury coach. When he and his wife journeyed to Chartres in the early autumn of 1979, though he spent money freely he tramped through cabbage fields. He dressed up and acted as the parfit gentil knight might have done ten pilgrimages later. Even his vocabulary changed: 'the word "vigil" suddenly presented itself.'

On this occasion he admitted that his idea of 'a stern pilgrimage in which many trials of patience and courage would have to be met' was a fantasy, and he frequently laughed at it. But it was a deadly serious matter too. When he arrived at the Channel he exclaimed in Holy Grail earnestness: 'What I most fear now is that I may have to turn back.' And when he reached the cathedral he felt that his 'entrance seemed more like an ordeal than a long-awaited pleasure: the first real test after so many fanciful ones on the way'.

Spiritually, the visit to Chartres seems to have been a great success. It is significant that what stands out most from his account of this pilgrimage is the incident of the schoolboy with his satchel who came through the north door of the cathedral, walked across its whole width 'and out through the south door, never once glancing to either side. Clearly this was his daily short cut home from school.'

Part of a Journey is long, but in one important respect it might have been helpful if it had been longer. A record of two years is not enough to show how external events may have provoked significant inner happenings. In his own diary *Like it Was*, Malcolm Muggeridge makes a comment which is relevant here. He speaks of St Augustine, 'living at a time rather like ours, barbarians sacking Rome etc. and taking little or no account of these events'. Toynbee does not take much explicit account of barbarians sacking Rome etc. either; the sinking of the Cambridge boat and the possible close-down of the *Observer* in '78 being the nearest he gets. There is no reason why he should be topical, but contemporary history must have affected his soul and his spirit in ways which would evade a relatively limited diary.

The importance, to those experimenting with eternity, of what time does and brings, is so apparent in Muggeridge's journals that his method – the chronological covering of decades – is worth comparing with Toynbee's. In 1936, Muggeridge, waking early in depression, was supported by the thought that 'the grey light just beginning to touch the sky had broken for aeons thus, and would break for aeons more'. Less than ten years later the bomb destroyed that kind of comfort.

When I was a student – about the time of Hiroshima – I was being taught that the prevalence of a particular kind of melancholy in the early seventeenth century was partly a result of the distress caused by the discovery that the heavenly bodies, previously thought to be immutable and incorruptible, were in fact as changeable as everything else. At the time this seemed to me very fanciful. By 1950 it no longer did. The knowledge that nowadays nobody can count on aeons of anything, such as dawn breaking on the earth – that is to say it might continue to break but there would be no one about in the quad – makes Muggeridge, and most of us, feel melancholy from time to time. It enters into Toynbee's thinking too, of course:

> Talking to Father C. at Tynmawr. He said he thought God would inter-
> vene at the last moment to prevent us destroying ourselves by nuclear
> war. Why did his confidence seem so strange and alien to me? For I also
> believe that God can intervene directly in the world. Yes, but not so
> simply and directly as that, or why is history what it is?

This is the expression of a settled fear. Even in Toynbee's skilful flashbacks there is no hint of a time when it was not there, or of the difference its presence made to him.

This said, one has to add that it is extraordinary how much information about his own past Toynbee does manage to work into this two-year journal; it is an almost complete autobiography. Take the visit to Chartres, for example, where while seeming to concentrate on his first glimpse of the cathedral from the train, he interpolates: 'I'd been to Chartres once, and many years before, but must have done no more than my usual ten-minute tour of the cathedral between drinks.' Incidentally, this glancing parenthesis gives a much livelier impression of his previous drinking habits than the allusion to the gutters of Babylon does. His account of a recent caravan holiday in the Wylie valley includes a useful aside about his memories of Wilton in 1941 at the time of his first marriage when he was an intelligence officer at Southern Command. It is all very deftly and economically done.

The construction of the book is in keeping with Toynbee's declared views about his own technique.

Ever since I began to plan *Tea with Mrs Goodman* – which appeared in 1947 – I've seen that for me the only way of writing is to string together a necklace of sharp occasions and to conceal as best I can any narrative or explanatory thread.

A necklace of more or less sharp occasions is exactly what *Part of a Journey* is. The narrative threads are there too; three of them in particular: the fluctuating progress of Toynbee's depressive illness, the decline and fall of the commune started by him and his wife in the house where they formerly lived, and his successive attempts to publish the final volumes of his verse novel *Pantaloon*. The first story is harrowing and commands one's deepest sympathy. The second is tragi-comic and brings one out in a rash of irritation at the unworldliness that courted so many troubles and humiliations. The third is even more agonising than the first: 'It *will* be recognised one day as the great work which I know it to be. (*Know* it to be? *Know* it to be!) But the real pain had only been postponed, and began to attack me quite viciously in bed last night.' The stories are not exactly concealed but they keep going underground; to their common source, probably. The searches for health, the good life and professional success are subordinated to the main quest, which is for goodness itself.

Yet the history of *Pantaloon* provides the sharpest occasions of all; for it is as a writer that Toynbee seeks God. The numerous reviews and articles of his own that he includes in this journal are no mere padding, I feel. Being a writer by profession and personality, he approaches God as a fellow professional: not a writer exactly, though he accords Him total respect as creator and author; more as the Great Editor in the sky, whose decision is final. And He reviews too.

Toynbee brings his own skills as reviewer into his search for God. He has what he himself calls 'an obsessive involvement with devotional and theological works', but he keeps his senses clear. He can smell from afar the mystical bilge which abounds in this kind of book. 'Slush' he says, and 'Windy poetics'; and he is right. He relates how once he even had to deny himself potentially helpful companionship, when it went along with poor writing. His effusive admiration of the spiritual autobiography of Lois Lang-Sims led him to suggest a meeting and friendship, but when she sent him her novel these overtures collapsed completely for it was very feeble and he could not hide his opinion. He records only one incident where his literary judgement was overcome by his moral enthusiasm: the case of James Kirkup's poem about Jesus which he publicly defended against the charge of blasphemy. The poem may or may not be blasphemous – I myself would say it is not – but it is such an indefensibly bad poem qua poem that it must have gone against his grain to support it at all.

Part of a Journey reminded me in so many ways of Thomas de Quincey's *Confessions of an English Opium Eater* (the first version) that when I had finished it I read de Quincey again. I heard the news of Philip Toynbee's death just as I had got to de Quincey's famous passage about such news being worse in summer:

> I find it impossible to banish the thought of death when I am walking alone in the endless days of summer; and any particular death, if not more affecting, at least haunts my mind more obstinately and besiegingly in that season.

De Quincey, in spite of persistent bad dreams, ended his confessions on a note of hope, and so does Toynbee. He concludes with a quotation from Pasternak which he must have felt to be a clincher. It is vague but clearly suggests resolution and enlightenment and possible peace of mind:

> Everything that happens in the world takes place not only on the earth that buries its dead, but also in some other dimension which some call the Kingdom of God.

Dissenters Divided*

To be the child of Dissent is as chic nowadays as to be of working class origins, and of course historically the two situations are frequently connected. In *A Gathered Church* Donald Davie boasts, very properly, of being the son of Baptists. I boast of being the daughter of Plymouth Brethren, which is, I claim, a dizzier and dottier background altogether. I also claim that it has absolutely nothing to do with literature.

To isolate and assemble the literature of the English Dissenting Interest, as Professor Davie sets out to do in his Clark Lectures of 1976, is very like getting up an anthology of poems by women. Neither religious belief nor gender has much to do with the ability to write. Obesity, say, or exceptionally bright red hair might have more.

Yet the ability to write well is what Donald Davie is discussing. Quite early in the book, and again in the peroration, he seriously maintains that a Calvinist aesthetic exists and that being a Dissenter is likely to endow the practitioners of all arts and particularly writing with the qualities of simplicity, sobriety and measure. He goes on to suggest that as all good art should have these qualities, Dissenters are in a very strong position.

It is a fascinating argument – indeed the whole book is fascinating – but there are no proofs; where literature is concerned, that is to say: Doreen Davie's beautiful photographs of Nonconformist chapels go some way to establishing the point about architecture. It is probably not important that two of the works which Davie singles out – Edmund Gosse's *Father and Son* and Matthew Green's *The Spleen* – are in fact written by dissenting Dissenters; at the time of writing Gosse was a lapsed Plymouth Brother and Green a lapsed Quaker. Those who have resigned from political parties or retired from professions often show more signs of their former environments in retirement than when they were active. But these two works do not really illustrate the general theme; and the writings of two still–loyal Dissenters, Isaac Watts and Elizabeth Gaskell, positively contradict it.

Isaac Watts was the writer of 'O God, our help in ages past'. As a poem

---

* From the *Listener*, 6 April 1978. Review of *A Gathered Church* by Donald Davie.

it may be simple, sober and measured but – and I hope I am not practising the holy nit-picking of my childhood – it is inaccurate and unobservant. Dreams do not die at the opening day, and the writers of the Old Testament (OGOH is based on a psalm) knew that, better than Freud. How devoutly Joseph's brethren must have wished that his dreams would do so. Certainly many of the doctrines of Dissent *are* inaccurate and unobservant but I do not think Dissenters have ever prided themselves on the fact and I do not think that is the point Professor Davie is making.

In the course of these lectures he administers a considerable amount of stick to Christopher Hill. Yet his own theories about Dissenting hymns, and in particular his insistence on regarding OGOH as a 'tribal lay', are just as perverse as anything Christopher Hill has imagined, even when, for example (an example that Davie does not in fact give) he presents Marvell's 'Bermudas' as a working song because the men in it are rowing a boat. (Try rowing to 'Bermudas'.) Davie dwells on the oral transmission of OGOH which has resulted in the dropping of some of the verses, but the cutting of a work which is direly long and repetitive needs just one person of taste or impatience, not a tribe. His point that the Dissenters for whom Watts wrote thought of themselves as a tribe is true, of course. The saved are a tribe. But they do not necessarily compile *Tribal Lays Ancient and Modern*.

Speaking further of Watts, and his hymn 'We are a garden walled around', Donald Davie makes another point I cannot agree with. He correctly describes the 'Song of Solomon' as 'one of the most intensely and unashamedly erotic pieces of literature that we know of', but seems to think that the metaphor of the marriage between Christ and his Church is the same kind of concept. But surely this mystical union is the deep peace of the marriage bed, whereas the 'Song of Solomon' depicts, in its own terms, of course, the hurly-burly on the chaise-longue.

Perhaps most difficult to swallow of all is the presentation of Elizabeth Gaskell as a Unitarian writer. The Unitarians were indeed what Donald Davie calls them, 'an enlightened intellectual minority' but there is no justification for his implication: 'It is generally conceded' (I have never heard *anybody* concede it) 'that even in her case, arguments and ideas, "causes" and propagandist intentions, lie up too close and manifest below the surface of her stories for us to think of her as a great novelist in the sense in which we are happy to applaud…' and then he names George Eliot. Nobody, I imagine, would dispute George Eliot's superiority as novelist to almost everybody else or our happiness in applauding her, but the description of Elizabeth Gaskell's writing methods fits her more aptly than it fits Elizabeth Gaskell; and her excellence does not spring from being a better Dissenter or a better unbeliever or a better anything than Gaskell except a better writer.

On Place

Furry Souls*

Quite soon now there will be only a few people still alive who remember trying to change their accents. I shall be one of them, I hope. I was four-teen before I realised I had a Devon accent. There was no way of knowing before. As a family we were forbidden by our religion to have a wireless or to go to the cinema, and the only local people who talked posh would have been the squire, the vicar and the doctor. As the twentieth-century equivalent of cottagers we never spoke to the squire, as Plymouth Brethren we never spoke to the vicar, and as patients we merely listened to the orac-ular pronouncements of the doctor, and an oracle is about as classless as you can get.

At the age of fourteen I changed schools and at the new one the head girl and several of the staff used what I now know was standard English. This was unnerving, chiefly because the phenomenon was linked with another phenomenon, the notion of middle-class behaviour. I had been brought up nicely but now I kept falling short. I was told off for eating an ice-cream cornet in the street. I was told off for saying in an imaginative composition that the hero while attending the opera ate a bar of fruit-and-nut chocolate. ('At the *opera*??!!') I was informed that no lady would hitch up her knickers in the middle of the sports field. So what were long thick black knickers *for*?

When in my last year in the sixth form it became clear that I was showing great promise and that my achievement in 'O' Levels had been no flash in the pan but a hard gem-like flame, the headmistress told me that, clever as I was, I would never get anywhere with *that accent* and therefore the staff after much discussion had decided that some money from school funds could be given me for a series of elocution lessons. So I went off to an elocutionist called Miss Rose Somebody. I suppose there are many possible ways of changing a person's accent. Hers was to make me learn by heart a set of poems of riveting soppiness and recite them to her without a Devon accent. I tried hard. I managed one about the west wind and one about not spoiling God's very perfect world and then I got to one about a rabbit who after various earthly tribulations that made my blood run cold was rescued by an angel who,

---

* From the *Listener*, 28 January 1971.

> carried in his arms
> A little furry soul.

It is physically impossible for a Devonian to say 'furry' in the approved manner, and the psychological strain of struggling with the wretched rabbit's rotten furry soul made me give up the whole idea, from my heart if not yet from my mind.

It all seemed so easy in books. Susan Nipper when she married above her station got along by calling her husband 'my dear' and saying little in public. Lizzie Hexam solved the problem by a simple effort of will when she decided she would not disgrace the disgraceful Eugene. Heathcliff and Hareton Earnshaw turned standard from one chapter to the next. Lady Chatterley's lover, it is true, made heavy weather of his accent but then he made an issue out of everything. Hardy's characters appeared not to care, though I have always suspected that Angel Clare, being a snob as well as a prig, was put off as much by Tess's country accent as by her sexual lapse, when it came to introducing her to his family and thoroughly acknowledging the marriage.

When I left university I applied to the British Council for a teaching job abroad and was interviewed, first by an important person and then by a more important person. While I was with this second interviewer his telephone rang and I could hear the voice of the first interviewer though not what he said. The man I was with became theatrically guarded and started using sentences with no pronouns in them. An objection was obviously being raised at the other end of the line but the words at my end made light of it: 'Oh quite slight really! Not so very noticeable. Doesn't really matter in view of general suitability.' And indeed I got the job. I now think it was lunacy to appoint someone with a strong regional accent to teach foreigners English and even at the time I felt, rather like Groucho Marx about his club, little respect for an institution that would admit me.

Being foreign is a well-known way of disguising one's origins, and of ignoring other people's. As Francis Hope has most aptly pointed out in talking about the Thirties: 'One of the attractions of the Spanish cause may well have been the classlessness which foreigners always miraculously acquire: the embarrassing gulfs between a socialist poet and an English industrial worker were transmuted to a picturesque starkness when the worker was replaced by a Catalan peasant.' In my case the Italians certainly seemed not to notice my accent and in the first week I started going out with a count – and they are not ten a penny in Italy as would-be sophisticates say. With my compatriots it was different. My years with the Council convinced me of what all my examination successes had failed to persuade me: that I was intelligent compared with some people. But apparently I still sounded rustic – at least I think it was my accent rather than any crudity of behaviour that made a colleague refer to me as a rough diamond. He was a Yorkshireman and just plain rough.

Back in England, much older, I have no complaints about the reception of my accent. It is sometimes admired, which I enjoy, but I have never been insulted by exhortations not to get rid of it, it is so delightful. When I did a broadcast about Hardy which included some searing remarks about his women characters, a friend said I sounded so comforting that they would certainly put me on the air when the Martians landed. I like the idea; it would be a far, far more socially useful thing than making penetrating comments on Hardy.

It is strange that a Devon accent should be soothing. The great Devonians, Raleigh and Drake, for example, were not famous for cosiness. Yet Drake's remark about the bowls has a nannyish ring; and Raleigh's couplet,

> And from which earth, and grave, and dust
> The Lord shall raise me up, I trust,

however much it may have been patched onto an early erotic poem, has the same quality. He certainly composed it in a Devon accent because it was the only one he had, to his dying day. His last speech rang out over Tower Hill with the authentic tones of East Budleigh.

All poets, major and minor, write, as Eliot pointed out, in the terms of their own voices. Somebody should read 'Ode to a Nightingale' aloud with a Cockney accent; perhaps somebody has. Certainly Basil Bunting's recent Northumbrian attempt at re-creating Wordsworth's Cumbrian accent was brilliantly suggestive. These are the masters, of course. But in a minor way I can bear out Eliot's comment myself. In my poem 'The Fifth Sense' I am speaking of someone dangerously ill in hospital:

> Lamps burn all the night
> Here.

The tone was intended to be desolate and menacing. The wounded man was an innocent victim, and wanted to be at home. But when I hear myself reading it, with 'here' coming out like the 'yurr' on a Widecombe cream dish and so making the hospital sound a womb-like refuge, I can see that this was what I subconsciously felt.

I now spend part of each year idyllically in Devon in a woolly beautiful valley not far from the village where I was born. But something has changed, if not my accent. When I show off in the pub there about having been born locally I cause genuine surprise. They obviously bracket me with the woman up the bungalows whose gnome rests eternally on its elbow and who comes from Potters Bar. When, back in Hampstead, I tell stories about my Devon neighbours and respectfully quote their views my imitation sounds phoney, with even a hint of Mummerset. And when the great Elocutionist calls I am afraid he will assemble furrier souls than mine.

Literary Cats*

It is not true that dogs like people and cats like places but the distinction is useful in itself and can be applied to the human race, half of whom apparently feel, like Ruth in the Bible: 'Whither thou goest I will go', while the others resemble Emily Brontë and cannot bear to be away from a much-loved place even when in the company of a much-loved person. Margaret Drabble's *A Writer's Britain* will have its deepest response from the Emily Brontës: a higher type of person altogether than the Ruths, though inclined to be awkward.

Anyone in her senses would enjoy the book. It is beautiful. The photographs, by Jorge Lewinski, are delightful, and very imaginative: I hope I am not being fanciful in noting that the grass in the churchyard at St Juliot, where Hardy so sunnily, for him, courted his first wife, is covered with frost. The literary references are so catholic and wide-ranging that every reader must be able to relate to something, and when literary matters, such as the pastoral convention, have to be explained to laypersons it is done with the tact of a good Radio 3 talk.

But there is more to the book than surface enjoyment; there is illumination. Margaret Drabble understands place and its demands, which are austere and the opposite of sentimental. In the last chapter, 'The Golden Age', she discusses the effect of environment on writers, not during their formative years (though she does that too) but when they have become professionals. Those who choose to live in the country – and a writer is one of the few people who really can choose where to work – may find

---

* From the *Listener*, 17 January 1980. Review of *A Writer's Britain* by Margaret Drabble. Photographs by Jorge Lewinski.

that its demands are excessive and that it cannot meet theirs. 'The countryside heals and saves, but some it cannot save' she says in tracing the life of Sylvia Plath and showing how a dream became a nightmare. 'Behind the cosy caricature of country life that she presents to her mother lies the reality of the moon and the yew tree; and the bee meeting which she describes in such cheerful terms in her letter is transformed in her poetry into a sinister sacrificial ritual'. The country was too much for Dylan Thomas as well. His diplomatic raptures to the patron who gave him his house at Laugharne are offset by his comment to Vernon Watkins: 'I'm not a country man; I stand for, if anything, the aspidistra, the provincial drive, the morning cafe, the evening pub.' Miss Drabble concludes this part of her argument with fine solemnity: 'death at Primrose Hill for Sylvia Plath, death in America for Dylan Thomas.'

The book's material is arranged thematically rather than geographically or strictly chronologically. The author impresses on us that it is a personal selection and is not intended to be, could not in fact be, comprehensive. Any account of the book, short of a lengthy essay, must be selective too.

I most enjoyed the chapter 'The Industrial Scene'. The survey of writers' reactions to the machine age is of great interest. They were very free with the word 'Satanic' (though in Blake's day it was probably not the cliché it later became) and with metaphors of hell. 'Devils proceeding to afternoon worship' was George Borrow's phrase as he watched the Workers of Merthyr Tydfil, yet in spite of himself he found the 'accursed pandemonium' impressive. It was a bitterly vexed question. Wordsworth opposed industrial development, on humanitarian grounds; Harriet Martineau welcomed it, on humanitarian grounds.

'The nearer to London Dickens gets, the more his love struggles with its disgust.' This and similar comments throw a bright light on the man who observed place more devotedly perhaps than any other novelist. In the North of England he can be single-minded: the horror revealed in his description of Coketown is quite uninhibited. How well this passage stands out of context, and repays the extra concentration: 'the piston of the steam-engine worked monotonously up and down, like the head of an elephant in a state of melancholy madness.' But when he gets home ambivalence fruitfully sets in again. 'The river Thames, which flows through his books, may be dangerous, dirty, corpse-laden, rat-infested and criminal-infested, stinking with drainage from graveyards and waste from slaughterhouses and gasworks, but it is also exciting, powerful, intensely alive.'

The Echoing Green*

Blaise Hamlet is bogus and beautiful. It is appropriately set in an estate which is just as beautiful and in some respects equally bogus. Blaise Castle itself came first. It was built in 1766 for the merchant Thomas Farr, on the crest of a hill four miles north of Bristol, and was quite frankly a folly. Its three circular towers, arranged in a becoming triangle as was fashionable at the time, never defended anybody or were attacked by anybody, except perhaps on grounds of taste. They did, however, attract the tourists who drove out from Bath at the time of its heyday in great numbers, especially the young people who were not there for the waters in the first place.

About Blaise Castle House, built in 1796 by William Paty for John Scandrett Harford, the Quaker banker, there is, essentially, nothing bogus whatever. It is a good-looking house, unaffected and almost austere, which suggests both the banker and the Quaker. But it has its moments. One of them is a romantic rather foolish little thatched dairy, designed by John Nash, too close to the house: even a token cow would have been a launching-pad for smells and flies.

The other exuberance is Humphry Repton's approach to the house. The long carriage drive that winds up through the gorge alongside a stream which in those earlier days may have rushed down it is superbly unnecessary. Anybody wishing simply to call on Mr Harford would have nipped in from the public road, on the same level, and been received at the modest though dignified entrance that visitors to today's museums still use. But, in having guests approach through the gorge, Repton was stunning them with his favourite precepts. Wooded hills were his signature, not bare ones with a clump on top like those of his master Capability Brown. Water was to stay in the bottom of the valley, not tumble picturesquely down from the heights. These ideas in themselves may sound prosaic but the theatricality which came from Repton's early passion for the stage, and his later experience of it as playwright and designer, carried him through to effects which must have made unsuspecting visitors, winding upwards and onwards between the stark white cliffs that emerged every so often from

---

* From *Wessex: A National Trust Book* by Patricia Beer, photographs by Fay Godwin, Thames and Hudson, 1985.

jungle vegetation, think they were heading for the Castle of Otranto at the very least.

In 1807 John Harford bought a six-acre piece of land in the nearby village of Henbury. It was called Greens, and it was a village green that Harford had in mind. The green had originated, quietly and practically, as a central clearing in an Anglo-Saxon settlement, intended for communal discussions and as a place to protect the old, the young, the weak and the four-legged against enemies. By the end of the eighteenth century it had become a focus of nostalgia and romanticism, as in Blake's poem, written in the 1780s.

> Old John, with white hair,
> Does laugh away care,
> Sitting under the oak,
> Among the old folk.
> They laugh at our play,
> And soon they all say:
> 'Such, such were the joys
> When we all, girls and boys,
> In our youth time were seen
> On the Echoing Green'.

Wessex villages tend to be nuclear or linear rather than 'green' as in other parts of the country, so the idea of deploying houses round a stretch of grass was slightly unusual in the first place, and the green which John Nash and George Repton, son of Humphry, established, departed even further from tradition, in shape; it was not the time-honoured triangle, it was hardly a geometrical figure at all though it fitted into a rectangle; and it had the wavy outline loved and much used by Capability Brown. In use, originally, it must have departed furthest of all. The idea that the cottages were made to face in different directions in order to discourage neighbourly gossiping is no doubt apocryphal, though as an idea it would have been consistent with the interfering paternalism of the times; the motive was probably love of asymmetry for its own sake. All the same it is clear that nothing very much was expected to happen on the green, or rather the lawn, of Blaise Hamlet; nothing traditional anyway. The tenants were to be retired servants of the Harford family: too frail by now to protect others, too old to wrestle or dance round the Maypole, too poor to attract pedlars, and too remote and small an audience for mummers and jugglers or even for a mystery play.

There was always a civil pretence of life on the green at Blaise Hamlet. Early Victorian engravings are at pains to include not only a person so ancient as to have no gender sitting on a bench, but also, say, a trim young matron accompanied by a child. The child is never rampaging about but being prettily helpful, at the pump, for instance. It was in the best tradition of the Picturesque that cottage-dwellers should be decorative. John Claudius Loudon, who summed it all up in his authoritative *Encyclopaedia of Cottage, Farm and Villa Architecture and Furniture* which began to appear in 1832, confidently expected that 'there would always be children playing and villagers passing to and fro, to contribute to the rural effect of the scene'. An earlier arbiter of the movement, William Gilpin, had also regarded as essential 'the occasional group of villagers supplying an additional embellishment to the landscape'.

But even if a group of elderly servants, who would certainly not have retired prematurely, could hardly have provided much indigenous go, there were perpetual invasions from the outside world, right from the beginning, for Blaise Hamlet made a very considerable impact, on both Englishmen and foreigners. It is true that excursions regularly came out from Bristol just for the frolic, as they had come from Bath to see the Castle, but the majority of visitors were serious, well-informed people, who wanted to learn something.

They must have learned a great deal. Building cottages for employees and tenants was something that landowners had conspicuously been doing for more than a hundred years, but increasingly their methods had come under fire. As often as not the new houses, of uniform design, were strung out on both sides of a road, and by the last decade of the eighteenth century, though most people agreed as to the end, this was widely felt to be the wrong means: lazy, obvious, insipid and unsuitable to the countryside. In *Essay on the Picturesque* (1794), Uvedale Price, whose name and views are usually coupled with Gilpin's, was eloquent in his criticism of such deadly regularity. But it was one thing to criticise and another to come up with a viable alternative. Some ill-advised things were done, on both sides of the argument, between the first stirrings of dissatisfaction and the building of Blaise Hamlet.

This was begun in 1810. The village green of Nash and Repton took up only part of the six acres Harford bought, but they fitted nine buildings round it; ten dwellings, for one was a double. Each was different, and in almost every possible way. Even lovers of the Picturesque might have felt that though they had prayed for variety this was ridiculous. The roofs were varied, in both shape and material; only three were thatched, strangely few at a time when everybody was being so lyrical about thatch, and the rest were tiled. Two gable-ends had holes suggesting a dovecote. Not only were the cottages set at apparently random angles, but each front door was in a different place. The windows were different, the chimneys were very different, in both placing and pattern. Even the lean-tos, sheds and privies were given personalities of their own. And, as a final touch, the naming was not consistent; most of the cottages were called after flowers and plants – Jasmine, Rose, Vine – but there had to be discrepancies, so one indicated shape – Diamond – and another its accommodation – Double.

There was something slightly perverse about the green itself, apart from its shape. Traditionally the village green had many attributes, some punitive – the stocks, the ducking stool, the whipping post – others more positive – the horse trough, the pump, the pound for stray animals. Blaise Hamlet had only a pump. Certainly any of the other things would have been most inappropriate in the circumstances, but a solitary pump does look artificial. Nash and Repton doggedly followed their star: the pump is placed asymmetrically. They were not responsible, of course, for the inscription carved on it later by Harford's son in praise of his father's liberality, but it is curiously in keeping. Strong in emotion and weak in syntax it is in itself a single-handed gesture against the age of reason.

The point about Blaise Hamlet is that it carries total conviction. It is not in the least surprising that visitors came and still come, and that its impact is felt to this day. As housing it is bogus. There is no sign of any thought for the people who were to live there or any idea that they might prefer a less poky sitting room to an imposing chimney or more light to gracefully overhanging eaves. But in being beautiful, unique and of powerful personality it is one of the wonders of the world, of which there are far more than the time-honoured seven.

Yet I often imagine – impertinently – a sadness about the place. The octopus of suburbia is flopping and heaving close by and might poke its tentacles through the trees at any minute. And twentieth-century notions of lower-case picturesque have actually got inside. The last time I was there I saw a cartwheel in one of the gardens, and a white-painted wrought-iron whatnot – a sort of plant tray on fixed wheels – in a porch, and dinky little flower beds outside a front door where, as the 1826 lithograph shows, none was intended. There is a feeling of something coming to a close, which makes the last verse of Blake's poem seem more relevant than the jauntier ones.

> The sun does descend
> And our sports have an end.
> Round the laps of their mothers
> Many sisters and brothers
> Like birds in their nest
> Are ready for rest
> And sport no more seen
> On the darkening green.

Selworthy Green, Somerset, though it is modelled on Blaise Hamlet, is surprisingly unlike it, in both appearance and atmosphere. This may be because there was a different motivation behind it. The land-owners who planned the earlier new villages and hamlets were at least as much concerned to show that they could afford it as to improve the lot of their dependents. In the course of the nineteenth century, genuine and often whole-hearted philanthropy began to creep in.

George Eliot wrote *Middlemarch* in the early 1870s but the action takes place forty years earlier, and Dorothea, the heroine, represents the new way of looking at things. The first time she really appears in the novel she is concentrating so intently on a drawing that only with difficulty can she join in her sister's talk of jewels, and the drawing turns out to be a plan for model cottages which she wishes to put up on her wealthy uncle's estate. She is quite untrained, and charmingly diffident about her design: 'I shall think I am a great architect if I have not got incompatible stairs and fire-places.' But in fact she is as well-prepared as any male landowner could be, for she has acquired Loudon's book, which could only just have come out, and studied it, as very probably she had studied earlier pattern books too of which there were a multitude, some sane, some crazy.

There can be no doubt about Dorothea's motive. She is always sincere, and never more so than when she exclaims:

'I think we deserve to be beaten out of our beautiful houses with a scourge of small cords – all of us who let tenants live in such sties as we see round us. Life in cottages might be happier than ours, if they were real houses fit for human beings from whom we expect duties and affections.'

or than when her sister, speaking of the cottages, has commented, 'It is your favourite *fad* to draw plans,' and she almost shouts, '*Fad* to draw plans! Do you think I only care about my fellow-creatures' houses in that childish way?'

By the time George Eliot wrote, the fictional Dorothea would have acquired counterparts in real life, for the female philanthropists had arrived. Indeed – to step outside the book – in her second marriage she would have met and perhaps worked with them. There were differences of tempera-ment: Dorothea went about her mission gently though ardently; Lady Waterford, Miss Georgina Talbot, Miss Mary Anne Talbot and Baroness Burdett-Coutts were all battleaxes. But the imaginary woman and the real ones had much in common, apart from the wealth and leisure which made their work possible. Their schemes were consistently governed by a wish that those they were re-housing should be as healthy and comfortable as possible. There was no emphasis on appearance for its own sake.

To mix literature and life once more: in *Northanger Abbey* when Catherine is visiting Henry Tilney's parsonage and admires a cottage in the grounds, his father General Tilney, mistakenly thinking she is an heiress, immediately says:

'You like it. You approve of it as an object. It is enough. Henry, remember that Robinson is spoken to about it. The cottage remains.'

The cottage, due for demolition, is now to be kept, as a pretty object. Three or four decades later, Lady Waterford would never have preserved a decrepit insanitary cottage, however picturesque, or have thought of it as an object. For her, the preservation of mere prettiness needed, as she once said, 'mixing up with a more onward march'.

This more onward march reached Selworthy quite early in the century. The builder of these cottages, Sir Thomas Dyke Acland, 10th Baronet, was a friend not so much of John Harford senior as of his son, so although Selworthy Green was created only eighteen years after Blaise Hamlet, the influence of a second generation was already at work. And as Acland did not employ an architect there was nobody to stand between his own notions and the final result.

He was a conscientious man and read all the right things. It is pleasant to know – rather than to surmise – that he had a thorough working knowledge of P.F. Robinson's *Rural Architecture,* one of the best of the pattern-books, which appeared in 1823. A copy full of his own underlinings and annotations was found in his library and can still be seen.

He must have agreed with Robinson that cottages should be 'objects of interest' and 'picturesque features in the landscape'; it would have been too outré not to, in those days. And, when it came to including the cottagers themselves in the effect, he and his wife went even further than some by dressing the pensioners up in scarlet cloaks. This sort of thing was done in other planned villages: at Old Warden in Bedfordshire the cottagers, it is said, were issued with red garments to match the paintwork. But no Acland went so far as to put them in pointed hats, as sometimes happened elsewhere.

To be part of an idyllic scene and gawped at by tourists might I suppose have gratified one or two modest egos, but not many, probably, especially when it became obvious, as it soon would have, that cows and sheep were being headed down specific paths so as to be in the production too.

Yet Selworthy Green does look less self-indulgent than Blaise Hamlet. The whole effect is not so formal and alien; the picturesqueness is not so resolute, more affectionate. In fact the cottages look very like what most people expect pretty cottages to look like. They are placed with conscious asymmetry, certainly. They are in many ways ornate – decorative thatch, decorative tiles, latticed windows, oriel windows, gables and porches – but not in every way: the chimneys though tall are perfectly plain. It is arguable whether or not they could properly be called *cottages ornés*, whereas there is no doubt that the Blaise Hamlet houses have to be.

Selworthy Green has natural advantages. It stands on a slope, and there is a church at the top, both very important elements in the Picturesque. It was, and still is, integrated with an attractive village. There is no suburban sprawl nearer than Porlock.

Two of the Selworthy houses are open to the public, one as a National Trust shop, another as a café – the rooms are relatively light and large – so there is some realistic coming and going on the green. People cross it to strike into the paths that burrow through the woods. Sometimes a thatch is being repaired, and then they pause to watch and appraise, exactly as our ancestors must have done. They knew more about it, of course, and had less time to spend on the way to their own work, but they must have screwed up their eyes and pointed in much the same way, and made remarks. This green still echoes.

The Trials of Farming Life*

How shall ye know seasonable time? Go upon the land that is ploughed, and if it sing or cry, or make any noise under thy feet, then it is too wet to sow, and if it make no noise and will bear thy horses, then sow in the name of God.

We will need to start drilling as soon as the weather improves.

The writer of the first of these passages is the great Fitzherbert, arbiter of sixteenth-century agricultural procedure. The second is Michael Morpurgo, author of the recently-published *All Around the Year*. His

* From the *Listener*, 4 March 1982. Review of *All Around the Year* by Michael Morpurgo.

comment, beneath Fitzherbert's, sounds like a subtitle to the Authorised Version, and it is almost all he says about knowing the seasonable time, though he goes into some detail about the preparation of the combine drill and the various stages of modern sowing.

Tusser was another of Morpurgo's sixteenth-century predecessors in the genre of books about the land. Communicating his views in slapdash verse, which he felt would be easier to remember than prose, he advised pruning out the newborn pigs in January:

> Of one sow at one time rear seldom past six.
> The few that she keep much the better shall be.
> Of all thing one good is worth starvelings three.

Here again, style and method have greatly changed. Morpurgo's comment is: 'A good sow can rear up to sixteen, so thirteen should not be too much of a strain.'

But though time and science have modified the traditions of both farming and writing, Fitzherbert, Tusser and Morpurgo still have much in common. For one thing they are all teachers. The first two make no bones at all about telling people what to do, whereas Morpurgo writes modestly and quietly in diary form, recording day by day the events he has observed and experienced on a farm in North Devon – Parsonage Farm, Iddesleigh, run by the Ward family. But beware teachers especially when they are trying to sound empirical. Morpurgo, who is in fact a schoolteacher not a farmer by profession, is just as didactic as the other two.

It is the strength, as well as the fascination, of his book that he is. His account of the farming year is vastly informative and the notes in the margins are encyclopaedic. It would benefit many categories of people: children (whom he perhaps has chiefly in mind as he directs the educational charity Farms for City Children), weekenders, holidaymakers, Marriage Bureau clients who ask for a farmer: almost everybody in fact except those who would like to cover the countryside with concrete.

The Marriage Bureau clients might well have a change of heart, for the trials of farming life are by no means glossed over. The farmer's teeth are kicked out by a stroppy cow; in the course of an extremely busy day he has to take the entire milking machine to pieces and sterilise it on the strength of a letter from the milk depot; he has to cope with Strip, White Scour, Bloat, Sheep-scab and Wooden Tongue, with white globules in the milk and pouches of pus in a cow's uterus; he is up half the night at lambing time; for much of the year he is wet-through and chapped with cold.

The trials of the animals are not glossed over either. Horrible things are done to them. Their sufferings are described by Morpurgo with vicarious resignation. When a cow is deprived of her calf: 'She will pine of course but that never lasts more than a day or two.' When the farmer castrates a litter of pigs: 'It wasn't a pleasant business but it was over very quickly and after a day or so they won't be bothered by it. He used a surgical knife and was careful to sterilise before and after the cutting.' Ah well, that's all right then.

But Mr Morpurgo takes the rough with the smooth for himself as well as for his charges. His heart is in his subject and he makes his temporary calling sound deeply satisfying, even noble, and his protagonists, animal and human, are all heroes. The welcome straightforwardness of his style is entirely appropriate to the absence of sukebind and the presence of hard cash. (He systematically quotes market prices and extremely interesting they are too.) And every so often an unaffected statement has more force than a purple passage: 'It is distinctly colder today and the swallows feel it.' 'The bells sounded well in the cold morning air with only the mist between the church and Dartmoor.'

The book is well-illustrated: with delicate drawings, by Robin Ravilious, and with unromantic photographs of people actually working, by James Ravilious.

If Shakespeare had supplied poems for later editions of Fitzherbert and Tusser, they would still have been Fitzherbert's and Tusser's books of course but the effect would have been decidedly distracting. Ted Hughes, who contributes twelve poems to *All Around the Year*, one for each month, is introduced in the text as a neighbouring farmer who offered the Wards some bales of hay in an emergency. Indeed he is and no doubt he did, but a poet of such stature cannot help rocking the boat. These poems are remarkably enjoyable, very much in the style of his *Season Songs*. Perhaps the most moving is 'Birth of Rainbow', which describes the first hours of a calf born on a day of sun and storm.

> The whole South West
> Was black as nightfall
> Trailing squall-smokes hung over the moor leaning
> And whitening towards us, then the world blurred
> And disappeared in forty-five degree hail
> And a gate-jerking blast. We got to cover.
> Left to God the calf and its mother.

Tenuous Claims*

As a Devonian, born, bred and resident, I am intrigued by the tenuous claims of most of the writers who are gathered into *The West Country Book*. The claims are not always made by themselves, of course – Jane Austen, I feel, did not think of herself as a West Country writer – but by the editor J.C. Trewin. The book does include some bona fide West Countrymen (Charles Causley, A.L. Rowse), but most are settlers (Colin Wilson, Daphne du Maurier, Sean O'Casey) or tourists (Dylan Thomas).

If the contributors were chosen by virtue of their subject matter rather than of their biographies, the case is even stranger. Agatha Christie's story 'The Regatta Mystery' is set in Dartmouth and Jane Austen's conversation between Catherine and Isabella in *Northanger Abbey* is set in Bath, but in fact they could have taken place anywhere. If placename-dropping is the key factor, the reader's ingenuity is thoroughly roused. Could not, for example, the visit of the housekeeper to Torquay in Wilkie Collins's *Woman in White* be included? True, there are no descriptions of the town and the demands of the plot would have been satisfied if she had gone to any other watering place, but never mind: Torquay is mentioned.

Certainly no considerations of literary merit seem to have shaped the collection which has really gone comprehensive. Winston Graham and Eden Philpotts sit with John Fowles and Thomas Hardy, while Dylan Thomas's piece must be one of the feeblest he ever wrote, even if he did spend his honeymoon near Penzance.

Many of the selections make the South West sound an extremely dangerous place, which presumably is not the overall intention, even though Exeter Cathedral *is* collapsing. Hardy's Henry Knight falls off a cliff in Cornwall; Austen's Louisa falls off the Cobb at Lyme; and Betjeman's doctor falls under a tram in Exeter. But this is hardly relevant for the West Country is intentionally put forward as a Never Never Land, where dangers are surmounted or where at least sadness is tolerable, a land of beauty, romance, nostalgia and gentle rustic humour. There is no room for such considerations as the rising price of fertiliser, the decline of the seaside land-lady, and the strike at the cattlecake factory. The only contributor who has

---

* From *South West Review*, November 1981. Review of *The West Country Book*, edited by J.C. Trewin.

any truck with reality is W.G. Hoskins, another genuine native, whose
excellent account of the social revolution in the Devon countryside is
included here.

The West Country Book is a truly handsome volume, beautifully
produced and illustrated. (The photograph of Widecombe-in-the-Moor
under snow, with sheep, is particularly lovely.) It is designed for those who
look rather than read and like all such books it should sell like hot cakes.
I certainly hope it does. On both emotional and aesthetic grounds Exeter
Cathedral has been dear to me all my life, and the proceeds of the book
are to be given to its Preservation Trust, a most worthy cause.

On Literature and Criticism

Ladies and Gentlemen*

The Young Rebecca is a collection of the writings of Rebecca West from 1911 to 1917, selected and introduced by Jane Marcus, with just the right amount of explanation and comment. In one respect it is an unfortunate title, suggesting as it does an item from the cast list of almost any black-and-white film about almost any celebrity, but in the respect that it makes a point of Rebecca West's youth, it is a good title. The first article is signed by her natural name Cicely Fairfield; she was so young that she had not yet yielded to whatever weakness it was that made her take a pseudonym, though she already had one in mind. She was nineteen.

She was young enough to bounce and snap at Mrs Humphry Ward. Three months after that first article and now as Rebecca West, she published another one in the *Freewoman*, the feminist paper financed by Harriet Weaver and edited by Dora Marsden. It is a good thwacking piece, cheerfully serious, in which she accuses Mrs Humphry Ward of lacking both honour and sense in her aggrandisement of 'the sheltered woman' who can be recognised by 'a smooth brow that has never known the sweat of labour; the lax mouth, flaccid for want of discipline; eyes that blink because they have never seen anything worth looking at; the fat body of the unexercised waster'. Oh dear.

Mrs Humphry Ward was a sacred cow with considerable secular powers of retaliation at her disposal. But the force of the writer's aggression, though characteristic, is perhaps not the most important fact to emerge from the article. I call 'The Gospel according to Mrs Humphry Ward' an article and not a review deliberately, and in this its title supports me, for though West is discussing *Robert Elsmere*, *The Case of Richard Meynell* and *Daphne*, the ethos that Mrs Humphry Ward puts forward is the only thing that really interests her. Even when she comments that on every relevant page the face of the heroine Catherine Leyburn 'works with emotion and is illuminated by a burning flush' she is not criticising the style so much as female working faces and burning flushes in themselves.

In 1912 Rebecca West was already using books in what has turned out

* From the *London Review of Books*, 6 May 1982. Review of *The Young Rebecca: Writings of Rebecca West 1911–17*, selected and introduced by Jane Marcus, *The Harsh Voice* by Rebecca West, *The Meaning of Treason* by Rebecca West and *1900* by Rebecca West.

to be, in the course of the century, a typically feminist manner, that is, gutting them for purposes of propaganda, She does not go so far as to falsify the text, as more recent feminist writers have done: Kate Millett, for example, in her discussion of *Villette* in *Sexual Politics*. But she is capable of ignoring it even when what she is writing is nominally a review, preferring to concentrate on her own paraphrase and such points as may arise from it. So compulsively tendentious is her approach to creative literature at this time, that when she announces her intention of reviewing a certain 'anti-feminist thesis' one assumes it is going to be a novel or a play, only to discover with surprise that it really *is* an anti-feminist thesis: Harold Owen's *Woman Adrift*.

It was natural that these pieces, having been written for the *Freewoman*, should be loaded. In 1915 and 1916, when West was contributing, principally but not exclusively, book reviews to the *Daily News*, the Liberal paper which, though radical in general, promoted many causes other than feminism, her method approximated much more nearly to that of literary criticism. Her comments on Arnold Bennett's *These Twain* and Ford Madox Ford's *The Good Soldier* acknowledge the presence of a medium as well as a message. There can be little doubt, however, that she enjoyed and still enjoys talking about content rather than form, and has no inhibitions about separating the two. The laurels of Pater and Wilde were still green in her formative years and their attempts to discredit meaning must have seemed to threaten her; but fortunately Pater kept contradicting himself and Wilde was far too silly. (His comment 'All bad poetry springs from genuine feeling' would strike a sympathetic chord in those adjudicating nationwide poetry competitions but in no one else probably.)

So she stuck to her guns. In 1974 she contributed an energetic essay to the *Times Literary Supplement* entitled 'And they all lived unhappily ever after', which begins 'Mutual understanding has never been the strong point of the sexes – an opinion it would be advisable to check by reference to the work of women imaginative writers.' So into the witness box come successively Edna O'Brien, Margaret Drabble, Penelope Mortimer, Doris Lessing, Iris Murdoch; to give evidence. In the case of three, perhaps four, of the witnesses nothing is said about *how* they give their evidence.

In the two years that Rebecca West was contributing to the *Clarion*, 1912 and 1913, she seldom wrote about books and so had no need to wring debating points out of works of art. The *Clarion* was a Socialist paper whose editor Robert Blatchford had been so impressed by her swashbuckling work in the *Freewoman* that he mentioned battleaxes and scalping knives in connection with it, and offered her a job. So, as picturesque warfare was what she had been hired for, this is what she provided. And now that books had been largely put away on the shelves her weapons glinted and her strategies were clear to all watchers on the hillside.

The cause was, unequivocally and unrelievedly, feminism. In these *Clarion* articles the specific grievances of women are shouted out, if not exactly for the first time (and in many instances not for the last time), at least with a freshness and immediacy that startles us, seventy years and several feminist waves later. (I began to wonder if we really were going to get the vote.) The personalities of suffragism are being thrown down flights of steps and into fountains, forcibly fed and hosed with icy water. West herself has been hit in the throat by a policeman whose Adam's apple was shaking with fury. She has just followed the coffin of Emily Davison who committed suicide by throwing herself in front of the King's horse.

Her account of Davison's career is nobly felt and phrased, but hagiographical to the point where the reader starts niggling, and about points which may not be central to the theme. Twice she rejoices that the executioner was an 'unmalicious brute'; my love for horses is well within bounds, but I am unhappy that a horse should be exploited as a kind of galloping guillotine. And though I share West's horror at the idea of forcible feeding I do not see that it can fairly be called 'unprovoked'. Like so many polemicists Rebecca West is in her best form when she can mock. Such an occasion was the publication by Christabel Pankhurst of an article about venereal disease. Quite apart from West's comments it does seem, from the quotations, to have been an ignorant and silly piece of writing. It sounds tactless, too. Pankhurst asserts that syphilis is the true cause of nervous illness. 'Perhaps,' remarks West, 'Miss Pankhurst is now puzzled at a certain coldness noticeable in those of her friends who have had nervous breakdowns.' Irritation even goads her into pitying *men* who have the disease; unless of course that is just sarcasm.

Sarcasm, very heavy sarcasm, is a mainstay of the young Rebecca's method. It is the voice of the nineteenth-century schoolmaster (Mr King, say, in *Stalky and Co*); the then fashionable voice of polemical journalism: if one has occasion to consult provincial newspapers of the time the sarcasm is sometimes so dense that it is impossible to see what point the writer is making. West's stylistic tropes and flourishes, too, that today would have her travelling on the fast lane to Pseuds' Corner, were in that more exuberant age perfectly acceptable as sober comment.

H.G. Wells liked Rebecca West's *The Harsh Voice*, which appeared in 1935 and is now reprinted by Virago. This would not be at all surprising – the four short novels of which it is composed were her most satisfactory fiction so far – if it were not for his previous denunciations of some of her books. In 1922 he called *The Judge*, which appeared that year, 'an ill-conceived sprawl of a book with a faked hero and a faked climax, an aimless waste of your powers'. In 1928, as his hostility seems to have been a belt-and-braces affair, he duplicated his abuse of *The Judge*: 'As a whole it is a sham. It is a beautiful voice and a keen and sensitive mind doing "Big Thinks" to the utmost of its ability – which is nil.'

Wells' admiration of Rebecca West's work had always flowed and ebbed in remarkably straightforward time with his personal feelings for her. Her review of his *Marriage* in the *New Freewoman* in 1913 ('Mr Wells' mannerisms are more infuriating than ever in *Marriage*... Of course, he is the old maid among novelists') had first brought her to his attention. 'I loved your clear hard-hitting generous mind first of all' he wrote a year later. Even after one of the things she had hit hard was his novel *The Passionate Friends* ('One feels as though one were going through a new country in the train and not liking it nearly as much as one had expected') he was able to call her comments 'first rate criticism'. In those years he voiced a reconciliation in terms of literary appraisal: 'You are writing gorgeously again. Please resume being friends.'

As the relationship deteriorated he very naturally began to confuse nasti-ness with integrity. He insisted that the wounding frankness of his remarks about *The Judge* was essential to the survival of even the little that remained between them: 'I've got no use for you at all as a humbugged pet woman. If I'm going to get a female pet I could get any number of prettier and more amusing pets than you.' After their separation, in spite of the inevitable disconcertments of aftermath, he turned quite nice about her novels. *Harriet Hume* appeared in 1929 and in fact he was nicer about it than most readers today would think called for. And he was still talking about love and work in interchangeable terms: 'It is just as though you were coming awake after years in a sort of intellectual trance.'

In 1935, lower-case was for him inadequate to describe the MASTERY displayed in the four stories of *The Harsh Voice*; and he pauses in his praise only long enough to compare her working methods with his: 'You have a richness. I am simplicity.' In spite of his apparent perception of the book's merits, he fantasises about the contents, imagining the murdered woman in 'The Salt of the Earth' to be Letty, one of his dreaded Fairfields, Rebecca's sister in fact ('I'm glad you've killed Letty'); and his singling out of 'Life Sentence' as the best story could be due to the fact that the hero, though he is a monster of weakness, is marginally less awful than the heroes of the three other stories.

They are a right crew, there is no doubt about it. Rebecca West is dramatising the rhetorical *Clarion*-call of her youth: 'Oh, men are miser-ably poor stuff.' To portray them she often employs devices similar to those of other women writers who have set themselves a similar task, even if, as is the case of Charlotte Brontë, they do not quite realise this is the task they *have* set themselves. Here is Mr Rochester, making a guest appearance in *The Salt of the Earth*:

> He murmured something under his breath, and bent his lips towards her. But she twisted out of his grasp.
> 'Why did you say that under your breath?'
> 'What did I say?'
> 'You know perfectly well what you said. You said "Forgive me".'

There are petty differences of course. Mr Rochester has bigamy in mind; Jimmy Pemberton is contemplating murder. And Alice picks up the 'Forgive me', whereas Jane Eyre rises above, though she records, Rochester's 'God pardon me.' But it is the same man.

The hero of 'There is no conversation' is Etienne de Sevenac. He is Mitford Man, seen plain. The irresistible Frenchman of Nancy Mitford's rather embarrassing fantasy – Fabrice, Charles Edouard – who knows how women's lipstick should be applied, how long to a millimetre their skirts should fashionably be at any time, and exactly what they really want, at table and in bed, better than they know it themselves, is shown, as perhaps we always suspected, to have got it all not just wrong but dead wrong. As a character in a novel he is splendid: conceited, kinky, silly and cruel. His very presence provides the plot: his total ignorance of everything forms a perfect three-stranded surprise.

The fourth story, 'The Abiding Vision', is said to be Rebecca West's own favourite. It is so dependent on melodrama and cliché, (from the failed businessman contemplating suicide to the tart with the heart of gold), that one could hardly understand this preference, if it were not for the appearance in the story of one of her cherished themes: the ideal of the Horatio-type woman who takes the buffets and rewards of love with equal thanks.

In the *TLS* article quoted above, Rebecca West bravely faces the fact that this woman, who at the beginning of the century looked as though she was about to emerge, was still, in 1974, a wishful thought. The first feminists had assumed that by this time women 'might be luckier in love than their mothers and grandmothers, and would take it better if they were unlucky. But this evidence is not forthcoming. After a course of study in Contemporary Women Novelists it is as if one heard a massed female choir singing 'Early one morning, just as the sun was rising, I heard a maid sing in the valley below, "Oh, don't deceive me, oh, never leave me, how could you use a poor maiden so?"'

Rebecca West's own early assumption had been that this ideal woman not only was about to come forward in strength but perhaps had always existed even if in isolation. It led her to some sweeping conclusions. In her biography of St Augustine (1933) she rightly describes as ugly and cruel the way in which the future saint's mistress was sent packing after a long and apparently happy relationship, but she insists on hoping for the best: 'After fourteen years of companionship with a violent and blundering man, the pain of separation might well have been assuaged, and even rendered unnoticeable, by the new-found pleasure of tranquillity, and the peace of the religious life may have seemed to her an exquisite self-indulgence.' I doubt it. She probably felt more like Heloïse.

In *The Abiding Vision* Rebecca West treats the theme with the utmost ambivalence. Lily the showgirl seems to businessman Sam Hartley, and through his eyes to us, to have the sort of independence within a sexual relationship that West wishes women to aspire to. During the negotiations that take place before Sam sets up Lily officially as his mistress, 'she was so magnificently free from emotion that he felt liberated to the point of soaring'. (Sam, it should be mentioned, knows what it is to be imprisoned emotionally; he is devoted to a devoted wife, who has got to look rather old recently.) But it is a business transaction; nobody is in love so it is not a real case of invulnerability. Sam loses his money, and Lily, now apparently in love, stands by him. Sam regains his money; Lily is still there but months of sacrifice have made her look old too. The story ends with Sam's abiding vision of the unlined face of a young girl dancing naked, and it will obviously not be long before Lily has to summon up some genuine invulnerability.

The Meaning of Treason, also re-printed this year by Virago, was first published in 1949. It has twice been brought up to date, once in 1965 to accommodate Burgess and MacLean, 'among others' as the blurb mildly puts it, and now with an introduction in which to receive Anthony Blunt. The book is much too well-known to review in the normal way, but this new prefatory statement is interesting in itself, and throws light on the already existing material.

Rebecca West collects traitors. Through four decades she has pinned down a startlingly large number of them. The genus has several species: scientific traitor, diplomatic traitor and so on. West is reminded of the course of the Industrial Revolution: 'at first such elementary forms as the spinning jenny: to be followed by thousands and thousands of machines of all sizes and shapes.' She has continued to admire 'the classic purity' of her aboriginal specimen, William Joyce. I had not thought of it before but she does make him sound rather like a spinning jenny.

Up to now Rebecca West has written about all her spies with the cool-ness and precision of a collector; the passion which presumably motivates collectors is well under control. *The Meaning of Treason* is vastly informative but I could not say that I understood spies any better after reading it, yet sometimes and especially in the William Joyce section I did seem to understand particular human beings better than formerly. The account of Joyce's progress in his own kind of treachery, though it does sound mechanical, is so convincingly specified that it explains the development of others whose treachery took a different form and was therefore known by a different name, if indeed it was classified at all: Branwell Brontë, for example, who had inspired in me nothing but a passing irritation before, but who, I came to think, had so much in common with William Joyce that Joyce almost interpreted him.

There can be no doubt about Rebecca West's moral disapprobation of treason. She undertook the subject in the first place, she tells us, because of the number of people who not only did not disapprove of it but who seemed to think it was of no importance whatever, and the experience of many years since has confirmed her wish to enlighten the public. Perhaps it is something about Anthony Blunt, then, which cools her evangelistic dislike of traitors – perhaps directing it to those who cover up for them – for she abuses him with a lack of verbal precision – so unlike her – which usually indicates a lack of thorough involvement. She calls him a blabbermouth. As far as I know I have never met a spy, but I imagine it is a spy's task to say in cold blood something he should not say to someone he realises should not hear it; as deliberate as that. Surely he is not just a foolish indiscreet talker, by either temperament or profession.

Or perhaps after forty years, she is simply tired of spies. She concludes this introduction by calling espionage 'a lout's game'. Some of her spies were louts all right: Donald Maclean, for example, who, as West describes, once in Cairo went with a friend 'in search of drink to the flat of a girl who worked as a librarian in the American Embassy and, finding that she was out, broke into the flat, took what drink they could find, and then smashed the girl's bath by throwing a radiator slab on it, broke some furniture, and dropped some of her clothes into the toilet bowl'. But, even granted that there is such a quality as moral loutishness, surely all spies are not as mindless as this.

★

On January 31st, 1900, as the ninth Marquess of Queensberry lay dying in his magnificent house in town, Emile Zola in France lovingly dusted the medal he had received a fortnight earlier for his services in the Dreyfus affair, and thousands of miles away Mafeking awoke to its hundred-and-first day of siege.

Almost any historical novel that happened to concern itself with the year 1900 might begin with similar words, the concept of simultaneity being dear to writers in this genre. Equally popular, in this case with downmarket historians, is the notion of a particular year; this has also been well used. In *1900*, Dame Rebecca West combines these two best-selling formulae to make an intriguing book which rises well above the level that they usually inspire, both in language and material. The publishers have done their part in creating a very handsome volume. The photographs are brilliant.

It is not essential to the 'yearbook' style that the writer should have been alive at the time, but it helps, even if she was only eight; not only because in that case an autobiographical element becomes possible without undue fantasy, but also because what a child inherits from the age in which it was brought up, and indeed from that of its parents' upbringing, is especially valuable as showing conditioning rather than observation.

In *1900* this asset is seen as early as the introduction. Mr and Mrs Fairfield were addressed, in an intelligent and courteous way, outside church one Sunday morning in Richmond by a 'good little man' ('such a nice man'). He was a hydropathist; if he had been an orthodox physician he could have been a dwarf without being called little, and it would not have been at all necessary to stipulate that he was nice. Mr Fairfield, to his credit, replied 'very civilly'. And soon they all met again. 'The good little man' was standing outside his house, one of the 'less proud dwellings' on the slopes of Richmond Hill as opposed to the ones on top, which he had draped with black to mark the death of Gladstone. The Fairfields, though they did not agree with his sentiments, were again very civil and 'smoothly expressed their sympathy', though once round the corner they voiced their fears that 'the good little man would probably lose some patients', Gladstone not having been universally popular.

Well, there is 1900 for you. And a decade later 'the young Rebecca' is still talking (in a *Clarion* article) with the condescension which had been instilled into her:

> There is really something very hopeful about the pert face of a Cockney beauty, smiling at life from under a wide and worthless hat with nodding spurious plumes... A similar idealism moves the waitress who, twittering like a little London sparrow, quite ridiculous, quite charming, carries on a flirtation under the sour gaze of her customers.

I assume that nowadays Dame Rebecca does not talk like this, nor that she is too surprised when people reply civilly to questions even when asked by little men. But in 1900 the middle classes, it seems, went on like this and it is 1900 she is attempting to evoke.

Dame Rebecca covers a great deal of ground in every sense except geographically. Europe is mostly France, but Germany and Italy are there too. An attempted assassination brings in the Middle East. An earthquake brings in South America. The United States tend to hover nearby with an expression of innocent wonder, occasionally asserting themselves with a Republican National Convention, a tram strike or a tidal wave. But on the whole the rest of the world exists only when Britain is fighting or governing it. But within these territorial boundaries it is a question of 'Enter Mrs Beeton and the Duke of Wellington' or 'Here comes Jonah, and the whale, and the sea'. Science and technology, literature and philosophy, fine and applied art, architecture and design, music and the performing arts are all covered or at least adumbrated.

The handling of all this material demands an eclecticism so extreme as to reach the borders of eccentricity, sometimes to cross them. It is as idiosyncratic to single out 'Nude in the Sun' as Auguste Renoir's contribution to 1900 as to exhume characters like Sir Charles Hartley from dictionaries of national biography and other works of reference. The interpretation is sometimes as unusual as the selection. Dame Rebecca's account of the Boer War is unlike any that I have ever heard put forward.

It is natural that the strongest passages of *1900* should be those where Dame Rebecca's personal interests, as distinct from her professional curiosity, are engaged. She describes the Dreyfus case with an involvement which is no doubt more complete because of this new aspect of the meaning of treason: the accused is not guilty and the accusers are the traitors. Perhaps the most memorable story of all is that of the woman at the meeting held by John Kensit, the Protestant reformer, as he considered himself, or 'rabble-rouser', as Dame Rebecca calls him, all too accurately as he was later killed in a riot of his own provoking. At question time the woman rose very diffidently to ask a sincere and mildly-worded question. She was not demanding votes for women; the high days of militant suffragism were still to come. She simply wanted to know if Mr Kensit would really not admit that a cross held in the hand could be an aid to devotion. Mr Kensit's reply was: 'Madam, you are dressed as a lady. Please behave as one.' Whether he was rebuking her for speaking at all or for daring to have views about her own private worship is not clear, but it is a remark to push a feminist, or indeed anybody, to extremes. It is one of the skills of *1900* that it so frequently and naturally shows the direction in which 1900 was heading.

New Women*

George Gissing was convinced that the year 1900 would make all the difference. Writing his study of Charles Dickens in the late 1890s he refers to his own generation as those 'upon whom the new century is breaking'. And one of the things the new century would bring was the New Woman.

To an extent, of course, as Gissing realised, she had already arrived. His chapter 'Women and Children' in the Dickens book is perhaps his most memorable statement on the subject. Nine-tenths of it is about women – the children come in for a few frail aperçus at the end – and his approach is wrong-headed, feverish and refreshingly outside the fold of traditional literary criticism. The table of contents would suggest that women are in themselves a feature of technique, parallel to 'Humour and Pathos' and 'Art, Veracity and Moral Purpose'. But Gissing, in fact, goes to the opposite extreme and discusses Dickens's women characters as though they were living people: actually existing termagants, for example, of whom a much-tried man could say 'It is difficult to believe that death can stifle them; one imagines them on the threshold of some other world, sounding confusion among unhappy spirits who hoped to have found peace'.

The tone is swashbuckling and with reason. It would be inaccurate to say that Gissing's married life was a failure. In a sense it was all too successful; he was looking for a neurotic woman and found three. But he was certainly not happy. He had inhibitions about punching the women in his own life, but he could lambaste Dickens's imagined ones and their creator himself for providing such a set of harpies, imbeciles and bores.

But his point was – and it fitted with the fact that he had just separated from his second wife – that all these evils were in the *past*. Even the imbeciles, even Mrs Nickleby who is certainly a test case, would have been different in 1898. 'Sixty years ago there was practically no provision in England for the mental training of women. Sent early to a good school,

---

* From the *London Review of Books*, 17 July 1980. Review of *The Odd Women* by George Gissing and *The Beth Book* by Sarah Grand.

and kept there till the age, say, of one-and-twenty, Mrs Nickleby would have grown into a quite endurable gentlewoman, aware of her natural weakness, and a modest participant in general conversation.' I doubt this very much, but the optimism is pleasing. The celibates, too, are looking up. 'Nowadays things are so different; it is common to find spinsters who are such by choice, and not a few of them are doing good work in the world.' It sounds dreary but is clearly meant to be cheerful.

A further tribute that Gissing makes to such progress is his statement that the women of his day did not read Dickens, feeling, in the modern way, that he was unjust to their sex. What they thought about Gissing's portrayal of them in his own novels it is difficult to say. On this subject his work is a minefield of ambiguities.

Nobody could accuse him of not knowing and understanding women, as he accused Dickens. (In his class-conscious way he is scornful of Dickens's early lack of experience of refined women: 'the damsels of Dingley Dell were probably as like ladies as anything he had seen.') But what *are* the readers to make, of say, Amy Reardon, the heroine or anti-heroine of *New Grub Street* (1891)? Every scene in which she appears implies both condemnation and justification. Is she a New Woman? She discusses such topics as the desirability of easy divorce, daringly exclaims 'Love is the most insignificant thing in women's lives' and replies with admirable spirit when her husband demands: 'Granted that I am not of a very sanguine nature, and that I easily fall into gloomy ways of talk, what is Amy here for?' Yet she gets her way by the methods of the harem. In the last chapter we see her reclining seductively on a settee cajoling her second husband into referring to the girl he has jilted as an ink-stained schoolgirl.

By the time *The Odd Women* was published in 1893 the cliché of the old maid had been even more thoroughly dented in literature than in life. The New Woman could be unmarried. Whatever people really thought, the idea of perpetual celibacy voluntarily assumed by the good-looking heroine of a novel (Trollope's Lily Dale, for example) had become quite chic. The shock was over; Gissing could be subtle.

The interesting thing is that he is not at all subtle. Rhoda Nunn, heroine of *The Odd Women*, is an amalgam of most of the stock elements which characterised the New Woman in fiction. She is healthy-looking rather than handsome; both her figure and her hands are described as 'strong and shapely'. She has 'a brisk movement'; she is no tomboy running about in her bloomers, but she strides along in the Lake District ('I could walk back again to Wastwater if it were necessary') and thoroughly enjoys the chicken sandwiches provided by the hero, Everard Barfoot, on the same occasion. She is not mealy-mouthed: 'What man lives in celibacy? Consider that unmentionable fact.' She discusses prostitution and free unions.

But what the portrait of Rhoda may lack in subtlety it makes up for in ambivalence, which after all produces a similar effect. Gissing's admiration appears to break down at several important points in the plot. He makes her show none of the female solidarity which should have animated a New Woman, or indeed a lower-case kindly woman, when one of her students who has run off with a married man and then turned to prostitution asks to be re-enrolled in her class. (Her hardness is represented as being of the head rather than of the heart but all the same it drives the girl to suicide.) In love, she is jealous and highly unreasonable; just like everybody else, in fact, but the New Woman claims not to be just like everybody else. When Everard Barfoot declares his love she abandons her principles about free unions and stipulates marriage or nothing.

It turns out to be nothing. When, in a kind of epilogue, the couple parts, one of the elements in Barfoot's waning enthusiasm is a consideration of class. Through his eyes, and possibly Gissing's, we suddenly see the New Woman as rather common.

> He began to think: If this woman had enjoyed the social advantages to which Agnes Brissenden and those others were doubtless indebted for so much of their charm, would she not have been their equal or more? For the first time he compassionated Rhoda.

It sounds like Fanny Knatchbull talking about her aunt, Jane Austen. Barfoot marries Agnes Brissenden.

There is no suggestion in *The Odd Women* that the New Woman is sexually unattractive, On the contrary: the worldly (as we are meant to think) Barfoot feels she might have very special attractions, and Gissing's first description of Rhoda includes a forthright passage to this effect:

> one became aware of a suggestiveness directed not solely to the intellect, of something like an unfamiliar sexual type, remote indeed from the voluptuous, but hinting at a possibility of subtle feminine forces that might be released by circumstance.

The apotheosis of the new sexual type had in fact taken place forty years earlier when in *The Woman in White*, Wilkie Collins offset his pretty, insipid, helpless heroine by a second heroine who was none of these things, the great Marian Halcombe, whose charm subdued not only the equally great Count Fosco in the book but also such men of the readership as Swinburne, and Edward Fitzgerald who named his new boat after her. It was difficult for the Rhoda Nunns of fiction to follow her.

But Marian Halcombe had no need to work. Though not rich herself she was half-sister to an heiress. Rhoda Nunn has to work, and this gives Gissing's portrait of her a particular tone. It also introduces us to other potential New Women, as she and her friend Mary Barfoot run a secretarial school. The pupils are strictly middle-class. ('Miss Barfoot hasn't much interest in the lower classes.')

The rakehelly tones in which Rhoda Nunn and her sympathisers speak about shorthand and typing make one half suspect satire and certainly recall the comment of the S.J. Perelman character who on taking a wife feels guilty that he has robbed the world of a shorthand typist. But even if Gissing is smiling at the women's missionary exuberance he clearly realises that their world of work is sadly limited and that even after the establishment of the Bureau of the Association for the Promotion of the Employment of Women in 1857 there was little range of choice for the educated woman.

They could teach, but the pronouncement of Harriet Martineau earlier in the century that only one in a thousand was fit to teach still applied and was more widely recognised as a truth, so that though the air of the Nineties was not as loud as formerly with the cries of governesses being trodden on, there must have been many a quietly crestfallen woman on whom it dawned that she was one of the nine hundred and ninety-nine.

Alice and Virginia Madden are two such. They are the oldest of a family of daughters left almost penniless by the premature death of their doctor father. It is with them that *The Odd Women* begins and ends. Rhoda Nunn is dismissive of them: 'The eldest can't teach seriously, but she can keep young children out of mischief and give them a nice way of speaking.' Virginia she writes off as childish. There is no question of their being invited to join the secretarial classes.

The case of the younger sister, Monica, is a different matter. True, 'it is a great absurdity to talk to her about business', but she has to escape from being a shop-girl. We gather what Gissing thinks about shop-girls when he is discussing the character of Fanny Dorritt in his book on Dickens. The shop-girl's 'sphere of action is extensive for we meet her not only in shops, strictly speaking, but at liquor-bars, in workrooms, and, unfortunately, sometimes in the post-office, to say nothing of fifty other forms of employment open to the underbred, and more or less aggressive, young woman.'

It is at this point that we begin to see the secretarial college in something of the rosy light in which its founders view it. Gissing's description of the draper's shop where Monica works is so depressing that the acquisition of office skills seems to lead to quite a haven of independence, reasonable hours and professionalism. The day of the comic female clerk, like Elizabeth Gaskell's Miss Galindo, is of course, for the New Woman, in the dark past.

Monica does not finish the course; it *was* absurd to talk to her about business. She makes a rash marriage which turns out disastrously. The moral of the Maddens is that not every woman can be a New Woman any more than she can be a saint or a creative artist. Many are called but few are chosen, and Gissing's New Woman is not very sympathetic to the unchosen:

'Rhoda, what comfort have you for the poor in spirit?'
'None whatever, I'm afraid. My mission is not to them.'

Virago have recently reprinted, in their Modern Classics series, a number of novels dealing with the situation of women at the end of the nineteenth century. Gissing's *The Odd Women* is one of them. Another is Sarah Grand's *The Beth Book,* published in 1897. One would expect the man's treatment of the subject to differ from the woman's, but though the two books are as dissimilar as they could be, the difference has little to do with gender.

From the point of view of late nineteenth-century feminists the great women novelists of earlier decades were lost leaders. Persuasively as they depicted the exploitation of women, they tended to be in two minds about the Woman Question as such.

Christianity confused two of them. Neither Charlotte Brontë nor Elizabeth Gaskell – devoutly religious themselves and members of clerical households – could rid herself of the debilitating idea that adversity was beneficial, especially for others. Much as Brontë and her sisters had suffered as governesses she was capable of writing to Mr Williams, her publisher, when he consulted her about careers for his daughters:

A governess's experience is frequently indeed bitter, but its results are precious; the mind, feeling, temper are there subjected to a discipline equally painful and priceless.

Elizabeth Gaskell felt much the same – that is, if we can take at all seriously her startling remark that Effie Ruskin would have been a nicer woman if she had ever had smallpox. Furthermore, the respect of both Brontë and Gaskell for the Divine Will was absolute, and in their day it favoured the exclusive domesticity of women.

George Eliot was in more than two minds about feminism. Unhampered by religion, she was, fortunately for the English novel, at the mercy of her own subtlety of perception, and felt the complications of the Woman Question far too keenly for simple commitment. 'It seems to me to overhang abysses of which even prostitution is not the worst.'

It is as though the New Woman was waiting for Sarah Grand. (She is said to have invented the expression, which may or may not be true.) Here is single-mindedness at last, but how much less persuasive it turns out to be than ambivalence. *The Beth Book* should be read alongside *The Odd Women* by anyone wanting a demonstration of the difference between a tract and a novel.

In Sarah Grand (Frances Elisabeth McFall, née Clarke) we have a writer of total conviction and limited imagination, who depicts a heroine, Elizabeth Maclure née Caldwell, of whom the same might be said. It is indeed an autobiographical novel. Grand makes no attempt to hide the partisanship she feels for her own image of herself and this blatancy is bound to alienate the sympathy of many readers, particularly when it comes to her portrait of the young Beth whom she clearly thinks of as cute, loveable, sensitive and misunderstood but who emerges as a tiresome, rather stupid child.

The book is a compilation, almost a manual, of stock feminist grievances, so predictable that it is not necessary to enumerate them; and as the story hangs on, or rather consists of, them, there can be no surprises: when Beth as a girl inherits a little money from an aunt we know she will be coerced into spending it on her worthless brother's education. The characters are similarly tendentious. The husband is a brute, but he is not just any brute; he is arch-enemy in the feminist war, being director of a hospital set up under the Contagious Diseases Act, against which Josephine Butler campaigned. He likewise practices vivisection and it is typical of Beth's inability to connect that her righteous horror when she discovers what he is doing is not tempered by any recollection of her own record of wanton beetle-squashing and rabbit-stoning.

But though Grand lacks imagination she has enough fancy to keep the book going, at considerable length, and to give it an appearance of vitality. It is one long daydream, the universal daydream that anyone can display instant genius without practice, technique, forethought or likelihood; as if, for example, a galumphing woman were suddenly to see herself dancing with a poetry and passion that made Dame Ninette de Valois bow her head in wordless homage. After a repressed childhood, a sketchy education, a degrading marriage and an abortive career as a writer, Beth suddenly realises herself, from one minute to the next, in public speaking. A great crowd rises with deafening shouts of applause and forces her to recognise her vocation. 'A woman of genius', cry the newspapers next day. What she actually said and to what specific audience is not stated.

Grand may have done harm at the time, for she conned women in the same way that Samuel Smiles conned men when he persuaded them that by means of self-help any man could, say, build the Scott Memorial or discover vaccination. In blustering across ravines neither Grand nor Smiles

seemed to see that as long as ravines were there many people would fall
into them.

Grand would certainly not have appreciated the content of a poem I
came across recently, by Margaret Bevan, in which a husband replies to
his wife's lament:

> But in forbidding you your dream career
> And binding you to stove and sink in Slough
> I'm helping you avoid what you most fear,
> Trying, and finding out you don't know how.

George Eliot acknowledged and respected that fear, and its cause. So did
George Gissing.

Very Like Poole Harbour*

This is a collection of fourteen stories by Mary Butts, a dedicated and
prolific writer who died comparatively young in the Thirties. She is one
of the current victims of the fashionable drive to exhume 'forgotten women
writers'. The category is dreary. Mary Butts is not.

Until very recently, it needed the temperament of an archaeologist to
find her books. In the libraries a request for them was received as an interesting challenge, and a well-motivated librarian would return from distant
stacks carrying, say, *Armed with Madness*, a novel; or it might be *The
Macedonian*, a fictional history of Alexander, the purple rubber-stamp
showing that the book went to war with the troops of fifty years ago.

Such searches may soon be unnecessary. In 1988 Carcanet reissued *The
Crystal Cabinet*, Mary Butts's account of her life as a child and girl in South
Dorset. And now, also from Carcanet, we have these stories, which first
appeared in the magazines and journals of the Twenties and Thirties. The
autobiography, in its idiosyncratic way, is a great success. The stories,
equally idiosyncratic but very uneven in quality, may not be quite that,

---

* From the *London Review of Books*, 5 December 1991. Review of *With and
Without Buttons* by Mary Butts, edited by Nathalie Blondel.

but their publication is welcome. More may follow. The years of invisibility are over.

Mary Butts did not live to experience the long period of neglect that befell her work after the Second World War, an oblivion not altogether easy to understand given the continued, if diminished reputation of her friend, the woman writer Bryher, of whom people said, 'Oh, yes, I *remember*', while of Mary Butts they said '*Who*?' From about the age of twenty to her death in 1937 Butts was probably as much in the limelight as she wished to be. She came from a privileged background. Her parents dressed the servants in red, perhaps not to match the paintwork as certain Victorian landowners did, but in much the same spirit. She always knew she would never have to go out to work. Her teachers (she was thoroughly, if not very wisely educated) congratulated her on the fact. So, with her family connections and the friends she acquired for herself and met through her first marriage, to publisher John Rodker, she could within reason command whatever pulpit, platform or stage she needed.

Once free of the security and conventions of her home and the violent claims that the countryside all around it made on her emotions, and having then sloughed off her marriage, she spent her time travelling round Europe, and for many years more or less settled in Paris. A list of her friends, lovers and associates during these two decades is impressive. Man Ray photographed her, Jean Cocteau sketched her, Ezra Pound and T.S. Eliot praised her work, Aleister Crowley exploited it. In the Twenties Harold Acton came across her in Paris, not exactly among 'the bevies of truculent women' who surrounded Hemingway and Ford Madox Ford but somewhere near.

> On the fringe of the Montparnasse bars were a few talented storytellers running to seed, like poor generous red-haired Mary Butts with her weakness for squalid parasites. She poured them drinks while she improvised the vivid stories one hoped she would write. Her real talent was akin to Anne Radcliffe, and she was born out of due time. All these people were segregated in self-conscious little groups.

In London on more than one occasion in the Thirties, Virginia Woolf reported conversations with Tony Butts, friend of William Plomer and brother of Mary, about his sister.

> She is a bad woman – pretentious – I can see no merit in her books – pretentious. She corrupts young men. They are always committing suicide. She has now married Gabriel Atkins – without any character. They were given 25 decanters for their wedding.

To those who have read, in *The Crystal Cabinet*, about Mary's total devotion to her young brother in childhood such a tone is sickening, but there is some comfort from Woolf herself, who, as she pensively notes, while listening to these ridiculous and disloyal maunderings was in fact speculating as to whether Tony looked more like a gnat or a jerboa. In any case, comments like those of Acton and Butts do Mary no harm. On the contrary, they make her look like the bright day that brings forth the adder.

In a consideration of Mary Butts's skill as a writer, *With and Without Buttons* is not a great deal of help. In all her work she clearly caught the taste of the period; certainly no magazine with any claims to modernity was long without a Butts story. Ezra Pound's enthusiasm for 'Green', included in this volume and far from being one of the best, is significant.

In some of her book-length work she showed considerable awareness of what she was doing. She may not always have been astute about what she was going to do, and she often deceived herself about what she had actually done: she thought, for example, that she was influenced by Dostoevsky. (Women writers of her day had a tendency to say this about themselves, usually in a tone of voice more appropriate to its being the other way round.) But sometimes she could see exactly what was happening and describe it. Halfway through the autobiography, she suddenly says: 'This book seems to write itself – winding in and out, like the streams of Poole Harbour, scouring their passages through mud to the mid-channel, and with the tide to the sea.'

Now that she mentions it, *The Crystal Cabinet* is very like Poole Harbour. There is a creative muddle about its currents which by no means obscures the outline and drive of the book, but does scramble the details: there is some confusion about the men called Freddy who at various times were married to her mother, and there is such a gallimaufry of aunts that it seems almost nit-picking to work out and remember which one it was who drowned. The method works well for this particular book: indeed you could say it represents the confusion of life itself when honestly looked back on.

Unfortunately, short stories should not really resemble Poole Harbour; they have neither the space nor the time to 'write themselves'. Unfortunately too, it is difficult, sixty or seventy years later, for the reader to decide whether anything unconventional in the writer's technique is the result of deliberate experiment or unconscious ineptitude. So when in these stories Mary Butts shows little regard for the ordinary everyday coherence that listeners and readers have always expected as a basic requirement for narrative, one can only concentrate on the text and wonder which it was.

In 'Friendship's Garland', for example, has she inadvertently lost, or deliberately ignored, the balance between physical and mental activity which traditional storytellers observe? Here, people bound across the room and throw themselves into cane chairs; they leap up and down baying like hounds; while, outside, the sun roars and a racing wind flings somebody down a steep road and blows her into the Tube. Meanwhile the thoughts of the characters, which seem potentially interesting and even subtle and which must be the essence of the tale since nothing much actually happens, are so understated as to be incomprehensible. This could be the point. But is it?

'After the Funeral', which has the makings of a strong story, presents another puzzle. A central character is unnamed for the greater part of the narrative. He does not seem to be a mystery man, and indeed when towards the end he is abruptly given a name it means nothing to anybody and sounds as though somebody quite new has come in. (Perhaps somebody has. I could be mistaken.) And who is Lionel? If there is no artistic purpose in leaving him unexplained why not identify him in a couple of words? Is it simply an indiscriminate wish to break the mould?

Throughout her career Butts's language could be obfuscating in much the same way. A little speculation may do us, the readers, no harm at all, but it is so distracting. Her first novel, *Ashe of Rings*, a fundamentally good yarn, rather on the lines of *Rebecca*, is stifled by a style which might be politely described as heightened. Here is the house: 'Through the afternoons it could be heard, sucking in its sleep, milky draughts, bubbles of quiet, drunk against the future when it should become a wrath.' And here is the heroine: 'She came into breakfast like a pale glass cup with a nasturtium in it.' It is easy enough to say 'Oh, my Gawd', but one must bear in mind that that was what many readers wanted and still do want ('Circumspice'), and that *Ashe of Rings* was published in several countries.

Mary Butts never entirely shook off the phoney poetics and strained lyricism which seem to have given her as much pleasure as they did her readers. But, as far as one can tell from a group of only fourteen stories, that style began to give way to another, plainer and more astringent. Certainly she must have realised from quite early on, even if not early enough, that one of her favourite subjects, magic, was particularly effective when conveyed by at least some down-to-earth language. 'With and Without Buttons', one of her first stories, involves a ghost, and she had the sense to say of her living hero: 'He was our next-door neighbour in Kent.' This quietly informative sentence, quite untypical of her writing at the time, was just right for what followed. Years later, in 'Mappa Mundi', a tale of the supernatural, though the dialogue is high-flown, the happenings are related as though they were the most natural thing in the world.

Two of the most accomplished stories in the collection are 'The House

Party' and 'From Altar to Chimneypiece'. They both deal with the English
and Americans abroad and specifically those who lived in or were based in
Paris at the same time as Mary Butts. She casts a very cool eye on their
behaviour, which ranges freely from deviation to depravity. As a child she
was carefully trained in habits of observation, and though her mentors
would presumably have been disconcerted by the uses to which she put
her training, it clearly took.

But some of the less accomplished stories can arouse more sympathy:
those in which she *seems* to divulge more about herself than she has
consciously observed. It is suggestive, surely, that a woman who would
have us believe that nature and the countryside are all in all to her and
constantly protests to that effect, should write so feelingly about the hero
of 'Speed the Plough'. He is a badly-wounded soldier who in convales-
cence is advised to take up agricultural work. He shows real aptitude for
it ('a born milkman'), but he can only find happiness in town making
expensive clothes for idle urban women.

And in 'After the Funeral', a lovely wayward woman, capricious but
unforgettable, has died abroad and is being brought back to London. In
the dark church the mourners wait for the coffin to arrive; there has been
a storm in the Channel. The mourners are mostly men. One is sobbing
uncontrollably. One suddenly pitches forward on to his knees. The air is
filled with love and grief... Well, we all have days like that.

Red Riding*

The Brontë trio and Marxist criticism were obviously made for each other
in much the same way that Hardy envisaged the *Titanic* and the iceberg.
The convergence of the twain was inevitable.

> Alien they seemed to be:
> No mortal eye could see
> The intimate welding of their later history.

---

* From the *Listener*, 13 March 1975. Review of *Myths of Power: a Marxist Study
of the Brontës* by Terry Eagleton.

But the Spinner of the Years said 'Now', and the consummation, as Hardy suggestively describes the collision, took place.

As far as Marx and the Brontës are concerned, the Spinner in fact said 'Now' some time ago and has frequently repeated it. The first number of *The Modern Quarterly Miscellany* which appeared in 1947 set out to define Marxist literary criticism by means of direct exposition, as in the first essay, and of demonstration, as in Kenneth Muir's 'Timon of Athens and the Cash-Nexus'. One of the most striking articles in this valuable magazine was David Wilson's 'Emily Brontë: First of the Moderns', which has been much referred to since. Mr Wilson gives a detailed account of social conditions in the West Riding at the time the Brontës were at Haworth and interprets Emily's *Wuthering Heights* in the light of these facts. 'We can see in the character of Heathcliff a true representation of the working men of her time.' Hindley is the capitalist oppressor who by degrading Heathcliff goads him into becoming a capitalist oppressor in his turn. *Wuthering Heights*, Mr Wilson concludes, could be considered as a source of the proletarian novel. Well, with respect, if you can believe that you can believe anything.

More persuasive is such an essay as A.L. Morton's 'Genius on the Border', to be found in his book *The Matter of Britain*, published in 1966. Mr Morton repeats, with generous acknowledgement, Mr Wilson's account of industrial conditions near Haworth. But he also describes the private social anxieties of Rev. Patrick Brontë which were the predictable result of his rags-to-cassock career, and it seems extremely likely that the father's insecurities on this score would, in such a claustrophobic household, be reflected in the daughters' work and indeed this influence can be quite satisfactorily demonstrated.

In his robust introduction to *Myths of Power: a Marxist Study of the Brontës* Terry Eagleton also describes the social problems and the class-struggles that the Brontë sisters were in a position to have observed. His account is accurate and fair except for his quickness to dismiss eye-witness accounts, such as those of Mrs Gaskell, when they happen to contradict his favourite contentions; after all, Mrs Gaskell was there. He outlines his critical method: it is not to be 'a crude one-to-one correlation of literary and social detail, in the manner of some vulgar literary sociology'. Good. He aims at defining the ideological structure to be found in the Brontë novels. That 'arises from the real history of the West Riding in the first half of the nineteenth century; and it is, I believe, imaginatively grasped and transposed in the production of the Brontës' fiction.' Splendid, except that I can believe no such thing (presuming that by 'real history' Dr Eagleton means the industrial revolution), certainly not about Emily. As A.L. Morton pointed out, Haworth was a frontier town; it was indeed at the edge of the industrial area, but to the west of it were, still are, only the moors, and I believe it was that side of the frontier that Emily grasped and transposed.

In his introduction Dr Eagleton is so insistent on the all-or-nothing nature of Marxist criticism which 'must refuse to occupy its modest niche within that formidable array of critical methods – mythological, psycho-analytic, theological, stylistic – which reflects the tolerant pluralism of a liberal democracy' that I am afraid he wouldn't like us to enjoy the book without entirely sharing his beliefs and assumptions. But in fact one does. It is spirited and imaginative throughout. A committed discussion of scrupulously-examined texts cannot fail to be interesting. I found the chapter on Anne Brontë the most rewarding. The relatively insipid *Agnes Grey* and *The Tenant of Wildfell Hall* gain from the application of pre-conceived ideas in a way *Wuthering Heights* cannot do. There are some illuminating comments on the characters such as the suggestion that Agnes Grey does not suffer as much as Charlotte's governesses do because her social feelings are not at stake, only her moral values, and these are firmly grounded.

Men and Women*

As a seventeenth-century bishop pointed out when he threw a stone at a dog and hit his mother-in-law by mistake, though the intention was imper-fectly fulfilled the effort was not wasted. Patricia Meyer Spacks does not seem to me to hit the target indicated by her title *The Female Imagination*. One infers from it that her book will examine the creative work of women and define what it is that makes their poems, their novels, their paintings, recognisably female quite apart from any clues offered by the subject matter. Such recognition we know can take place. Dickens spotted instantly that George Eliot's *Scenes of Clerical Life* was the work not of the pottering old clergyman suggested by George Henry Lewes but of a woman. He supported his opinion with a few reasons but clearly what he – and only he for some considerable time – had spotted was the female

---

* From the *New York Times Book Review*, 11 May 1975. Review of *The Female Imagination* by Patricia Meyer Spacks.

imagination. Today certain readers can say unerringly whether a poem is by a man or a woman when there is absolutely nothing in the theme to give the game away.

How do they know? Mrs Spacks does not really tell us, though the blurb on the jacket suggests she is going to. Sometimes she gets near the problem. In speaking of Virginia Woolf's *A Room of One's Own*, for example, where the subject matter is of course explicitly feminine, she points out how the dithery belle-lettrist style positively enacts the insecurities Virginia Woolf was enduring and describing: an excellent point, especially as we can make comparisons with similar styles in the work of men. E.M. Forster's style in *Aspects of the Novel* is dithery too, partly because the book was a transcript of a series of lectures and partly because he had his own insecurities, but he sounds like a man. Later on in *The Female Imagination*, after an interesting discussion of Dorothea Brooke's frustrations in *Middlemarch*, Mrs Spacks comments: 'The complicated pessimism of George Eliot's attitude towards society exemplifies the characteristic tone of women writing on the subject.' I should so much have liked her to discuss this tone further and to compare it with the tone of men who are pessimistic about society.

I have no right or desire, however, to carp at the fact that this valuable and enjoyable book does not tell me what I wish to know. There are too many things about it that I heartily applaud. Kate Millett's wrong-headed interpretation of *Villette* and her general exploitation of literature for her own ends have already been combated but the point was worth making again and Mrs Spacks makes it with spirit. Her discussion of some of the better-known nineteenth-century novels from a feminist viewpoint is also admirable, because although this has already been done too, her comments are usually sound and frequently novel. For example, she gives Daniel Deronda's mother the full treatment she deserves. Too often that poor lady is presented as a tiresome puppet whose existence is necessary for the dénouement, both in supplying Daniel with the information he needs to spur him to his final actions and in giving some plausibility to his presence at Grandcourt's drowning. She now emerges, quite properly, as a woman who has made a highly unconventional choice: weighing her duty to her son against a wish to pursue her career she has ditched the former in favour of the latter. Mrs Spacks is good about Emma Woodhouse too. Most readers have noticed that in many ways Elizabeth Bennet resembles her father but probably not that Emma resembles hers. Mrs Spacks points out that, dissimilar as they are, they have the same kind of selfishness: an illuminating comment.

Some of her interpretations are controversial. To my mind she overlooks the true artistic reason for the grotesque dog-bite incident in *Shirley*. Surely it was inserted largely to establish the identity of Shirley with Emily

Brontë. We should hardly suspect there was a connection between the two women if it were not for the dog-bite, apart of course from the fact that Charlotte Brontë said there was. I cannot agree either with her remark that it is 'outside the conventions of the Victorian novel to hint that a man and a woman might inhabit a single bed'. When George Eliot makes Gwendolen Grandcourt sleep with a dagger under her pillow, put there for the express purpose of murdering her husband when a suitable moment arrives, she is quite firmly tucking them up together.

I am not too happy about the way Mrs Spacks incorporates into her own argument the comments of her students. They sound too much like the comments we all used to make ten, twenty, thirty years ago, which is a depressing thought, however you look at it, but that is a quibble. What remains with one principally after reading this book are the splendid portraits of women through the ages who have been the protagonists, whether pathetic or triumphant, of the Woman Question. The seventeenth-century Duchess of Newcastle can think of no better way to establish her identity than to impress on the readers of her short autobiography who her father was and who her husband was. A century later Mrs Thrale, devoted to her mother and compliant to two husbands yet unloved by her children, is bewildered that her lifelong efforts to please should have brought so little return. But wholesomely, she is not only bewildered but very cross about it. In our own century Mabel Dodge Luhan, so defiant in the assertion of her personality ('her narcissism loud and relentless') has gone down to history chiefly as the friend of D.H. Lawrence. Beatrice Webb has been luckier; she battled her way successfully through the neurosis caused by the conflict between what she was expected to do and what she felt like doing, and has certainly not gone down to history as the wife of Sidney Webb. It is fine gallery of portraits, and their eyes follow us about.

No Deliverance from Dorset*

For readers who are disposed to think of William Barnes as a Dorset poet, Andrew Motion's *Selected Poems* is the ideal guide. Dispensing with a critical introduction, Motion prefaces the poems he has chosen with such information as the comments of Barnes himself on Dorset speech, and a table of the salient dates in the poet's life. The poems themselves are followed by three appendices containing further background material: 'A Dissertation on the Dorset Dialect of the English Language' by Barnes himself, Hardy's preface to his *Select Poems of William Barnes*, and appreciations of Barnes's work by Coventry Patmore, Tennyson and Gerard Manley Hopkins; the whole wound up by a scrupulous set of textual notes.

What more could readers want? The trouble is that they could want less, and, specifically, might well do without the assumption that Barnes *was* a Dorset poet. It is stated unequivocally on the back cover that 'Barnes wrote his greatest poetry in the vernacular of rural Dorset.' This is not much to go by, in fact; it is modish nowadays (it was not always so) for anybody who has anything to say about Barnes to say just that. But Motion himself seriously supports the comments, as is plain from the bias of his selection. Barnes wrote about 500 poems in dialect and about 400 in Standard English. Motion represents this output by seventy of the former and twelve of the latter.

In 1908, Hardy did not see it like that at all. In his preface, he seems more concerned with the differences between 'lyrical' and 'meditative' verse than those between verse written in Dorset and in Standard English. Of course, he understood Dorset speech and Barnes's use of it, but he went so far as to say that Barnes 'really belonged to the literary school of such poets as Tennyson, Gray and Collins rather than that of the old unpremeditating singers in dialect'. By 1950, the notion of Barnes the Dorset poet must have been well in the ascendant, for Geoffrey Grigson in his *Selected Poems of William Barnes* is at pains to shoot it down; pains gladly borne, the tone of his spirited introduction would suggest. He does not, of course, attempt to deny that Dorset had some influence on Barnes. 'He was narrowed by Dorset', he roundly says. 'Yet Dorset,' he continues, with a

---

* From the *Times Literary Supplement*, 2 December 1994. Review of *Selected Poems* by William Barnes, edited by Andrew Motion.

cleverly botched appearance of even-handedness, 'for all its indifference kept him safe, as Clare was kept safe in his asylum'. But he flatly denies that Barnes was a 'rustic aberration', which is what a Dorset poet would be. Later editors seem not to have taken much notice of Grigson, which is a mistake. In 1972, Robert Nye published a volume which claims, as Motion's does, that Barnes 'wrote best in Dorset dialect' and in which the selection favours the dialect poems to much the same degree as Motion's. Nye's book has many good qualities. It includes a glossary supplying trans-lations of words which Motion has either overlooked or thinks we ought to know. But the introduction shows some confusion of mind; Nye exhorts us not to approach Barnes as a Dorset poet, but to dwell on his Englishness – his selection having done exactly the opposite.

Naturally enough, Nye and Motion, being editors of slim selections, do not set out to discuss at any length whether or not Barnes really should be regarded as a Dorset poet; they simply demonstrate that they think he was. The excellent two-volume collection edited by Bernard Jones, which appeared in 1962, does go into the matter, ably and at satisfactory length. His views are expressed in something of the rallying tones of Grigson, who twelve years earlier had declared: 'Just as Barnes kept in Dorset during his life so he has been kept in Dorset ever since. The point is to deliver him.' Jones is less swashbuckling but firm: 'To keep Barnes for Dorset is to set greater store by birthplace than by poetry.' With even greater firmness, he states that 'the general picture of a peasant poet... was never really shown up as the deception it was'.

This deception was not practised only by those who somehow felt the need of a Dorset poet and created one in the image of what they imagined a Dorset poet should be. Barnes joined in; in fact he led the way. Jones points out that for years it was commonly held that Barnes spoke Dorset in his everyday adult life. 'He did,' agrees Jones, 'as a performance.' One has only to consider his career to realise how very unlikely it was that, once away from childhood, Barnes would not have tried to 'improve' (as he would certainly have considered it, though in social terms only) his way of speaking. 'He was a successful Jude Fawley', wrote Philip Larkin, reviewing Jones's collection, and, if we can imagine Jude as anything but obscure, that indeed sums up Barnes. As a country schoolteacher, it was his duty to train his pupils in Standard English (in East Devon, it is still advertised in some school prospectuses as a desirable accomplishment) and therefore to speak it fluently himself. Later, as a country clergyman, it was his duty to address the gentry in the mode to which they were accustomed.

As to his writing in dialect, he pretended that it was spontaneous. 'I cannot help it', he once rashly stated, and around this remark a pantomime dialogue has been going on intermittently ever since: 'Oh, yes he could';

'Oh no, he couldn't.' The answer is that, yes, he could help it. He wrote poetry in Standard English until he was in his early thirties and for the last twenty years of his life, and on many significant occasions in between. But if the compulsive dialect writing was an act, or if, as some critics have suggested, it was an extension of a philological exercise, it could still be his 'greatest' work, as Motion's book claims.

We are given little chance to judge for ourselves; the book provides too few poems that are not in dialect, fairly chosen though they are, and after so many poems in Dorset, the few in English are bound to seem genteel and affected. The only way, and we can easily take it for ourselves since our editor has decided not to, is to compare any couple of poems which exist in both Dorset and English: 'The Mother's Dream', for example. Barnes wrote it first in Dorset and later 'translated' it. In fact, there was little to do except indicate that the pronunciation of the original was no longer required and to standardise a little of the grammar and syntax. I cannot myself feel that the poem loses or gains anything by being Englished. When the dead child reproves his mother for extinguishing by her perpetual weeping the lamp he is carrying in heaven, the Dorset boy says, 'Your tears put en out', and begs her not to 'murn', whereas the English boy says, 'Your tears put it out/Mother, never mourn', which helps to make it a different poem, in that we see and hear different people, but not a better or worse one.

The value, indeed the legitimacy, of dialect poetry is a subject that has been much discussed, and Barnes's work has been in the thick of it, causing not only acrimonious debate but double thinking on the part of the debaters. Gerard Manley Hopkins, while hotly defending Barnes's use of it, admitted that he thought it to be 'a sort of unfair play', and Grigson, in the act of delivering Barnes from being a Dorset poet, conceded that in Dorset dialect he was at his best. We the readers, struggling to enjoy the Dorset poems, glossary in hand and notes on pronunciation at the ready, must wonder for whom they were written. Would those whose mother tongue was Dorset have recognised in print those strange-looking words – a'mwost, stwone, gookoo – which they had *not* learned to write at the village school? And would not those who had got on to grammar be puzzled by an eclogue which talked about fattening a vowel?

'The first difficulty,' says Bernard Jones, 'is deciding what the Dorset dialect is.' It is the last difficulty too; it pervades everything. It certainly raises further questions, such as why Hardy's Dorset dialect and Barnes's are so different; Dorchester and Sturminster Newton are not that far apart, and neither were the ages of the two poets nor their social standing. It has to be a question of personality. I have tried 'translating' famous lines from other poets into Barnes's Dorset: 'Hwome be the zailor, hwome vrom zea', for example, and 'Ees, I do well mind Adlestrop. The neäme', and they do not sound like anything except somebody fooling about.

This century-long Dorset-versus-English contest can be settled only by a consideration of the needs of the poet, which are paramount, and the taste of the various anthologists, compilers and critics for whom he has provided such very worthwhile employment. Helen Gardner, in her *New Oxford Book of English Verse* (1972), liked Barnes well enough to include four of his poems, but they are all in Standard English. Philip Larkin said thirty years ago: 'The time when Barnes is read as an English and not a Dorset poet has been slow in coming, if indeed it has come at all.' His melancholy proviso still applies, as Motion's book suggests; but in the recurrent drive to get William Barnes appreciated, in whatever capacity, it is relatively unimportant.

Jo's Other Sisters*

Little Women is a treatise on the repression or suppression of the instincts. The March household fizzes with bottled-up violence. Marmee, by her own account, has been a lifelong sufferer from murderous impulses, which she has remorselessly – and wrong-headedly we would of course now think – schooled herself to check by a system of folding her lips tight together, going out of the room and giving herself a little shake for being so weak and wicked. In this campaign of suppression she has enlisted her husband who puts his finger on his lips and looks at her with a kind but sober face when she is about to break out. The little women themselves are surprisingly aggressive: that is, their aggression is perfectly consistent with realism; the surprise comes from the way it is glossed over. It is true that Jo's attempt to murder Amy, when she lets her skate on ice she knows to be thin, is given proper weight, but Jo's dropping of the infant Amy into the coalbox, thereby permanently flattening her nose, is presented as a comic accident. Amy's burning of Jo's irreplaceable book of stories is treated leniently and when darling Beth ('Little Tranquillity') lets her canary starve

---

* From the *Times Literary Supplement*, 14 May 1976. Review of *Behind a Mask: the Unknown Thrillers of Louisa M. Alcott,* edited by Madeleine Stern.

and he is found 'with his little claws pathetically extended, as if imploring the food for want of which he had died', we are expected not to censure, but to condole.

Behind a Mask, edited by Madeleine Stern, consists of four novelettes written by Louisa M. Alcott in the 1860s, the decade which culminated in the publication of *Little Women*, inside the four righteous and cosy walls of which she was to be encapsulated for ever. In these four stories hardly anyone suppresses anything except for reasons of calculated self-interest and with an eye to the main chance. Adults hurl their fellow-creatures into deeper gulfs than coal-boxes and imperfectly frozen lakes. Siblings have no inhibitions about attacking each other. In the title story Edward sees the girl he loves turning to Another, who happens to be his brother Gerald.

> In a paroxysm of blind wrath, he caught up a large pruning knife left there by the gardener and would have dealt his brother a fatal blow had he not warded it off with his arm. The stroke fell... The blood poured from a deep wound in his arm, showing by its rapid flow that an artery had been severed.

But the stories are by no means totally amoral, though the bounds of morality are much more widely spread than we are accustomed to in nine-teenth-century fiction. It is true that whereas in *Little Women* everyone spends twenty-four hours a day trying to be good, in *Behind a Mask* most of them devote themselves to being bad. We see Jean Muir, heroine of the title story, sitting up late at night in her room, drinking, as she works out her unedifying plans. But there are limits. There is a moral Tom Tiddler's ground where people may go too far and get caught. The heroine of 'Pauline's Passion and Punishment' sets out to avenge herself on a faithless lover, and is getting along splendidly with her nasty machinations, apparently with the author's entire approval, until she oversteps the mark and, as the title states, is punished. Sir Jasper in 'The Abbot's Ghost, or Maurice Treherne's Temptation' also goes too far. His card-sharping and forgery, in which he implicates and ruins his innocent cousin, end in his being thrown from his horse and killed.

However vindictive and self-seeking the heroines may be there is some-thing touching about the way they have a code of their own and how they play the game at last. Jean Muir and Edith Snowdon, of 'The Abbot's Ghost', cunningly and cynically entrap old men for their money and social position. But when these little women promise to be good wives we believe them and feel comfortably certain that their elderly husbands (actu-ally Sir John Coventry is only fifty-five) will in the autumn of their days enter an exciting Indian summer. It is disarming: if Becky Sharp had been kind to Rawdon we should have forgiven her everything.

The liveliness of the women characters and the spirited part they play in the sex war contribute greatly to our enjoyment of the books. And they do not have to be hoydens. Assuming, if necessary, a touch of rouge and a few strategically-placed false teeth, they can be beautiful graceful nineteenth-century women. But the stories have other virtues, including brisk dialogue, strong plots and genuine suspense: Jean very nearly fails, Pauline very nearly succeeds. And there is always someone to identify with; who wants to be Marmee nowadays or Jo? The backgrounds are all made exotic, whether the action takes place in the tropics or England. Ghosts, blood and thunder know no frontiers.

And there is an abundance of all three. Alcott owes a harmless, indeed a flattering, debt to the worst excesses of the nineteenth-century British novel, and particularly to those of Charlotte Brontë and Dickens:

> The winter dusk gathered early… A loud, long shriek echoed through the hall. The young ladies clung to one another aghast, for mortal terror was in the cry, and a deadly silence followed it.

It is implausibly explained that a servant is having a fit. The gentlemen appear on the scene, to take charge, counsel and console. Surely they are headed by Mr Rochester in his dressing gown.

We owe Madeleine Stern gratitude for providing us with a thoroughly enjoyable experience. She also offers us a helpful introduction. Some of her phrases are rather unfortunate (Alcott 'took her pen as her bridegroom' and thereafter 'lived in her inkstand') but her account of the circumstances in which the stories were composed and of the periodicals, such as *Frank Leslie's Illustrated Newspaper*, in which they were first published, is very interesting.

Poesy's Face*

The Midsummer Cushion represents perhaps the greatest disappointment, as distinct from tragedy, of John Clare's life; and the disappointment certainly contributed to the final tragedy.

In 1831 Clare was thirty-eight, and the author of three published volumes of verse: *Poems Descriptive of Rural Life and Scenery* (1820), *The Village Minstrel* (1821) and *The Shepherd's Calendar* (1827). The first book had sold briskly, securing for the poet public recognition and the attentions of the great. The other two had not; success had receded on the tide of fashion, leaving Clare puzzled and sorrowful ('I sit sometimes and wonder over the little noise I have made in the world') but not incapable of initiative. He prepared a manuscript consisting of 361 poems and chose a title that alluded – most appropriately, he thought – to 'the very old custom among villagers in summer time to stick a piece of greensward full of field flowers and place it as an ornament in their cottages'. He finished the necessary copying in 1832 and set to work, with sufficient energy and common sense, to find subscribers. The result was almost total failure.

Nobody seems to know what happened to this manuscript immediately after Clare's death in 1864, but since 1893 it has been in Peterborough Museum. Anne Tibble, assisted by R.K.R. Thornton, now gives us the volume as originally planned by Clare, complete with illiteracies and misspellings. I cannot see how perpetuation of these departures from the norm can do anything better than distract the modern reader, but Mrs Tibble declares it to be essential and her past contributions to Clare studies give her some right to pronounce. Her insistence on the verbatim leads her to include one poem, 'The Wryneck's Nest', twice, simply because Clare copied it out twice, presumably by mistake as the differences between the two texts are not poetically significant, at least not in the way that, for example Blake's emendations were.

The fact that *The Midsummer Cushion* has not been printed in its entirety before does not mean that the poems have not been available all this while. In fact, two-thirds of them have been. Clare himself dipped into the collection. So have twentieth-century editors, led by Edmund Blunden in his *Poems Chiefly from Manuscript* (1920).

---

* From the *Listener*, 15 February 1979. Review of *The Midsummer Cushion* by John Clare, edited by Anne Tibble.

If this present volume needed any justification, it could be pointed out that it was assembled at a key moment in Clare's life, a half-way stage at which (so the most enlightened of his doctors later declared) his development might have taken a much happier turn if success and money had come to his rescue. He was already suffering from mental instability but seems not yet to have been irreparably damaged, and his first committal to an asylum was still four years ahead.

The poems give a clear picture not only of Clare's enthusiasms at this time – his nature poetry was never more fervently accurate – but also of his anxieties, and also of the distresses which might seem topical and transitory but which in fact extended themselves into his eventual long decline. It was now, for example, that he most reluctantly moved with his family from the house where he had been born. The new house was superior in every way, but for Clare, as he shows with a dejection which was still coherent in 'The Flitting', that was not the point; he was being uprooted:

> Here every tree is strange to me
> All foreign things where'er I go.

Another bad experience which naturally involved him poetically in these years was his setback as a poet. His original welcome to the pantheon had been succeeded so soon and so irrationally by rebuff that he had come to the conclusion that his poetry itself was diseased. In 'Decay, a Ballad' he exclaims:

> O poesy is on the wane
> I hardly know her face again.

But this doleful acceptance is not his only approach to the subject. He attempts to be strong and philosophical about it, asserting in 'To a Poet' that the critics can be sick too. This attempt to rise above neglect plays havoc with his verse, and leads to what happens in a poem written some eight years later, 'To Wordsworth', which ends:

> Wordsworth, go on – a greater poet be.
> Merit will live though parties disagree.

To the genuinely optimistic this is a statement of fact. Parties, some of them most unpleasant ones, are always disagreeing about poetic merit, yet it does survive. Clare, however, though with great reason to wish it, had little capacity for believing it, and the couplet has collapsed.

Many of the reflective poems in *The Midsummer Cushion* are weakened by this same reluctance of his to speak as he finds. On the subject of Woman as opposed to women, for instance, Clare can be derivative and affected. In 'The Enthusiast', an otherwise fine poem, his remarks about the ability of woman to make earth divine and cause life its rudest cares to resign, have, unfortunately, more to do with literature than with life. He sounds rather like MacHeath relaxing in the company of The Sex after a hard day robbing coaches. But Clare's admirers get used to such unevenness and indeed feel privileged to put up with it.

At the same time the two real women in Clare's life seem real indeed in *The Midsummer Cushion*, which represents a pivotal point in his portrayal of them. Both Mary and Patty are transformed from what they once actually were to him, but though his feelings may be heightened they are not distorted. The women have not yet become delusions; they are more like dreams, a very vivid dream in the case of Mary. Patty is fading; there is little heat and much formality in the poem addressed to her but she is not yet the stranger whom he was to resist when she jumped out of the cart to greet him on his escape from the asylum. As usual it is Mary, the lost love of his early youth, who provokes the most interesting poetry. He is now some twenty years away from her; he knows she exists in the past though in 'The Enthusiast' he conjures her up with a radiance beyond that of sober memory. But she has not yet thoroughly become the 'first wife' which she never really was, much less the only wife, to whom he was travelling so painfully on his journey from the asylum, though she had been dead for three years.

On Lives

Two Hares and a Priest*

'Who do you think will close the door after you? Pushkin?' The question, which Elaine Feinstein quotes in her introduction to this excellent biography, is one which apparently might still be asked by a Russian mother of a careless child. No British mother would say anything like it, if only because she could not think of a figure with comparable evocative power: writers here are hardly household names. She would certainly not use that of the greatest Russian of them all. Some of us call our cats Pushkin but that is about as far as it has gone.

Our shortcomings as readers seem not to be entirely our fault. Feinstein makes it clear that there was a dearth of accessible books in Britain about Pushkin at the time she started to write hers; the classic biographies were out of print and seldom to be found on the shelves of public libraries although some might well lurk in the stacks. In a good working bibliography she lists what is available in the rest of the world. A considerable proportion comes from the USA, and the rest, largely and predictably, from the scholars of Moscow and St Petersburg.

In a substantial note to the introduction Feinstein recommends, though with reservations, books which would instruct us, if we could get hold of them – or if they were translated into English. One piece of guidance given in a book she recommends has important implications: in his biography, *Pushkin: The Man and His Age* (1994), Robin Edmonds strong-mindedly refrains from even attempting to introduce Pushkin's poetry to readers who have no Russian, and helpfully fobs us off with the diplomatic and historical background of Pushkin's life. Feinstein also mentions David Magarshack's biography respectfully for what was at the time – 1967 – its up-to-date research but reprovingly for its lack of notes and references. (In fact notes do often appear in Magarshack's book, as parentheses in the text, and there is an efficient index.)

One other reference Feinstein makes leads to questions of style. In 1950 there appeared an English translation of Henri Troyat's *Pouchkine*, which, though commendable in some ways, is, she tells us, 'written like a popular novel with freely invented dialogue'. And it was most probably not only

---

* From the *London Review of Books*, 13 May 1999. Review of *Pushkin* by Elaine Feinstein.

the dialogue that was invented: *Pouchkine* is clearly the product of the ever-popular school of biography immortalised by one author's comment in a Life of St Teresa of Avila that 'St John of the Cross bit his lip.' If Feinstein has ever come under the influence of this school, which I doubt, she has long since renounced it. When she wishes to give us a telling visual detail she selects, if not from actual documents then from very strong probabilities: when Natalya Goncharova and Pushkin were betrothed she 'gave him her cold timid hand'. This is more plausible than St John of the Cross biting his lip: a formal betrothal would have involved the extending of hands and made most girls timid, while Moscow in April would have made their hands cold. It is not a banal comment.

Though there is a suitable detachment about Feinstein's style in general, her tone has considerable variation. Her indignation at the unkindness with which Pushkin's mother, Nahdezhda Osipovna, consistently treated him makes the reader's blood boil too and it goes on simmering until, on her deathbed, Nahdezhda says 'sorry' to her son, at which point it boils up again. (Pushkin, a generous man, was quite touched by her penitence.) When she describes historical events, however, Feinstein keeps calm. In her account of Tsar Paul's overthrow in 1799 (the year of Pushkin's birth) in favour of his son Alexander, her tone is neutral. Alexander had apparently been assured that no harm would come to his father but 'in the event' Paul happened to be strangled amid the confusion. Easily done.

Pushkin's looks are an important part of his story. This of course is the case with all of us, but Feinstein works his appearance into her narrative with particular deftness. He was a great-grandson on his mother's side of an African slave who had become a protege of Peter the Great. He inherited several African characteristics, such as hair, features and skin colour, and this seemed to annoy his mother, though perhaps no more than everything else about him. He himself was, or appeared to be, proud of his African features, and they clearly caused no annoyance to the women with whom before his marriage he was a marked success. His allusions to God's help in his sexual exploits were either a manner of speaking or a ribald joke, or perhaps a sign of how little he needed it.

Whatever his real opinion of his own looks he was certainly obsessed by the subject. He perpetually doodled sketches of a male profile. All the drawings were alike: looking to the left and with a firm outline from the top of the brow to the tip of the nose, which suggested a ski-slope. The details of the heads show many variations – a tonsure, a patch of natural baldness, side-whiskers, a professional collar, a cravat – but the profile, checked against authentic portraits, is always his. His height, specified by his brother Lev as being 'no more than five feet', was what seemed to bother him most. It bothered others, too. A highly suitable girl whom he wished to marry refused him partly on the grounds that he was not tall enough. When it was a question of fame not marriage people were tactful. In a well-known group portrait of Russian writers, the composition is diplomatic. Pushkin stands fairly well back and the ground seems to slope up in his favour; and he is placed next to the fattest of the writers so that he looks slender rather than short.

Of the sketches that Pushkin drew in the margins of his manuscripts, most harrowing are those of the hanged Decembrists, mostly his friends. By name at least the Decembrists are probably better known in Britain than Pushkin himself. They were failed revolutionaries, always popular. Hanged men look tall. Not for nothing did the dreadful word 'stretched', meaning hanged, enter the English language in the sixteenth century. The pitiless bungling with which these particular executions were carried out – some of the ropes broke and the process had to be repeated – would have made the word more horribly accurate. Pushkin put his heart into the drawing of these men and for the rest of his life mourned their fate and that of the other conspirators, again mostly his friends, who were sent into exile.

> The helmsman perished and the crew.
> But the abating tempest threw
> Me, the mysterious bard, ashore,
> Of all that ship the only one;
> I dry my wet robe in the sun
> And sing the songs I sang before.

The lines are from the poem 'Arion'.

Any account of Pushkin's life has to make much of the Decembrists. At many points he came very close to them. Feinstein traces this association with due emphasis, starting from the days when, still not twenty years old, he wrote poems such as 'Ode to Freedom', which the burgeoning movement for political reform used as rallying cries.

> Fallen slaves, take heart like men
> Listen to these words and rise.

These were also the days when he freely alluded to tyrants and the voice of history and, though his friends tried to shut him up, had a habit of shouting anti-Tsar jibes in the theatre.

For such seditious behaviour he was, unsurprisingly, sent into exile, and was only too thankful that it was to South Russia and not Siberia. After that he was to become more or less a professional exile. (To lose one's liberty more than once looks like carelessness.) In the course of the next five years he met fully-fledged Decembrists and consolidated his links with old school-friends with whose ideas, approaching those of the Decembrists, he had always had great sympathy. These friends, old and new, appreciated his support and felt that he would be a good person to have beside them in a coup – he was no coward. But he was a dangerously indiscreet conspirator at the planning stages. His friends all said so and he was never taken into anyone's confidence.

The military coup so long anticipated took place on 14 December 1825. Pushkin was at that time at Mikhailovskoe, his family's estate. He had set out for St Petersburg two weeks before, nobody knows why, but turned back in mid-journey, again nobody seems to know why. He said it was because his path had been crossed by two hares and a priest. As he was known to be superstitious this story was taken quite seriously. In any case the auguries of disaster proved to be reliable. The coup failed miserably. As Pushkin later scrawled near the relevant sketches in his notebook, 'I, like a clown, might have hanged'; 'clown' was an odd word in the circumstances.

When readers come across a poet who was five feet tall they are bound to think of Keats. Feinstein does, and could have developed the theme further, for there are other similarities between the poets. There are also striking differences, two in particular: first, class and background, and secondly, taste in poetry. Pushkin, who had been introduced to the work of Byron in his South Russian exile, initially and for a long time adored him. Keats, though he spoke enthusiastically about Byron and quoted him with ease, did not. He had to endure the irritation of being mentioned in the same breath. As he wrote to his brother and sister-in-law, 'You speak of Lord Byron and me. There is this great difference between us. He describes what he sees. I describe what I imagine. Mine is the hardest task.' Rather a good way of calling a fellow poet facile.

Neither Pushkin nor Keats thought that his own appearance disqualified him from demanding exceptional beauty in the woman of his choice and neither expected, or apparently wished, her to be intelligent or capable of appreciating poetry. Pushkin, generalising about women and literature, jotted down a few eloquent reflections. 'Poetry slides over them without touching their souls; they are insensitive to its harmony... Listen to their literary judgements and you will be surprised by the distortion and even the crudeness of their understanding... Exceptions are rare.' Feinstein comments: 'He did not woo any of the exceptions as a wife.' Neither did Keats. Fanny Brawne did notice that he loved her only for her beauty and made a 'half-complaint' about his attitude. But she was never able to put it to the test: Keats died much younger than Pushkin.

A final similarity between the two poets is the way in which Natalya and Fanny were discussed in later years, as having been frivolous, irresponsible, silly and a drag on their talented menfolk. Fanny came out of this better, having turned into nothing worse than a mildly derogatory legend, which was finally dispelled by the publication of some of her letters. Well into the twentieth century, however, Natalya has been the object of considerable contempt: Anna Akhmatova, for example, often became vituperative about her. Comparatively little has been said about either Pushkin or his wife in this country, but in a recent broadcast Gwyn Williams described Natalya as a 'good-natured bimbo', not a very fierce comment but not a tribute one would choose to have on one's tombstone. Well-informed about the problems of Natalya's upbringing, Feinstein is balanced in her presentation of her importance.

The Pushkin marriage started off with impeccable behaviour on both sides, apart from her lack of interest in his work, which was no surprise. As time went by, however, her main, almost her only, ambition was to shine in society: to receive an invitation to every prestigious ball and to attend them all, sumptuously dressed and universally desired. She succeeded, and danced her way through several pregnancies, though Pushkin begged her to stick to quadrilles else she 'might miscarry on the 105th step of the Tsar's staircase'. All this sounds innocent enough and quite possibly was, but it led to trouble, and by stages which Feinstein skilfully examines, to the duel in which Pushkin was killed. She has cast considerable light on these circumstances by making use of the substantial collection of letters discovered earlier this decade and published in St Petersburg in 1995. The writer of the letters was d'Anthès, the duellist who shot Pushkin and who had been accused of being Natalya's lover.

Unlike Robin Edmonds, Feinstein does not shirk the challenge of introducing Pushkin's poetry to readers who know no Russian, though she is able to deal with many topics relevant to the poems, such as Pushkin's sense of history, without necessarily referring to his poetic techniques. In the chapter entitled '*The Bronze Horseman*', for example, she sets out the historical and political issues involved in the great flood of St Petersburg, briefly outlines the story of the poem, and then, for the greater part of the chapter, returns to pure biography. The Tsar comes into it, interfering with Pushkin's work as usual, and so do Pushkin's domestic affairs, with the arrival in Moscow of his two sisters-in-law, one of whom is to play a strong part in the action. There appears to be nothing about the style of the poem or what it sounds like.

There is, however. It is in the translation. Feinstein presents a great many English versions of Pushkin's poems, or extracts from them. Some of them are her own translations, others are by Antony Wood, A.D.P. Briggs and

D.M. Thomas, all experienced and with idiosyncrasies of their own. The considerable variety in the way the translators work suits Pushkin's own versatility. The lines Feinstein quotes from her own rendering of *The Bronze Horseman* demonstrate how plainly he could write, without any figures of speech, and convey a strong impression that we are hearing Pushkin's tone. Here is poor Evgeny looking for his sweetheart when the flood is beginning to die down and finding that her house and she herself have been swept away.

> Here is the place where their house stands
> Here is the willow. There was a gate.
> That has been swept away. But the house?

The epilogue to Feinstein's biography first rouses indignation at the spiteful refusal of his country's authorities to honour Pushkin's death or allow others to do so, but goes on to evoke feelings of triumph at the establishment of his reputation, which has survived, and at times even seemed to dominate, the Soviet era. Anna Akhmatova is given the last word. With her usual animation she points out that the people who in the days of Pushkin's greatest popularity considered themselves to be major figures compared with him are now identified, if at all, as 'contemporaries of Pushkin'. Those characters who thought so much of themselves are now to be found, probably with their dates wrong, in the indexes to editions of Pushkin's work.

Mixed Marriages*

'I believe the description of himself, me and our marriage to be a fiction' writes Ursula Creagh (who twenty years ago was Mrs Alvarez), in the current number of the *London Review of Books*. The second chapter of A. Alvarez's *Life after Marriage: Scenes from Divorce*, romantically and not very originally entitled 'Myself when young', consists of his account of their

* From the *Listener*, 10 June 1982. Review of *Life after Marriage: Scenes from Divorce* by A. Alvarez, and *The Marrying Kind* by Brenda Maddox.

brief married life and certainly does sound unconvincing as fact. Particularly hard to believe is the famous scene – I feel it may become famous in its way though possibly not the way he meant – in which the bride's first and only recorded words on the day after the wedding are (à propos of the toast he has so kindly brought upstairs for her breakfast) 'You didn't cut off the crusts.' Even his reply: 'Pardon?' sounds strangely Coronation Street (to English ears) for someone who aims to handle words so finely.

A note of petty insult pervades all his references to her. She herself writes with much greater dignity, though with reasonable resentment. In the previously-mentioned article she attributes his spite to his natural wish for a repetition of the bestseller status accorded to *The Savage God*. 'The fact that our marriage was a drab and commonplace failure like countless others was plainly quite unacceptable. No one was going to buy *that* book.' So up came the images of a brainy sensitive accomplished young writer and an uneducated insensitive virago.

The crusts became a leitmotif. Several pages after the first mention:

'The crusts. You have to cut the crusts off to let the steam out.'
'Pardon?' I said.
But she did not reply, then or ever.

Well, she has now.

Alvarez's original intention, he tells us in the preface, was 'to write a book on divorce rather like my study of suicide: a kind of critical meditation, with some history and philosophy, but above all literary and personal'. Even though later he felt inclined to modify the method, giving greater weight to private conversations, 'without benefit of theories or statistics', the formula is in fact much the same as before. Searching Roget for some polite alternative to the word hotchpotch I have come up with gallimaufry or perhaps pot-pourri.

His version of his own first attempt at marriage is followed by a chapter on Lawrence and Frieda whose joint spirit 'brooded unnaturally, as a model and as an inspiration' over it. His hero and heroine sound, as they nearly always do in books, no more than rather tiresome, but the sufferings of the Weekley children make highly distressing reading. After this, by means of one of those tenuous chronological links beloved by historical novelists ('in 1911, the year before Frieda eloped with Lawrence, Edith Wharton published a story "Autres Temps"... ') we arrive in New York to over-hear a conversation – one of those without benefit of theories or statistics – between the author and a woman whose Bostonian grandmother Charlotte had been the model for Edith Wharton's heroine Mrs Lidcote. The encounter is embellished with the sort of imaginative details (beloved by biographers) that nobody could possibly have known, about scenes that took place in private over half a century before ('Charlotte fluttered her hands, smiled sweetly... ') but adds nothing much to the general theme.

Alvarez now turns historian and we are presented with a panorama of divorce through the ages. Much of it is usefully informative; though clearly many of the readers are going to be either ignorant or foreign, for surely an English person likely to read the book would know roughly where Henry VIII stood in the matter of divorce.

The versatility of the writing is extraordinary for after this we arrive at Alvarez the Novella. The stories of Leo and Emma, on their way into divorce, and of Katherine and her 'touchy English husband', on their long march the other side of it, are both very grippingly told. The book ends with a tone poem.

Brenda Maddox's advice to homosexuals who are about to marry heterosexuals is, on the whole: don't; though she mentions interesting exceptions. *The Marrying Kind* tells us all that we ever needed to know about married homosexuals – if we did – except the really relevant thing which apparently nobody knows: what made them homosexuals in the first place. The tone throughout is sympathetic and knowing in a woman's page kind of way. There is no eavesdropping or looking through keyholes; there is in fact no call for any sort of prying as in the series of interviews which form the core of the book the subjects seem hell-bent on revealing all.

The very first sentence gives the feeling of the whole book:

> Chain-smoking peacefully, sipping Perrier, oblivious of the flirtatious young waiter with the prep school accent, a lawyer sits in a New York restaurant searching his mind for memories of his marriage.

Mrs Maddox interviewed a great number of homosexuals, male and female, and the heterosexual women and men they married. In some cases she has given them false names, but by no means all; when it comes to some statements, such as those of Hallam Tennyson, for example, she is explicit. She claims that in no case has she altered the person's actual words and I am sure this is true. What amazes me is that she seems to believe what everybody says even when she knows nothing else about him or her. She is one of the believing kind.

Remembering and Forgetting*

In *Souvenirs* Roy Fuller both claims and demonstrates that he can remember very little about the events of his earlier life, which is in a way unfortunate as they are the subject of the book. He was born in 1912, to a fluctuating middle-class environment, and spent his youth for the first eight years near and in Oldham, after that in Blackpool. This account of his home life, schooling and professional training is wrapped in a cloud of unknowing (which would have been a good title if it had not been used already) and at many points the reader cannot help wondering if such an extensive lack of recall is quite the best preparation for the writing of an autobiography: 'I seem to think... ', 'I will guess... ', 'I do not know... ', 'nothing remains in my memory of the occasion', 'a context that now escapes me'.

Whether or not this is a good method, it is perfectly deliberate. Mr Fuller prefers ignorance even when speaking of events that could easily be verified. His Aunt Minnie 'became Matron (or possibly merely Assistant Matron) of the Manchester Royal Infirmary.' Well, which? I should have liked to know whether Aunt Minnie got to the top or remained at the last col. 'My grandfather died, I think in 1937.' It would not have been a labour of Hercules to have unearthed the date. Alternatively he need not have hazarded a date at all.

But Roy Fuller believes in the innate significance of forgetting, a view which is at least familiar to twentieth-century readers. Whether it is sympathetic or not depends on the context. When it is a question of the names of stations on the railway line from Manchester to Oldham, guessing rather than checking is quite an interesting game. When he says of a schoolfriend, however, 'I rather think he was killed in the War' his imprecision sounds heartless.

The book is thoroughly artful. It has to be, with such gaps in the material. Fuller compensates for what he calls his 'morbidly defective' memory in three principal ways. Firstly he makes a feature of this handicap, almost a leading character. He discusses its mysterious birth: it does not proceed, as he once thought, from his training as a lawyer, nor is it systematic enough

---

* From the *Listener*, 21 February 1980. Review of *Souvenirs* by Roy Fuller and *The Reign of Sparrows* by Roy Fuller.

to be the offspring of self-justification. But it is interesting and does him credit. Secondly, he avoids sustained narrative. There is, he explains, chronological progression but essentially the work is a set of variations. Thirdly, he makes ample use of the journalistic device (described by Claud Cockburn in his own autobiography) where a question asked in genuine ignorance manages to suggest positive knowledge: 'Could she even then have been suffering from her terminal illness?'

Complete anecdotes by the very nature of the method we cannot expect. We have to keep on the alert for glimpses and make the most of them. At one point we catch sight of the author as an articled clerk watching guiltily from his office window some unemployed friends in the street below:

> a feeble procession I had helped the National Unemployed Workers Movement to organise but which it was tolerantly recognised I was in the wrong social position to join myself.

There is one approach to a set piece: the post-war meeting of Roy Fuller, by then a recognised poet, with Edith Sitwell:

> She was of such an eminence that selected guests were one by one invited to sit by her. As I once waited in the wings, as it were, William Plomer whispered to me: 'Isn't she exactly like Max Miller?' There was certainly some resemblance in the long nose and smooth skin, but the association was really made plausible by the poet's wearing a species of white bowler hat.

The Reign of Sparrows, Roy Fuller's new collection of poems, is very much a companion volume to *Souvenirs*. The title is taken from 'Hedge-sparrows and house-sparrows', one of the poems published a few years ago in a pamphlet by Ceolfrith Press and included in this book. It is a charming poem. The concern is genuine but by its nature ineffectual, in the same way that our Heavenly Father's notorious sympathy for sparrows cannot, or at any rate does not, afford them any actual protection. The mature Fuller seems to be looking down from above as the young Fuller did on the vulnerable demonstrators in the street below: a member of a different species and therefore unable to join in.

Characters from the autobiography reappear in the poems when there is a point to be developed; for example, the violinist of the orchestra at the Metropole, Blackpool, who killed himself when his wife died. 'Odd fate' comments Fuller in 'To George Woodcock, in his and the author's sixty-fifth year',

For someone utterly *moyen sensuel,*
Although response to Bruch's *schmalz* (our own
Not least) must always put us on our guard.

It is pleasant to meet again the poem 'Crisis' that won the *New Statesman*'s
Prudence Farmer Poetry Prize in 1976. Here we have the true Fuller
modesty, both of subject matter and personal stance. At the time of the
competition the judge did his best to point out depths but it remains an
engaging poem about a man buying a pair of trousers at a sale. But the
modesty is an almost complete defence, especially when embodying a
compliment to the 'courteous ladies of the West Countree'. We feel it is
all we need to ask, which is a pity.

A Professional's Diary*

'Floreat Bloomsburga' wrote Raymond Mortimer to Virginia Woolf in
the early Twenties, the heyday of all three. One of the most significant
events in this second volume of Woolf's diary, which covers the years 1920
to 1924, is the removal of herself and her husband from 'beautiful and
lovable' Hogarth House in Richmond to the Bloomsbury with which she
already had such a complication of ties, and such a quizzical involvement.
('How good, kind, tender and clever we all are!') It is easy to share her
horror of the 'long, cold, exhausting journey' back to Richmond after
theatres and dinner parties but it would be impossible, after the changes
fifty years have brought, to appreciate without her eloquent guidance the
enchantment of London as entered from Tavistock Square. 'I step out upon
a tawny coloured magic carpet and get carried into beauty without raising
a finger. The nights are amazing, with all the white porticoes and broad
silent avenues.' 'I must here break off to go to the post, down that
wonderful lamplit street.'

But of course Bloomsbury was not only a pretty face. It was god-like
in being a spirit; and it is the heat of Virginia Woolf's portion of this spirit

---

★ From the *Listener*, 24 August 1978. Review of *The Diary of Virginia Woolf Volume
II*, edited by Anne Olivier Bell.

that scorches the inhabitants and works of other districts – which might as well be Sioux territory – particularly South Kensington. ('I detest the mixture of ideas and South Kensington.') Her wonderful description of the 'party to discuss Ireland' given by Naomi Royde-Smith ('never did I see a less attractive woman') is radiantly malicious: the clergymen whose attitude seemed to be 'See how free and playful and advanced we are – yet we have not sacrificed niceness. We are people of the world. Very open-minded. Not mere intellectuals – no – look how nicely we dress'; Lady Rhondda, a cut above the others, more of a solid bulldog; Rose Macaulay chipping in with her witticisms at which 'everyone laughed loud, as if Rose had done the thing they expected'. Woolf comments, rather unnecessarily, 'I disliked it all a good deal' and then sums up: 'There's no bite about these people. I thought of Bloomsbury. But then in Bloomsbury you would come up against something hard – a Maynard, or a Lytton or even Clive.'

You would indeed. Never can these men have been better described than she describes them, particularly Lytton Strachey. She may have fallen asleep twice while he was reading aloud the opening chapters of *Queen Victoria*, but she missed nothing else.

It is difficult not to be envious of the privileges that Virginia Woolf enjoyed. To hear, in the course of a few days, T.S. Eliot reading *The Waste Land* at your own fireside and to sit at your own dining-room table discussing the progress of *Passage to India* with E.M. Forster is the apotheosis of privilege. Yet from time to time many readers may experience, as I do, a perverseness of spirit that makes one prefer to identify with the wife of the Vicar of Rodmell whose chief drama, according to the conversation so witheringly transcribed, was that the shop had sent her a plain cake instead of a fruit cake.

There is so much that is robust and even swashbuckling in the diaries of these years that it is tempting to quote from such passages to the relative exclusion of the painful entries, for though Woolf speaks in the matter-of-fact tones of someone who has no wish and no need to exaggerate her suffering ('all the horrors of the dark cupboard of illness once more displayed for my diversion') some of her accounts are unbearably distressing, for example, the description of the wet windy night she went to meet Leonard at the station and her wild irrational terror when he was delayed.

As the diary of a writer this volume could hardly be more illuminating. At a basic level she gives information of a sort which would answer all the questions that alert non-writers ask after public readings: about sales, hours of work, reviews and all the practicalities. Yet she also reveals attitudes which would be incomprehensible probably to the uncreative and certainly to amateurs: a professionalism which asserts that successful work is 'the prime function of the soul', and an inventiveness which knows itself to be powerless without a complete mastery of technique.

The period of time covered by these diaries includes the writing and publication, in 1922, of *Jacob's Room* and the writing of *Mrs Dalloway*, which she finished in 1924. On the progress of both works she frequently comments, recording both Leonard's praise and her own doubts. Of *Jacob's Room* she writes in March 1921: 'I am not satisfied that this book is in a healthy way. Suppose one of my myriad changes of style is antipathetic to the material? Or does my style remain fixed? To my mind it changes always. But no one notices. Nor can I give it a name myself.' In November 1924: 'I am driving my way through the mad chapters of Mrs D. My wonder is whether the book would have been better without them. But this is an afterthought, consequent upon learning how to deal with her. Always I think at the end, I see how the whole ought to have been written.'

The editor, Anne Olivier Bell, points out in her introduction that whereas Virginia Woolf as letter-writer regards herself as not being on oath, as diarist she is comparatively truthful. Only comparatively, however. When she relates the story of the young man who fell off the roof at Alys Russell's dance and was killed, her editor notes that the account is substantially true, as though it might well not have been. And Woolf's account of Mrs Humphry Ward's funeral was a complete lie, as I imagine she must have known. 'It appears she was merely a woman of straw after all – shovelled into the grave and already forgotten. The most perfunctory earth strewing even by the orthodox.' In fact, as Mrs Bell tells us, Mrs Humphry Ward had 'a tremendous send-off'.

Woolf speaks of her diary as 'a kindly blank faced old confidante' but this is disingenuous too. Her frequent use of 'as I say' proves that this is communication on a wide scale, not self-expression or a strictly limited confidence. She is speaking to the public, but one at a time, in the manner of a good radio broadcaster.

Mrs Bell has managed the footnotes admirably. She appeals to us to imagine that information we might consider superfluous could be valuable to others; this puts us on our mettle but is not really necessary. There is only one annotation in the entire book that seems to me superfluous: the gloss on *The Beggar's Opera*. More important is her decision, in this volume, to omit nothing, and this seems right too. It must have been tempting to exclude remarks which defy justification, like 'The fact is the lower classes *are* detestable.' But in the total context Virginia Woolf admits to more than anyone could accuse her of. Her honesty about her jealousy of Katherine Mansfield is heroic.

Volume II of *The Diary* is hauntingly impressive. To meet with anything like it we may have to wait till Volume III.

It's a Battlefield*

'Loved him, hated her', or vice versa, is the most interesting attitude for any writer to adopt when narrating a love story that ends in discord; the six-of-one approach would be boring. In this case it is very much vice versa and *Your Isadora* is a very interesting book. In the introductory chapter Francis Steegmuller gives a useful account of the work of his protagonists, Gordon Craig and Isadora Duncan, before going on to describe their romance, and in this account he accords Craig his full due as stage designer and producer, speaking of his achievements with respect and of his complicated and often self-defeating personality with sympathy. It is later on, when Craig is hurting Isadora, that Mr Steegmuller becomes a partisan, committed and caustic.

In fact we are not shown Craig, as a creative artist, behaving so very badly. He was arrogant and explosive, but often with reason: to have part of one's stage design lopped off by carpenters because it didn't fit the theatre would infuriate anybody, and he was not the only creative artist to be unable to work with others. And Bernard Shaw's remark, quoted in the book: 'Gordon Craig has made himself the most famous producer in Europe by dint of never producing anything' is seen to be more amusing than true.

It was as lover and father that he failed. At the time of his first meeting with Isadora, in Berlin in 1904, he was thirty-two and already the father of eight acknowledged children by three women, all of whom he had more or less abandoned, though they had not all abandoned him. (When Craig gave women up they tended to hand themselves back to him.) He led Isadora an ugly dance. Though he was always generous about her as an artist, he was generous in no other way, not with his company nor his compassion, and certainly not with his money; here again it was very much vice versa. When she was lonely he recommended solitude; when she needed support he sang the praises of renunciation. He wrote insulting and jeering remarks on the loving letters she sent him and left them for posterity to read.

More than two hundred of Isadora's letters to Craig, previously unpublished, are printed here. They are not great literary compositions, though

---

* From the *Times Literary Supplement*, 31 January 1975. Review of *Your Isadora* edited by Francis Steegmuller.

some of the earlier ones have a beautiful shape and movement on the page, rather like a dance. It is perhaps unfair to find her baby talk irritating, as she is not addressing us, but a grown woman who refers to herself as 'Topsy me' who is 'wery wery sick' and says to her lover 'You is the most Wonderfullest man in the world' and 'Me comes to Berlin if you telegraphs' makes one feel that babies have a lot to answer for. Some of her more cloying sentiments, such as 'There are *no* complications which Love cannot make simple' and her perpetual references to Beauty make one yearn for a little astringency, but she was not a great writer or a great thinker and never pretended to be.

She was a great dancer. The inevitable weakness of any book about her (or indeed any film, as long as actresses who cannot dance are given the part) is that this cannot be adequately conveyed. In reading about her one has continually to remind oneself that she was an international star, a household word, a woman after whom a great many people and things were named, including long scarves of the type which strangled her.

This is not to say that no such book was needed; on the contrary. Mr Steegmuller has assembled his material skilfully. The letters form the chief part of the book but he connects them with narrative links, with quotations from Isadora's *My Life* and Craig's book *Topsy* (which needless to say give luridly conflicting accounts of such incidents as their first meeting) and with drafts of letters that Craig wrote, though he did not necessarily send, to Isadora. The story so constructed moves from early and brief happiness to the birth of their child Deirdre; then to what must have been the second worst happening of Isadora's life: Craig's brutal rebuff of her in Florence; then to her liaison with Singer and the horror of the drowning of her two children; and finally to a summary of her last seven years during which it seems she and Craig never met.

One document which is put to particularly good use is the autobiography-cum-diary of Kathleen Bruce, who later married Scott of the Antarctic and later still Lord Kennet. She gallantly kept Isadora company during the last weeks of waiting for the birth of Deirdre at the Villa Maria, a small house by the sand dunes on the north coast of Holland. Her comments cast a dollop of cool commonsense into the heady love potion concocted by Isadora, and break the spell woven by Isadora's own account of herself and Craig and their relationship. Kathleen Bruce disliked Craig who though 'he was to be treated as the Messiah' had 'low-bitten nails which betrayed the brute in him'. At one point, however, she does him justice by acknowledging as Isadora did not, that he was in the house at the time of the birth. How, if at all, he participated she does not say; it is hard to imagine him helpfully boiling up kettles of water. But though, according to her vivid account, he was frequently, during his stay at the

Villa Maria, as bleak and tempest-surrounded as Mount Everest, at least, like Everest, he was there.

As a dancer Isadora Duncan was outstandingly calm, serene and self-contained; everybody said so who saw her in her professional capacity. In her letters and in her private life she was none of these things for long. Certainly her conflicts were real, and enough to banish such qualities. She longed for motherhood yet realised that a baby would stop her dancing, temporarily and perhaps permanently. She longed to bind Craig to her by devotion yet could not for one moment contemplate sacrificing her art to this end. Perhaps the most touching of her difficulties was her almost total inability to admit that all was not well between herself and Craig. She went on blessing him for his wonderful letters at a time when, if the drafts are anything to go by (and presumably they are), she can have been receiving little comfort from them. Isadora Duncan might never have heard of the sentiment that once is happenstance, twice is coincidence and three times is enemy action. Craig was always telling her either how weak or how strong she was, depending on his own mood and needs at the time. Her revealing letters show that it was both her strength and her weakness that she could not or would not recognise enemy action.

Randall Jarrell's Cruelty*

Randall Jarrell's letters in the volume so entitled tell us as much about his generation as they do about himself and are therefore doubly welcome. The biographical commentary provided by editor Mary Jarrell, the poet's second wife, is skilfully organised, highly informative and quite startlingly detached.

I had already read and enjoyed Eileen Simpson's *Poets in their Youth* which speaks of almost exactly the same set of people – John Berryman, R.P. Blackmur, Randall Jarrell, Robert Lowell, John Crowe Ransom, Delmore Schwartz, Allen Tate, Robert Penn Warren and others – and I found it rewarding to contemplate the two books together.

---

* From the *Listener*, 13 February 1986. Review of *Randall Jarrell's Letters*, edited by Mary Jarrell.

Eileen Simpson has no hesitation in describing as a group the poets on whom she concentrates. She quotes and endorses Lowell's lines about Berryman:

> Yet really we had the same life
> the generic one
> our generation offered.

She has a strong point. A composite Poet-in-his-Youth of about Randall Jarrell's age (he was born in 1914) would in the course of time graduate, teach at university, take part in the Second World War either as combatant or conscientious objector, win literary prizes (the Pulitzer, the Bollingen, the Academy of American Poets award), contribute original work to, review in, edit or simply feud with, the appropriate magazines (the *Nation*, *The New Republic*, *Kenyon Review*, *Partisan Review*), be appointed Poetry Consultant to the Library of Congress, go into analysis, experience breakdown, and die prematurely, possibly of his own volition. And of course know all the others and write letters to them.

Randall Jarrell did nearly all these things. Yet – and in this too he resembled the others – he stood out as a most distinctive individual. Both he and his wife state categorically that he was not gregarious. But he very often speaks as though there was a flock somewhere around: from his greetings in an early letter ('Give my love to Cenina and Cleanth and Tinkum and Albert') to later letters in which he writes to Robert Lowell about how Blackmur did a wonderful review of Trilling in *Kenyon Review*, to John Crowe Ransom about how he can hardly wait to see Robert Penn Warren's long poem 'Brother to Dragons', part of which Ransom is printing in *Kenyon*, and to Warren about his nomination of John Crowe Ransom for the Academy of American Poets award.

One of the things at which Jarrell excelled them all and for which he became widely known was the ferocity of his criticism. In 1948 when he was first teaching at the Woman's College of the University of North Carolina (where eventually he was to end his career) the whole question of how he could be as cruel as he was, if he was, received a thorough airing in his letters as well as in print. The review he wrote for the *Nation* of Conrad Aiken's *The Kid* concluded: 'There is something a little too musically ectoplasmic, too pretty-pretty, about Mr Aiken's best poems; but one longs for them as one wanders, like an imported camel, through the Great American Desert of *The Kid*.' This review, mildness itself by the standards of at least two British hatchetmen, provoked a violent response from Aiken in which he spoke of attempted murder and of Jarrell as 'this self-appointed judge and executioner', suggesting that he was 'condemned in advance to condemn in advance, and therefore to look with glee for faults about which he can be funny rather than with love for virtues that can be praised.'

This particular accusation was one that Jarrell had already denied, in a letter to the *New Republic* some years before, in connection with Aiken's work, and he denied it again now, in a letter to the *Nation*. Not everybody was convinced. John Berryman roundly said, 'He was immensely cruel, and the extraordinary thing about it is that he didn't know he was cruel.' But, he explained, Jarrell hated bad poetry so much that he could not realise that human beings wrote it.

From his letters it appears to have been not quite like that. Robert Penn Warren said of him in his student days, 'He was overwhelmed by the spectacle of human dumbness', a comment which he was to echo in a wartime letter to his first wife: 'If this world were cleverer I'd be happier.' His attitude seems to have been not so much arrogant delight that he was brighter than other people as sadness that they were stupider than himself. If this is so it makes marginally more amiable his otherwise appalling remark about his students: 'The average North Carolina girl talks as if she were an imbecile with an ambition to be an idiot.'

In a youthful letter to Edmund Wilson, Jarrell declared his belief in a very precise difference between poetry and prose: 'A poem doesn't exist till it's written but prose is what you think or say anyway.' This is intelligible, not to say simplistic; but it is infinitely arguable, and the argument is relevant to *Randall Jarrell's Letters*. So many poems, sent with letters, are included in this collection and the material presented in prose is so often treated simultaneously in poetry that Jarrell's dictum is being put constantly to the test.

To take an example: in 1943 during his months of military training at Chanute Field, Illinois, Jarrell spent a short leave visiting the University of Illinois. Whilst there he wrote a poem 'The Soldier Walks under the Trees of the University' and this he sent to his wife within hours of its being written. To read it now embedded in the surrounding letters is to recall the advice traditionally offered to adult actors about the dangers of appearing with children and animals.

The poem has a weary composure and a predictable philosophy which may well be part of war but which makes it come across as something you might think or say anyway. Whereas Jarrell's prose descriptions of army life and the occasional respites from it – in Texas and Arizona as well as at Chanute – steal the show: energetic, unrehearsed, almost blurted out, as though they had not existed before they were written. And so, except for the occasional self-conscious *mot*, do most of the other letters. Jarrell's dividing line may have fallen in the wrong place or he may have been mistaken as to what was on which side of it.

Some Other Lady?*

The publishers make no claims as to the authenticity of this book, which purports to be the diary, written between 1933 and l948, of a German woman living in Germany with her husband, a high-ranking Nazi, during this period. There is no mention of a translator. The writer tells us that she knew very little English at the time, and if she later acquired enough to translate from the original herself it would have been interesting to know that this is what she had done. And politic on the part of the publishers, too, for it would have engagingly explained some of the stylistic banalities. We are given no details of the provenance of the diaries. There is no caption that identifies the young woman depicted on the jacket with Hitler's arm round her (or somebody remarkably like Hitler; he is not identified either). Presumably the implication is that the photograph is of the writer but it is impossible to relate it to the exceptionally beautiful blonde girl, compliments to whose loveliness are so frequently quoted by herself in the course of the book.

The book ends with a note informing us that in 1948 the writer married an American and moved to Texas, where she still lives, and gives the dates of birth of her two daughters. It concludes: 'Her former identity is not generally known and for this reason all names except those of public figures have been changed.' But from the wealth of detail given she would not be difficult to trace.

So we are left, virtually, with Hitler, Göering and Goebbels. The story that emerges is a tragic one which, tragically, must have been only too common under the Nazi regime and indeed other regimes throughout history: the death at the hand of his masters of a man who was at first fanatically loyal to them and at last a dissenter. It deserves the most serious and honest treatment in the telling. In this case the sadness of the story cannot conceal the fact that the book reads like an inept novel in diary form or a diary titivated by hindsight.

The writer's prescience is quite uncanny. 'I would like to meet the Doktor myself!' she says when Goebbels is mentioned and eventually there she is copulating with him (from the noblest of motives). 'He was like a

---

* From the *Listener*, 9 February 1978. Review of *Nazi Lady: The Diaries of Elisabeth von Stahlenberg 1933–1948*.

rapacious ferret, all over me. In such a hurry he didn't take off his clothes, only mine. There's a bruise on my breast like a prune.' Dear Diary! (Later she forgives herself: 'Elisabeth von Stahlenberg, forget it! It meant nothing except that it saved your husband's life.') At another point she idly makes a note of the address of a family-planning clinic in the States. Little did she know that fifteen years later she would be going to the States to live.

It is almost as if she knew who was to be in the news in the late Seventies. She and an English friend go to lunch at the Osteria Bavaria hoping to see the Führer. 'The owner put us at a table where we could see the door and everyone coming in. "This is where the other English girl always sits," he said, and Liz says she'll ask among her friends and find out *who* it is.' Sure enough, Unity Mitford – for it is she – appears some pages later.

Into the diary together go frivolities and solemnities in a way that might be expected to produce a just-like-life effect but in fact give the opposite impression:

> Liz has taught me how to make English Trifle, she says you need the special ingredient Bird's Custard, and is going to ask her mother to send me a tin and if she goes to London will bring me one back herself. We're all going to go to Nuremberg for the Rally, so she won't go till after that.

In case the prospect of such political profundities should daunt readers I add that there is a description of a kitchen-table abortion ('There was a moment of such excruciating agony that I screamed') and much talk about contraceptives, in and out of season, mostly in season, I admit, as when the heroine arranges to meet Goebbels: 'Remember,' she tells herself, 'to wear your French perfume, your crêpe de chine underwear and your Dutch cap.'

At the end the writer muses, 'It's really as if it all happened to some other lady.' Quite.

Merry Wife of Windsor*

The most terrifying comment made on the Abdication may well be that of Lord Beaverbrook, writing twenty years after the events in which he played such a prominent part: he is convinced that if the British people had been less absorbed in the affair of Edward VIII and Mrs Simpson the energy thus saved might have been used to avert world war. Possibly the same remark might be made today, for popular, even best-selling, books and plays are still being written about the protagonists.

One of the first books about Mrs Simpson, as she still was, must have been Edwina H. Wilson's *Her Name was Wallis Warfield*, for it was published, in New York, in December 1936, before the issue was decided. ('Suppose – just suppose – an American girl should become Queen of England!'). The volume is worth looking at, for it sets the style of much that has been written since, and the tone is of an unpretentious idiocy which is engaging rather than otherwise. Everything British is explained as if to educationally sub-normal Martians.

There is a great deal, of course, about following the dictates of one's heart and people drawing other people to them like magnets, but that is only the background. What is irresistible to the readers (the book went into three printings in a fortnight) is the account of Mrs Simpson's furs, nail varnish, jewellery and accomplishments e.g. 'She can complete a jigsaw puzzle in half the time the average person takes.' The readers need not despair, however; 'those who envy Wallis Simpson her success' are given hints to guide them, such as: 'A wise hostess never entertains at the same time her bridge-playing friends and those who shun the game.'

All this is accurate and well-researched, no doubt, but in one respect Edwina H. Wilson is wrong. In spite of her assertions that whatever happens Mrs Simpson 'IS queen – QUEEN OF ROMANCE', her subordinate clauses give her away: à propos of *their* first meeting she writes, 'It was – at least it may have been – a night to make history'; clearly if Mrs Simpson does not bring it off, the waters will close over her. In fact, they never have.

Writers concerned with the politics of the Abdication obviously do not

---

* From the *London Review of Books,* 16 October 1980. Review of *The Duchess of Windsor* by Diana Mosley.

indulge, at any length or at all, in revelations about Mrs Simpson's favourite colour. Lord Beaverbrook, in *The Abdication of Edward VIII* (published in 1966 though written earlier, and arguably the best book on the subject) gives an account of his first meeting with Mrs Simpson which is not dismissive – in fact it is quite eloquent and certainly intriguing – but is appropriately succinct.

> She appeared to me to be a simple woman. She was plainly dressed and I was not attracted to her style of hairdressing. Her smile was kindly and pleasing, and her conversation was interspersed with protestations of ignorance of politics and with declarations of simplicity of character and outlook, with a claim to inexperience in worldly affairs. Throughout the evening she only once engaged in political conversation, and then she showed a liberal outlook, well maintained in discussion, and based on a conception which was sound.

Whether the emphasis is on politics or on gossip, the body of literature about the Windsors is large, repetitious and with a few exceptions boring. (If one has occasion to study it, a good way of keeping oneself going is to concentrate on how very variously a concept can be expressed provided the language is competently loaded; for example, Stanley Baldwin said of Edward VIII 'He has the secret of youth in the prime of age', whereas Ernest Simpson just called him Peter Pan.) In contributing *The Duchess of Windsor*, Diana Mosley has set herself a harder task than most. Her aims are good or at least interesting; their realisation was impossible.

There is bound to be an element of moral judgement in any account of the Windsors, but the Duchess has had the worst of it. The Duke, after the first accusations of dereliction of duty wore off, has been blamed principally for silliness, which is commonly supposed not to be a moral quality. Geoffrey Bocca's *She Might Have Been Queen* (1955), for instance, bears out the title by recording the long series of fatal mistakes made by the King/Duke at the time of the Abdication; it reads like a nightmare school report to the effect that Windsor could have done better. The Duchess, on the other hand, has been saddled with the Seven Deadly Sins, except perhaps Sloth.

If people feel that the Duchess should be defended then it is obviously correct for them to make the attempt, and Lady Mosley would seem a natural for the task, possessing qualifications for both the political and the personal approach. She is connected with a long tradition of knight-errantry on the Windsors' behalf: Sir Oswald led his Blackshirts through the East End in support of the King. And her own political views dispose her to a lenient interpretation of such incidents as the Windsors' respectful visit to Nazi Germany. She has known the Duchess for many years in France and can supply all the details about table decorations, weight-watching and centre partings that readers are still assumed to need. But an apologia at book length tends to defeat its own ends, unless there is some new material or a powerful argument. A repetitious listing of good qualities is not enough, especially when some of the claims strain credulity: I cannot believe that Mrs Simpson divorced Mr Simpson for his own good. The best method, surely, is the one used by A.J.P. Taylor in his editorial foreword to Beaverbrook's book: he feels that Mrs Simpson was unfairly blamed; he says so and says why, briefly.

Lady Mosley's other aim is 'to try and discover something about the woman who inspired such a deep and lasting love and the man who lavished it on her'. She clearly thinks that deep, lasting love, and especially this particular example of it, is a freak that calls for investigation, but it may be that, like the ability to dress well and serve good food (talents of the Duchess's about which she is particularly repetitious), it is more common than she supposes. But if a deep, lasting love really has to be regarded not as natural but as some kind of infatuation or obsession then it is not much good examining the object of it. It certainly seems to have been a happy marriage; Lady Mosley, with a rare approach to shrewdness, points out that photographs in which the Duke looks sad were mostly taken at family funerals.

In any case, as some people defy photography, the Duchess seems to defy any description which is simultaneously favourable, interesting and convincing. In the early Fifties both Windsors published memoirs, and neither the Duke's account of his wife, in *The King's Story*, nor hers of herself, in *The Heart has its Reasons*, makes her seem even tangible; but as both books were written by ghosts that may account for it.

The Duchess of Windsor is a curiously unworldly book. Lady Mosley really did have special knowledge of her subject; there is footnote after footnote saying 'in conversation with the author' and 'in a letter to the author', but her confidential informants seldom tell her anything very penetrating, and they are clearly a communicative set, for over the years they must also have told it to the women's magazines, the popular press and most of the rival biographers. Some of her other informants are 'ordinary people' as in 'Nothing that happened afterwards ever altered the love that ordinary people bore King Edward VIII.' I suppose these ordinary people are the ones that British election manifestos address as being the objects of the candidate's deepest concern; and I do not imagine that Lady Mosley knows many of them. I know several, and they tell me she is wrong, on this point and on many others.

She is on the wrong tack from the start; from the epigraph, in fact, which reads: 'The more alive one is, the more one is attacked.' She has apparently come to the conclusion that any form of criticism necessarily indicates that the criticised person has superior vitality and extraordinary talents. It is a comfortable belief, and would be a life-saver if the case was one's own, but when applied generally it can lead to misinterpretation. Lady Mosley really seems to believe that the infrequency of the Duchess's visits to England was master-minded by 'those in the know' who feared her, perhaps throne-toppling, popularity. 'What if the Duchess, with her breezy, friendly manner, went down all too well?'

Lady Mosley is so vehement in her denunciation of spitefulness, as directed towards the Duchess, that it is no surprise at all to find her being spiteful herself: about George V, about George VI, and particularly about Queen Mary: 'It is easy to understand why it was Queen Mary who most resented the Abdication. She was imbued with a sense of the importance of being royal, and she never recovered from having been a Serene Highness among Royal Highnesses.' As an Englishwoman living in France, Lady Mosley is ready with a special set of sneers about the way the Royal Family dress: 'The Duchess in her Paris clothes looked like the denizen of another planet among the flowery toques and pastel over-coats.'

I was quite startled to find how much these jibes annoyed me. I was at school at the time of the Abdication and we were unmoved by the event except as an occasion to exchange jokes at the back of the gymnasium. (Q. Why has the King bought a tin-opener? A. Because what he wants is in Cannes.) Nor have I been particularly concerned since. But Lady Mosley's book makes me feel, after more than forty years and in the presence of infinitely more important controversies, that I ought to be taking sides.

Memories are Made of This*

I was well into Giles Gordon's *Aren't We Due a Royalty Statement?* before I noticed that other readers were taking the book seriously, often to the point of denunciation. Up to then I had been assuming that it had set out to be an ingenious spoof, a sort of hoax or parody which had failed to make its intentions thoroughly clear; and that was nothing to be censorious about. But all leg-pullers have to declare themselves eventually, otherwise there would be no point, and as I read on it dawned on me that Gordon was not going to declare any such thing. But there is so much to support my original impression that I have still not been able entirely to give up the idea that the book *is* a spoof.

There is a kind of innocent absurdity about it, which belongs to the very nature of a good spoof. To begin with, having firmly introduced his book as an autobiography, Gordon puts on a consistent act of not being able to remember a thing, which in the circumstances seems a 'smidgen', as he would say, foolish. He cannot recall the name of the funeral parlour where Tennessee Williams lay in state, nor can he remember the venue ('some pub in Fleet Street') where he was to meet Gore Vidal. Probably it had been so with us had we been there, but we might not have thought it necessary to say so, especially if, like Gordon himself, we had not in the event bothered to visit the funeral parlour or actually speak to the live celebrity. The motif of forgetfulness is heard throughout the book. Gordon held an umbrella over Judi Dench on her way 'to I think it was Heal's in Tottenham Court Road'. He made some changes to an article by Ronald Harwood but as to what they were: 'I really can't remember.' This motif could be a useful technical device in another context but in this case it can only be a motive: to cut the great and famous down to size.

It is difficult to catch the intended tone of this book partly because Gordon presents himself as essentially a man with a keen sense of humour, and you never know where you are with people like that. He laughs in the wrong place at a friend's poetry reading. He giggles at names like Rees-Mogg, and splits his sides at the list of those who supported Count Tolstoy (ha ha) in the recent painful court case: Prince Dmitri Galitzine, for

---

* From the *London Review of Books*, 16 December 1993. Review of *Aren't We Due a Royalty Statement?* by Giles Gordon, *Yesterday Came Suddenly* by Francis King and *Excursions in the Real World* by William Trevor.

instance, and Princess Tatiana Metternich (ho ho). He finds his jokes good enough to repeat, like the one about Sue Townsend: 'creator of Adrian but no mole.' Confronted with such a merry madcap I see that I have no sense of humour at all, and am rather glad about it. On the other hand, in reading this book, I must be missing a lot of jokes. When Gordon speaks of other writers, 'including he who was to become Lord Archer', and a little later tells us that he was employed to teach Prince Andrew to write *grammatically*, I am at a loss. I feel there must be a joke in there somewhere.

Of course it is a perfectly acceptable ploy for a writer to be deliberately silly but I simply cannot decide whether or not this is what Giles Gordon is doing. When he speaks of syllabics as 'a briefly fashionable, and easy, way of writing verse by counting syllables' is he (I am assuming he knows better) being naughtily provocative or is he inventing a comic pig-ignorant character, the Alf Garnett of the world of literature? When he reveals how 'Prince Harry even let my baby daughter Lucy sit on his horse' is he lampooning people who talk like that, or is he talking like that? And then there is the mystery of his sneering. He mocks the writer of the farming column in Private Eye who, he says, 'eager to reveal his pseudonymous identity at one of their parties, introduces himself as Old Muckspreader'. (A natural and friendly thing to do, I would have thought.) Does he forget, or is it meant to be funny, that he himself is extremely eager to make sure that we all know about his own contributions to the *Eye*?

Any autobiographer who has a well-defined role, even at a lowish level, in any particular environment can reasonably be expected to give an interesting and informative account of it. We really can learn a lot from Giles Gordon about the British literary scene of the present and the recent past. The facts are there, rather too many of them sometimes: his article, as it must be called, on PLR, which is embedded in the text, contains material which deserves to be known but could more easily be acquired from a reference book. Length rather than depth is his object and many of those who would read the book might expect the latter and not need the former. It would make a splendid present for a visiting Martian. Gordon deigns to remember enough to provide a great many personalities to look out for – or to mention, should they have died. He gives an accurate portrayal, for instance, of Edith Sitwell and her ill-bred public manners. But here comes a drawback. He makes no real suggestion as to the quality of her work or the possibility that it might be good enough to counterbalance her arrogant rudeness. I do not think for a moment that it was but some do and an alien might and should be given a chance. Gordon's portraits, of course, have to be highly selective as to detail; but his choice in this respect is often unsure. Having described, quite relevantly, Arnold Goodman as 'physically a dauntingly large and hairy man', he adds that there was a Goodman brother who 'was smaller in stature'. Now I come to think of it, though, that might interest an alien.

Francis King, in his autobiography *Yesterday Came Suddenly*, writes as straightforwardly as he has always done. Every so often in the course of his long career as a novelist critics have spoken of the detachment of his style, nearly all of them meaning it as a compliment. For most of his formative years and on into middle age, King was an expatriate, born in Switzerland, spending his early boyhood in India, and in manhood working for the British Council in Italy, Greece, Finland and Japan successively. This long exile – and most of it, the British Council part, was voluntary – would affect anyone's prose style, unless of course it was the other way round, the temperament behind the prose style being the prime mover. It is significant that when he said, half-jokingly, that he felt so much at home in Japan he must in a previous existence have been Japanese, an English friend commented that it was a pity he hadn't remembered more of the language. When in 1966, at the age of forty-three, he returned to England he made Brighton, where he settled for some time, sound just like a foreign country, where they do things differently and you have to try to learn the language but not get too involved.

Detachment in an autobiography is a mixed blessing, but the calmness of King's style is rather welcome when he is speaking of both his own homosexuality and that of the men he met while working abroad. There were a great many. Indeed the reader's first impression is likely to be that the British Council in the Forties and Fifties was, by way of its staff, visiting celebrities and general contacts, only a few citizens short of a latterday Sodom. This turns out to be not quite true; a closer reading shows that in fact gays were numerically outmatched – just – by staid heterosexual husbands. It is a question of treatment. King almost invariably describes the married couples as kind – a word he cruelly overworks – and not much else. His presentation of the homosexuals, on the other hand, is lively and explicit. He refers to a respected member of the teaching staff as 'an inveterate cottager', and recounts how he arranged for Anthony Blunt, who was giving a lecture tour for the Council in Greece, to meet and assess young men ('That one's rather jolly', 'I rather like that one over there') and sometimes paid them on his behalf, a part of the proceedings about which Blunt displayed great delicacy.

He has nothing detailed or penetrating to say about the politics of the countries he lived in while working abroad, many of which were going through periods of desperate readjustment. He can give harrowingly vivid descriptions of the squalor that war had brought to many of the towns and cities he knew, but his accounts of governmental politics tend to be cursory.

His attention is caught by people. He may not explore their minds and hearts but he sees the full surface.

Back in England he soon assembled and carefully cultivated a kind of floating salon of compatriots, of both genders and varying sexual tastes, most of them known writers such as J.R. Ackerley, Ivy Compton-Burnett, L.P. Hartley. They were nearly all middle-class, by birth or advancement, and middle-aged, and as by now they are nearly all dead as well, the series of spirited portraits which forms much of the later part of King's book has an intriguing tone which is both racy and funereal. He has already told us that he likes his women friends to be difficult and in London there seems to have been no lack of choice. The sketch of Olivia Manning is one of the best. He presents her irritating, often unpleasant vagaries with something like affection.

It is part of King's technique that when he has something nasty to say he quotes somebody else as saying it: a device that is several years older than Methuselah but still seems to work. He relates that when at a British Council gathering a newcomer asked if Ronald Bottrall was handsome, Roger Hinks replied: 'Well, that all depends on whether you're attracted by men with eyes on the tops of their heads.' It was perhaps rather unwise of King, after that, to include a photograph of Bottrall which shows his eyes to have been in the normal human place. But the inclusion was probably an oversight for King would certainly not set out to discredit one of Hinks's sallies, which he admired excessively, as he did those of Maurice Bowra. His appreciative quotation of their spiteful and meaningless quips seems to indicate that he mistook inaccurate bitchiness for wit.

King's book is mercifully free of the pretence of amnesia which Giles Gordon flaunted and which has been creeping up on the reading public for some time. Penelope Mortimer's parade of forgetfulness, for example, in her recent biography *About Time Too*, knows so few bounds that the only fair comment can be *Private Eye*'s: 'Every time she says she can't remember something the reader simply thinks then why on earth am I paying you to say so?' Francis King permits himself the occasional admission of failure to recall, yes, but not all this disingenuous forgetting.

Knowing as we do that the authors of the three autobiographies under review all write or have written fiction, are all living in England, and have covered much the same period of time, we might expect them to have something in common when they turn to fact. We should be wrong. A tinker, a tailor and a soldier, living in various centuries, might well have more in common when it came to writing their life stories. It could be said, I suppose, that Giles Gordon and Francis King, though very dissimilar, stand in much the same part of the field, but no one could deny that

William Trevor in *Excursions in the Real World* is somewhere else, in a world that seems more real then theirs.

In the first place his use of memory, or perhaps one should say his relationship with it, sets him apart. He does not pretend to remember and, more significantly, he does not pretend to forget. He accepts that in this book he must renounce invention. It is an anthology of memories rather than a straightforward narrative but it begins traditionally: 'My earliest memories are of County Cork.' The chapters are arranged in more or less chronological order. In his introduction he turns the whole enterprise over to memory, explaining that this faculty alone has chosen the real people he depicts here; in an excellent clause he describes them as those 'who for one reason or another have remained snagged in the memory'. Later in the introduction he states his approach very clearly by identifying himself as 'the figure whose memory has been tapped in order to provide these forays from the territory of fiction into that of reality as it was'.

I think it is not fanciful to see this voluntary passivity expressed in Trevor's syntax. He certainly uses the passive tense or an intransitive verb much more frequently than he does in his fiction. In the schoolroom 'poster paint was produced', 'errors and aberrations were corrected'. On holiday abroad, 'postcards are written'. And – best example of all – in Venetian churches, '*lire* drop into ecclesiastical boxes'; look, no hands.

Of course, as Trevor says himself, 'in any record of personal fascinations and enthusiasms, the recorder cannot remain entirely in the shadows,' and this is certainly true in his case. Not all his fine qualities as a writer of fiction can come through into the new territory of fact – not all fiction's techniques are appropriate to autobiography – but many do. One of them is what might be called, if it were not too dull a word, decorum. After the outpourings of biographers who insist on deluging us with more than we wish to know, his delicacy is telling. It enables him to deal with sensitive material – the harrowing deterioration of his parents' marriage, for example – with no loss of eloquence.

Memory could, and presumably did, put forward many important names for him to drop if he wished, but he markedly has not used them. Any writer in search of lost time can exercise his right of veto. Almost the only authors Trevor speaks of are Somerville and Ross; they are allotted a four-page chapter and one of Lucy Willis's engaging illustrations. He never met Ross; she died before he was born. He might just have met Somerville who lived on to be ninety-one, but he says nothing of it here. Trevor's memory of them must be attached to something they were or did in their prime, something which made an impression on him later. Perhaps, for him, they represented the fraught theme of Anglo-Irishness whose implications were made even more complicated, one imagines, by the fact that

Trevor, too, was a Protestant. Somerville and Ross, daughters of the Ascendancy, considered themselves to be totally Irish, whereas the Irish they wrote about with such patronising mirth did not consider them to be Irish at all. This situation might well snag in Trevor's memory, though he writes temperately.

One of the most real of the 'real people' whom Trevor presents is Miss Quirke, the girl who 'had been found in a farmhouse at Oola, a few miles from Tipperary, where she'd been vaguely waiting for something to happen'. She was employed to teach William Trevor and his brother at their home before they went to boarding-school; she taught a stimulating hotchpotch of skills and information, not much of it apparently suited to the immediate needs of untravelled schoolboys, like the names of Parisian streets and the history of the electric chair in America. Looking back, Trevor says that 'learning was never again to be as calm or as agreeable as it was in that upstairs room with Miss Quirke'; and the boys half-suspected this at the time. It is a delightful description; the tone made me think of the 'lovely Miss' of D.J. Enright's schooldays as he evokes her in his poem 'And two good things'. As with many of Trevor's fictional characters, Miss Quirke is mysterious, at first because she is seen through the eyes of young boys but at the end because the adult author asks: 'Did she simply slip back into the County Tipperary landscape?' Although we are in the real world we feel uneasily that that is exactly what happened. After all she was 'found' there.

Now that this new book has told us so many of the facts of Trevor's life, we can see how time has worked with memory to create episodes and situations in his fiction. In the story 'Matilda's England', for example, surely his distress at the disintegration of his parents' once happy marriage has surfaced in the feelings of the child Matilda, whose glad though not fully conscious awareness of the harmony her parents enjoyed is broken for ever when her father is killed in the war. Trevor's ability to represent the passing of time is as keen as ever in this new world. Social mores process in front of us. A man kisses a strange girl: 'she'd have slapped his face in the Fifties and taken him to court in the Nineties, but in the Sixties ... everybody laughed.' His dexterity in passing from today to fifty years ago is as marked as it has ever been. In the way we all take through the dark wood William Trevor is one of the few who can look round at the past without bumping into a tree.

All and Warts*

Who deserves a biography? I suppose that in the eyes of God either everybody does or nobody. But in this imperfect world there is hot and eccentric
debate as to who does or who does not qualify. There are no objective
criteria, it seems. The zeitgeist and not the Holy Ghost is the arbiter here
on earth, and in the last few years one of its favourite subjects has been
minor women writers who have quite recently died and on whom other
women writers have become fixated.

Rosemary Sullivan's *By Heart* gives an account of the life and work of
Elizabeth Smart. The life story, which in this case has to mean love story,
is essentially trite, though the biographer does everything she can to keep
us on the edge of our seats. Her book starts at the 'historic moment' in
1937 when a rich and pretty Canadian girl walked into Better Books in
Charing Cross Road and, reasonably enough, picked up a book, after
which, again rather sensibly, she began to read it.

> The poem may have been 'Daedalus': 'The moist palm of my hand like
> handled fear ...' The words seared. On the spot she would have memo-
> rised them by heart, for she did not read books; she engrammed them.
> Who was this George Barker, so passionate, with such a roar of
> authority?

Typically, Sullivan does not think it matters whether the poem was
'Daedalus' or not; she could easily have found out, from Smart. Nor does
she reflect that there is no way of memorising except by heart; is she aiming
at a steamy pun on the title of the book or is it just tautology? She does,
however, answer her question and tell us who George Barker was, many
times in the course of the book. The information she gives is probably
necessary to many readers, for he is much less well known nowadays than
he was in the Forties, but it sometimes gives the impression of having been
selected almost maliciously. She quotes, for example, an anecdote told by
Jay Landesman, the American publisher, about Barker's visit to New York
in the Fifties, which shows the British poet,

---

* From *PN Review*, May/June 1992. Review of *By Heart: Elizabeth Smart, A Life*
by Rosemary Sullivan, and *Anne Sexton* by Diane Wood Middlebrook.

leaning against the mantelpiece and the Beat poets at his feet because they thought he was the end, their god. George bent down towards Ginsberg with a cigarette in his hand and said 'Light me, Jew.' It was uproarious, perfect George, and they loved it.

But after all, Smart's biographer could not be too scrupulous about George, totally absorbed as she was by her heroine's tale: how Elizabeth decided that Barker was to be the poet–lover of her life, how she tracked him down, broke up his marriage, had four children by him and then seemed to lose interest.

This banal story may seem to some readers not to rate four hundred pages but Elizabeth Smart, naturally enough, would have contemptuously disagreed. It was her way of life – it had to be – to assume that there was something dreadfully wrong about anybody who did not take her as seriously as she took herself: 'I am the obsessional type. Which type are you? If you are the butterfly type you will never forgive my intensity.' She certainly got the right biographer, for her requirements, that is. Many of us, though we may never have thought of ourselves as the butterfly type, might find her, as described by Rosemary Sullivan, invariably tiresome and frequently absurd. The question of forgiveness we would probably reserve for some more serious crime.

But along the protracted path of the narrative there are some rewarding backgrounds. Those reared on *Anne of Green Gables* will be quick to recognise the *mores* of Avonlea, suitably urbanised, in the Ottawa of Anne's grandchildren. And those who had any contact with the Soho of the Forties and Fifties will respond, in one way or another, to the biographer's account of the district's pubs and clubs and the posturings of men and women who imagined they were daring to be themselves at last. Of course these are not first-hand descriptions by Sullivan; it is the hopefully shocking voice of Smart that we hear as she tells of the wit and glories of the Soho which had liberated her: 'You can't reply pompously when greeted by "Hello, cunty."'

In her character as lover Elizabeth thought of herself as Dido, without the pyre. As a writer she simply thought of herself as a genius, going along with any illustrious name that suggestible critics might put forward as a comparison. Her literary judgement was undeniably frail. She could speak of Virginia Woolf and Mary Webb in the same breath as writers of equal merit, the important connection between them being that they had both stimulated her own work. Yet one has to remember her immediate recognition (if the Better Books story is true) of her literary affinity with George Barker, which was deadly accurate.

If her life hardly entitles her to a long biography, does her writing? The decision must rest on her only well-known work, *By Grand Central Station I Sat Down and Wept*, first published in 1945, a book of just over a hundred pages. It is a fantasy which follows the course of Smart's early involvement with Barker, though in the air many thousand feet above it; significantly, she started the book before she started the relationship. Her other prose books could not support any claim to a biography and only very indulgent friends could recommend her poetry.

But *By Grand Central Station*, though it has had a mixed reception over the years and many brickbats, has also received outstanding compliments. Some of them have been demonstrably inaccurate: it has, for example, been called ahead of its time, whereas it is a typical product of the Forties in full gush. It has also frequently been called a prose poem, whereas there is no such thing. And some of the adjectives lavished on it – 'raw', 'original' – are decidedly arguable.

But there is no gainsaying the extravagant praise with which many respected critics and writers, nearly all women, have greeted it: with effusive statements that there are only half a dozen such masterpieces in the world and that sort of thing. What really startled me was Beryl Bainbridge's assertion that the book was one of the factors that made her want to be a writer.

Such opinions must be given proper consideration, however much one disagrees. It is certainly right that the book should be kept in print. Readers will no doubt go on swooning with delight over it, especially as it becomes increasingly dated. But does it justify a biography for its author? I should have thought not.

Diane Wood Middlebrook's *Anne Sexton* is a very different proposition. In the first place it is better written. The style is both persuasive and seemly. The author can describe hysteria – the usual diagnosis of Sexton's illness – without becoming hysterical herself, and she lightens her account with as many dabs of humour as the unhappy story of madness and suicide permits. Her methods as a biographer are of a higher standard too. Sometimes she lapses into biographical speculation: 'One of the magazines she may have been reading as she twirled her hair into snarls that day in January 1957 was …'; but not too often. In the second place, she chose a much stronger subject. Few would say that Anne Sexton was a great poet, not even in a poor season, and it was a very rich season: her work could not reasonably be thought to stand beside that of, say, Robert Lowell, W.D. Snodgrass and Sylvia Plath. But she and her work were of significance in American poetry in many ways, all of which her biographer discusses.

It is a pity that there has been such a noise about the fact that Dr Orne, Sexton's principal psychiatrist, released the tapes of their sessions for the purposes of this biography. Such a breach of confidentiality should indeed be considered seriously by those concerned, but it is somehow extraneous to the impact of the book as a whole, even though the practice of psychotherapy in the USA at that time is at the heart of the narrative. Middlebrook relevantly brings out its dominance of the society in which Sexton moved. Over here, still, any member of a family who is in therapy is something of a freak, whereas in the Sexton story the freak was the one who was not. The many psychiatrists who treated Anne over the years come through as individuals, but also collectively, as a blend of correctness and malpractice, incompetence and dedication, just like any other body of professionals. Their chief sin, as I see it, is their notion that poetry is therapy. We are left in no doubt of their ubiquity and, presumably, their power.

Readers can forget the tapes and concentrate on what makes this biography not only justifiable but valuable. Middlebrook's vivid presentation of the American poetry scene in the Sixties could serve as a coda to Eileen Simpson's *Poets in their Youth* and so, more specifically, could her account of the rise and fall of confessional poetry. The subject has been too scantily covered, at least over here. In Britain we felt its practical repercussions, in that poets who chose not to write in this mode were derided, both at readings and in print, for being cold-hearted, prissy and (the final insult) academic. But there was little in the way of intelligent comment about who was confessing what to whom or about the poetic techniques (free association, for example) which were used.

Anne Sexton was proud to be called a confessional poet, though she would rather have been *the* confessional poet, and Middlebrook's thorough appraisal of her work is just what she would have wished and what we definitely needed. Not that it leaves us much the wiser as to what Sexton meant by confession, except that it had little to do with truth, fact, guilt, penitence, honesty or reality, as those words are commonly understood and as the word 'confession' normally suggests. 'Disclosure' would be more accurate.

There was always a lack of privacy about her and her poetry. At readings it was obviously her duty to show off in some way, but whereas the affectation of reluctance and reserve is the act of some poets, hers was straightforward self-display, which, given her beauty and her flamboyant clothes, was a wise choice. It did not go down well at the Royal Festival Hall in 1969 but was highly acceptable in general.

And for her, the actual writing of poetry, which could have been a private function, was not. She had prolonged sessions with a friend on the telephone, keeping it off the hook and whistling down it when she was ready to talk over the next bit. She discussed her work at the top of her voice at every available workshop and creative writing class. She sent her poems, as she finished them, to as many pundits as she could claim to know and they usually modified and altered them for her. Those who say about certain literary periods of the past – the age of the ballad, for example – that poems cannot be written by a committee should think again.

Diane Wood Middlebrook said recently in an interview that she found her biography of Anne Sexton a joy to re-read. She is right to be pleased. Memorably, she added: 'I worked my ass off understanding that woman.' Perhaps that is the answer to the question as to who deserves a biography: anybody who inspires a first rate biographer to work his or her ass off.

The History of Publicity*

I had not expected another book about Edith Sitwell quite so soon. There will presumably be one in nineteen years' time, as in 2000 the correspondence between the poet and the painter Pavel Tchelitchew is to be resurrected. But as recently as 1978 we had John Pearson's *Façades*, a substantial study of all three Sitwells including a very thorough account of Edith – there could never be much difference, from the point of view of material, between a book about the three siblings and a book about one of them – and now we have Victoria Glendinning's 357-page *Edith Sitwell*. In life Edith Sitwell got far more publicity than her poetry ever justified and she is still getting it.

In her foreword Victoria Glendinning seems about to tackle the important question of how good or otherwise Edith Sitwell's poetry actually was. Not that she is attempting a literary study, but she presumably realises that if she is not writing a book about a great poet she is writing a different book altogether: a case history. Disappointingly, she shies away from the question, falling back on the unreliability of the judgement of literary critics, the inevitable conditioning of all poetry readers, and finally on Stephen Spender's comment: 'In the long run poems survive because people fall in love with them.' On these grounds she believes Edith Sitwell's reputation to be secure 'in the hearts and minds of individual nonacademic

---

* From the *Listener*, 6 August 1981. Review of *Edith Sitwell* by Victoria Glendinning.

readers.' They are rather shaky grounds. In the twentieth century a list of the poems that people have fallen in love with and which have found a place in the hearts and minds of individual, and indeed collective, nonacademic readers would, I suspect, make dismal reading.

I believe that objective standards do exist. This sets me right back in Noah's Ark, I realise, but after all Noah had to make some highly influential value judgements, so I am emboldened to say that Edith Sitwell was not the greatest. She was the Mohammed Ali of the poetry scene in assertion only. But there was plenty of that:

> Mr Thomas is a young poet of genius, and Mr Turner is a well-known and practised poet, but Miss Ridler, though, I believe, a nice young person, is not qualified to discuss poetry with me. And Mr Fuller, to whom the last clause of the above sentence also applies, not only writes verses which to my mind are of no consequence, but has also had the presumption to be impertinent to me. To ask me to discuss poetry with them is like asking Sarah Bernhardt to discuss the art of acting with some nice – or nasty – young person who has appeared twice in some remote and sparsely-peopled, dusty provincial theatre.

She was outraged when a review in *Time and Tide*, by Norman Nicholson, discussed a book by Kathleen Raine together with one of hers, and to Raine's advantage.

> Is it not disgraceful? I resent nobody's success. But it is a little much that I should be insulted to bolster up this lady's-maid poetry – underbred, undervitalised, undertechniqued, messy and *déplaisant*.

I daresay that deep down where it really counts all this shows an insecurity which should evoke nothing less tender than compassion, but I find it unattractive.

Part of the trouble is that Edith Sitwell was low on originality while acting as though she was high on it. But even if she was not as great as she thought she was – nobody could be – she could not possibly be denied a place in twentieth-century poetry, and in fact she is included, and indeed very fairly represented, in all the anthologies except those in which she refused to appear because she had fewer pages than somebody else.

Dame Edith herself would have had no hesitation in attributing my comments to envy, and in one respect I do envy her. Few people attract such a sympathetic biographer as Victoria Glendinning. She is clearly partisan, which is very reasonable, indeed essential, in the circumstances. She did not start on her task with such a firm bias, for she says in the foreword: 'I have ended up with a great respect for her, and a very protective feeling.' This protectiveness is evident, and if not totally persuasive it makes one feel intermittently guilty.

Victoria Glendinning does not treat her subject with the kind of charity that would belittle them both and that would, if it were ever to prevail in general, make Judgement Day a very dull affair. She puts Edith Sitwell's insane arrogance and vindictiveness on the whole fairly before us. Some of the most damaging evidence she does leave out, such as the incident, which John Pearson includes, where Sitwell tried to persuade Ian Fleming to use his influence on the *Sunday Times* to get a bad review for a poet she disliked. But this omission may be the result of selectivity rather than partisanship. On the surface no account of a life could be less hagiographical but underneath I think we are being invited to contemplate a kind of saint, one of those who irritatingly stand on pillars and have only themselves to blame for their tribulations.

Any book about the Sitwells is half written from the start, as there is a great fund of tall stories on which a biographer can, and usually does, draw. They are all suspect, and most are demonstrably untrue. I like the story of the 'fight' between Roy Campbell and Geoffrey Grigson outside the BBC in 1949, when according to Edith the former attacked the latter for speaking ill of her work. So Grigson had; that bit is true. The rest is a farrago of lies and exaggerations. Edith had for some time experienced a wish to be fought over, and the fact that the 'fight' – in reality a minimal encounter – was not about her at all, did not hamper her in the least, After all she had been able to imagine – because she needed to – a crowd of outraged philistines with threatening umbrellas after the first performance of *Façade*. In both these cases there were witnesses to give a different version, but even when there was none, the stories usually have some essential improbability; for example, the threadbare tale of how at the age of four she had replied to a friend of her mother's that when she grew up she was going to be a genius; apart from the fact that the anecdote obviously comes out of the Young Somebody kitty, it is unlikely that in the Victorian age anybody would ask a little *girl* what she was going to be when she grew up.

Victoria Glendinning uses a great many of these stories, as John Pearson did before her, but the fact that they are custom-built, by Edith herself in accordance with her own wishful thinking, makes them more valuable to her than if they were factually accurate. They are as good as dreams. Edith was quick to mock the sexual dreams of Helen Rootham, her ex-governess and friend, and described in her autobiography how Helen was given to relating them in male company, but her own funny stories – including that one – were equally, and one assumes unintentionally, revealing.

F.R. Leavis's comment that the Sitwells belonged to the history of publicity rather than that of poetry is almost threadbare by this time, but Victoria Glendinning quotes it, as every biographer must, for it is the key to the situation. Her conclusion is, like that of judicious critics before her, that Dame Edith belonged to the history of both. Yet it is the publicity she concentrates on, from the sedate readings in the presence of Royalty to the barnstorming tours of America in the presence of absolutely everybody. We even get detailed and vivid descriptions of the Emperor's Clothes in all their brocade ostentation.

It is only every so often that Victoria Glendinning essays comment on the poetry, and when she does she reveals an anti-intellectual bias – forecast in her early use of the word 'nonacademic' – as in her reaction to Julian Symons's (perspicacious, in my opinion) criticism of 'Still Falls the Rain'. In this attitude the biographer follows her subject: 'People *will* mix up poetry and intellect.' So Keats who, according to Dame Edith, 'had no brain', made it to Parnassus nevertheless. I think they both misunderstand. When it comes to the writing of poetry, nobody, I imagine, ever supposed that intellect was enough, but few would deny that it helps. If Edith Sitwell had had a finer intellect she would have been a finer poet. And her judgement of her own work and that of others would have been less disastrously wrong.

But however much one may disagree with the points it makes, this biography is a wonderfully good read. Pace Leavis, the history of publicity is much more fun than the history of poetry, and, come to think of it, he never said otherwise.

Jane for Janeites*

A Portrait of Jane Austen is the ideal Christmas present for Janeites. Like the announcement of the birth of Mrs Palmer's baby in *Sense and Sensibility* the information may be of the greatest interest to those who know it already.

It is a handsome book. The illustrations are all interesting in themselves

---

* From the *Listener*, 10 November 1978. Review of *A Portrait of Jane Austen* by David Cecil.

even if some of them are connected only tenuously with the text: a view of Covent Garden Market, for example, is included because Henry Austen lived for a time in Henrietta Street. (Incidentally, never before have I been able to get Jane Austen's brothers and their wives so thoroughly sorted out as now.) Cassandra Austen's watercolours – the famous back-view of her sister and the less well-known portrait of Fanny Knight – have in their amateurish way a great deal of charm and liveliness, particularly the portrait of Fanny, while the drawings done by another niece, Anna Lefroy, depict with considerable skill Chawton Cottage, Chawton Great House and other buildings associated with the family. On the subject of the book's appearance there can, in fact, be only one complaint: the print on pages 166 and 169 is sadly jumbled, though I believe one is not supposed to mention such things nowadays.

Janeism is of course a religion, possibly the most flourishing in Britain today, and for its adherents Lord David Cecil has provided admirably. The book compiles accepted facts and doctrines, and – very properly, given its purpose – has no truck with madcap innovations. Even the passages that comment critically on the novels are, as Lord David explains in the foreword, virtual or actual quotations from a lecture he gave in 1935; he has been staunch to his basic views for forty-three years. Again as in religion, the book caters for mixed abilities. The sophisticated will not feel insulted by it, yet the less well-informed are reminded, very courteously, that in those days 'there were no telephones or radios or daily posts and the horse was the fastest means of travel'. They are also told that Marianne Dashwood is one of the two heroines of *Sense and Sensibility*.

I certainly do not mean to imply that Lord David has no personal point of view. He puts unusual stress on the fact that Jane Austen was 'a child of the gentry' and is anxious to clear up any misapprehensions on the point: 'Critics, ignorant of social history, sometimes speak of Jane Austen as coming from the middle class and as such lumped together with George Eliot and Dickens. In fact their families would not have been on visiting terms with Jane Austen's.' So, farewell then, George Eliot and Dickens.

Lord David is also anxious to prove that she was personally attractive, almost as if plainness would have diminished her both as a woman and a writer. He has to flout a great deal of evidence. There is no authenticated portrait that shows her to be pretty. He also has to disregard comments by a cousin, Philadelphia Walter, and by an admirer of her work, Mary Mitford. He is at his most ingenious when grappling with the famous comment made by Miss Mitford's mother that the young Jane was 'the prettiest, silliest, most affected husband-hunting butterfly she ever remembered'; he accepts 'pretty butterfly' and dismisses the rest. His assumption is that a woman who was soon to portray Isabella Thorpe and Lucy Steele

could not have been silly, affected and husband-hunting herself; but surely
with a novelist this does not follow at all.

I admire partisanship and I admire Jane Austen; and I do not think it
matters, to us, in the least what she looked like, unless her appearance
affected her work which I see no signs of its having done. But I am uneasy
about Lord David's treatment of her relationship to the society in which
she lived, a matter which was bound to affect her work. A key document
here is the letter written by Fanny Knatchbull, formerly Knight, many years
after her aunt's death. It is a nasty letter but that is hardly the point. Lady
Knatchbull speaks with all seriousness and in some detail of her aunt's lack
of refinement, breeding and sophistication, and of her own opinion that
if it had not been for the visits of both the Austen sisters to Godmersham
they would have been 'very much below par as to good Society and its
ways'. Lord David quotes from the letter but dismisses its comments as
proceeding from jealousy and snobbery: 'This is the only convincing explanation.' But another convincing explanation is that there was truth in what
Fanny Knatchbull said.

There is evidence that Jane Austen was not as much in tune with the
society in which she found herself as the *Portrait* would have us believe.
Contemporary observers (whose accounts are quoted by Lord David only
to be explained away) commented on her gaucherie and taciturnity in
company, and this may well have been caused by honourable and intelligent resentment at the limitations of her role in life, especially when
poverty and spinsterhood had clipped her wings.

There is weighty evidence in the novels themselves when they are taken
in conjunction with what we know of Jane Austen that she was compelled
to live something of a double life, or at least to observe a double standard.
We know, for example, that when she was speaking without disguise, in
her letters to Cassandra, she sounded not like any of her heroines or other
good characters but exactly like Mary Crawford, and in *Mansfield Park* it
is on Mary Crawford's head that she empties the vials of her moral indignation when Mary talks racily or honestly. How solemnly Edmund and
Fanny are made to look down their noses at Mary's little joke about Vice
Admirals, which is mild compared with the way Jane Austen talked when
she was being herself.

Pigglejams and After*

Most of the letters in the first section of this volume are addressed to John Middleton Murry, soon to become Katherine Mansfield's husband. It was the beginning of 1918 and she was twenty-nine. He was doing war work in London and she was in the south of France nursing an illness which had not yet been firmly diagnosed as consumption. She wrote to him every day.

The Hotel Beau Rivage answered few of her dreams and changed many of them into nightmares. Not long after her arrival she had her first haemorrhage and from then on lived in dread that, as she put it, the consumption was going to gallop. Incessantly smoking the cigarettes that Virginia Woolf and other friends kept sending her, she sat reading Keats, and watching her handkerchiefs as desperately as he had watched his. She snatched at the first signs of spring and clung to the beauties of the external world, while her own internal world darkened. 'Great big black things lie in wait for me under the trees and stretch their shadows across the road.'

She turned against the hotel; the french (usually lower-case) made too much noise in the lavatory. She turned with special emphasis against her friends: the Woolfs were *smelly*; Lady Ottoline Morrell was *corrupt-corrupt*. She turned against her doctor: 'He is such a *ponce*.'

The war had not spared her. She could not rejoice at victories: 'my mind fills with the wretched little picture of my brother's grave.' He had been killed in 1915. And since then the war had not only damaged her health and seeped into her writing but would, she feared, prevent her return to England. It very nearly did. She was held up in Paris for nearly three weeks at the height of the bombardments.

The second section, which covers the five months after she finally got back, shows her reunion with Murry and their wedding. But almost immediately she set off again, this time to Cornwall, as he was convinced that the flat in Fulham was bad for her. And a new series of letters began.

The tone was different. Baby talk had dominated the earlier correspondence: Wig would tell Bogey that she was a well girl and though in her pigglejams at the moment was soon going out with her bastick and

---

* From the *Sunday Telegraph*, 8 February 1987. Review of *The Collected Letters of Katherine Mansfield Volume II*, edited by Vincent O'Sullivan with Margaret Scott.

praps a few sangwiches to buy something scrumbuncktious. Strictly speaking it had not been baby talk at all, for that presupposes an adult at one end of the dialogue, but whatever it had been, it was withering away. A sick, frightened, lonely woman was beginning to send out unaffected appeals for help.

In the third section the tone changes again. When Mansfield returned to London it was to a house in Hampstead which she liked and where she was looked after by an adequate staff. Her principal correspondents were now women, old acquaintances whom she had rehabilitated. Corrupt corrupt Lady Ottoline had become her dearest dearest friend. Murry was now editor of the *Athenaeum* and they lived in as much of a literary whirl as was consistent with her failing health and the awkward temperaments of the litterateurs.

Her comments on these gatherings range, though not far, from caustic to bitchy, and are most enjoyable. My favourite glimpse is of Aldous Huxley, who 'lay upon the sofa, buried his head in a purple pillow and groaned over the horrible quality of Smollett's coarseness'. I was also greatly taken by Dorothy Brett's expressed intention of getting a black frock like Katherine's as it didn't show the dirt.

In 1919 with another English winter approaching she was advised to go abroad again. In September she set off for Italy. This time she left a will.

Here this volume ends. We have experienced nearly two years in the life of a writer, following the fortunes of some of her best-known stories and discovering her, often startling, literary tastes. (Her views on Eliot, Pound, Joyce and Laforgue are those of the hypothetical man on the Clapham omnibus.) We are given no great insights of the kind to be found in the letters of Keats but we do get, and it is impressive, a vision of a true writer for whom work was both life and salvation.

Vincent O'Sullivan and Margaret Scott are excellent editors: alert to primary sources, up-to-date in their scholarship and, in the case of O'Sullivan's notes, sensitive to what readers do and do not need.

Hippy Wordsworth*

I approached these three books with feelings of relief, having, as it happened, just heard a description of the proceedings of the George Eliot Centenary Conference held at Leicester this July, where, it appears, structuralists, anti-structuralists and post-structuralists all flailed about trying to hit each other, where hermeneutical dons developed arguments about technique which were applauded for their strenuous density, and where, if all else failed, the heroine of the occasion was compared with other writers with whom she seemed, and still seems, to have no earthly connection. I needed to turn to the concept that there are readers who peacefully enjoy the literature of the past, and if they want help, prefer something helpful.

Hunter Davies, I say without fear of contradiction, is no hermeneut. In writing *William Wordsworth* his intention was to provide an up-to-date general biography of the poet. It was to cover the whole of his life; it would include no literary criticism and would not be addressed to scholars, whose cup is full and running over already, and who in any case tend to address each other. In all these particulars he has succeeded; and he was quite right: there was no such book before, and there was a place for it.

He clearly hopes that his audience will include young people, not the ones who go on to read English at university but those who have somehow been brought to the conclusion that the heights, and indeed the slopes, of Parnassus, are not for them. His hope I heartily endorse, even though it sometimes results in a told-to-the-children approach, as in his explanation of Pantisocracy: 'It is hard not to smile at the idealism of it all, though if you too happen to be young and idealistic and radical, you perhaps won't smile but think it perfectly wonderful.' And his wooing of the young and untried can sometimes lead to falsification, as when he explicitly presents the household at Dove Cottage as a hippy community, failing to point out that the Wordsworth family circle was, to an unusual degree, literate, articulate, intelligent and industrious.

Davies's vocabulary is ardently demotic: nobody, young or old, must be put off, so Wordsworth cannot do anything as academic as compose;

---

* From the *Listener*, 31 July 1980. Review of *William Wordsworth* by Hunter Davies, *Keats and his Circle* by Joanna Richardson and *Shelley and his World* by Claire Tomalin.

he must spout. The idiom and slang cover a wide range of style and period: in his departure from eighteenth-century poetic tradition Wordsworth was, according to Davies, thought to be 'slumming and deliberately letting down the side'; and the Wordsworths gave Coleridge's wife 'a bad press'. Everything in the way of contemporary manners and customs is explained, as if to a Martian, but where the action is concerned, we are occasionally invited to prophesy: 'You've guessed, of course, where they are going. To see Annette.' Sometimes the informality defeats its own ends. I am perplexed as to how Wordsworth could do 'the most amazing walks and mountain climbs all round the Lakes single-handed'. I can see that Nelson might.

Davies's stylistic mannerisms may or may not irritate the readership; they cannot damage the real strength of the book, which is that it gives, as no esoteric scholarly study could, a thoroughly good journalistic account of how it all happened at the time. We know so well, for example, that *Lyrical Ballads* was one of the most important publications in the history of English poetry, that it is refreshing to be reminded of the casual, almost unedifying, nature of its appearance: we are shown Wordsworth and Coleridge compiling it in haste in order to take advantage of Cottle's offer of thirty guineas, which they needed for a trip to Germany, and then starting on their travels without waiting for it to come out. Graphic too are the descriptions of how the book offended, whom it offended particularly, and how it gradually won acceptance.

Although Hunter Davies abstains from literary criticism he rightly allows himself to comment on any literary manifesto that the poet himself puts forward. His gloss on the 'emotion recollected in tranquillity' statement is remarkably sensible and discerning.

Joanna Richardson's *Keats and his Circle* is not so much for the general reader as for buffs – either of Keats or portraiture or both. It is a sumptuous album of portraits, far-ranging in its choice of subjects: over sixty people are depicted, some of whom have fairly marginal connections with the poet, e.g. Lewis Way, the 'great Jew converter' in Keats's phrase, at the consecration of whose chapel Keats had been present, and others who though they knew him only for a short time rendered him important services, e.g. William Ewing, the ivory carver, who meeting Keats in Rome during his last illness, showed him considerable kindness and attended his funeral.

It so happens that I myself have never cared too much about the appearance of, say, Keats's sister's children in old age, and perhaps it is not just lack of curiosity on my part, for the album interestingly shows how little reliance can be placed on likenesses taken in the past, by whatever method. In two miniatures and a silhouette Benjamin Bailey has three completely different noses, while an ambrotype – a photograph on glass – said to be of Fanny Brawne in the 1850s, when she was in her own fifties, shows a woman half that age.

The portraits are arranged alphabetically, which means that, though the notes supplied beneath each one are exact and ample in that specific connection, the album as a whole cannot give the chronological or the thematic view of Keats's life which the less experienced might need.

Claire Tomalin's *Shelley and his World*, companion to over thirty similar volumes (Brunel, Gilbert and Sullivan, Louis XIV and Wagner as well as the predictable English writers) in the Thames and Hudson series, is a model of its kind. It is well-organised, well-illustrated, elegantly written and sensitively informative: highly recommended, in fact, for any reader who has become interested in Shelley's poems and wishes to know about their social and biographical framework.

On Society

Sadey Ladies*

If ever anybody was justified to say 'I did it my way' it was the Marquis de Sade, not simply because his worst crimes existed in fantasy, the only area where people can really do anything their way, but because his way as a pornographer was different from that of other pornographers. As Angela Carter argues in the first chapter of her high-spirited book *The Sadeian Woman*, he not only goes further than most of them, to become 'a terrorist of the imagination' but he really believes that society and human nature, which he shows as monstrous, *could* in fact be transformed, a belief which, Ms Carter thinks, is alien to the pornography of most ages, certainly to that of our own.

Up to now feminists writing in English have not made as much use of Sade as they might; specifically, that is, for Germaine Greer in the 'Hate' section of *The Female Eunuch* has discussed many of the themes (loathing, disgust, abuse, resentment) with which he too was concerned, while the first chapter of Kate Millett's *Sexual Politics* shows by means of quotations from twentieth-century writers – Miller and Mahler – what happens when men have the whip hand.

In the non-pejorative sense of the word Angela Carter's book is tendentious. She makes no attempt to treat Sade's writings as literature, only as pornographic literature, and as she points out 'there is no question of an aesthetics of pornography. It can never be art for art's sake.' Honourably enough, it is always art with work to do. Neither is she concerned to examine the tenets of this 'illiberal philosopher', as she calls him, intellectually.

Working on the assumption that readers know nothing of Sade beyond what the dictionary tells them, she recounts at considerable length and from various versions of the novels in which they appear, the respective careers of Justine and Juliette, the two principal Sadeian women (though she discusses others as well). They are sisters and opposites, who starting from the same circumstances go in completely different directions, Justine to be oppressed, hunted and humiliated, consistently at the mercy of a sexuality she consistently denies, Juliette to achieve every kind of sexual and material triumph.

---

* From the *Listener*, 5 April 1979. Review of *The Sadeian Woman* by Angela Carter.

The main part of the argument is now well under way, for Angela Carter wishes to demonstrate that from these two characters descend recognisable twentieth-century types of women. Justine, as portrayed by Sade, 'marks the start of a kind of self-regarding female masochism, a woman with no place in the world, no status, the core of whose resistance has been eaten away by self-pity.' Juliette, on the other hand, 'is a woman who acts according to the precepts and also the practice of a man's world and so she does not suffer. Instead she causes suffering.'

Looking around for Justine in our own age, Ms Carter takes her chief examples from the film industry. She sees Marilyn Monroe as the 'living image' of Justine and goes into great and sometimes fanciful detail to establish the resemblance. She sees Mary Pickford, Mae West and Marlene Dietrich as women whose screen personae deny their real sexuality as Justine wilfully denied hers in that they are presented as being, respectively, too young, too old and too foreign for it to be apparent. Juliette, she considers, has 'fewer spiritual great-granddaughters', though she was perhaps the prototype of the vamp, and certainly she was the first token woman.

Which of these two Sadeian women should we wish to be? Neither. We are not to imagine that Juliette is the one to lead us out of bondage. Guillame Apollinaire thought she might be the New Woman who would renew the world, but, in Angela Carter's words, 'a free woman in an unfree society will be a monster', and this is what Juliette is, an outstandingly wicked person. 'I do not think I want Juliette to renew my world' says Ms Carter, mildly in the circumstances, though she adds, 'her work of destruction complete, she will, with her own death, have removed a repressive and authoritarian superstructure that has prevented a good deal of the work of renewal.'

Sade emerges from this book as a slightly more admirable character than he is usually supposed to be. 'Give the old monster his due,' cries Angela Carter. And part of Sade's due is that though he gave people hell in his fantasies, and, to a lesser extent, outside them too, he had glimpses and actual moments of goodness. Those whom he saved from the guillotine during the Terror by refusing on principle to sign their death warrants were probably not too censorious about the viciousness of his novels.

Another part of his due, and this is very relevant to the message of *The Sadeian Woman*, is that he wished women to be free in a way that Justine and Juliette could not be, that is, in a free society where women would automatically be liberated. In one passage, which Angela Carter quotes, he urges us to throw off our chains. Admittedly, his vocabulary trips him up. Modern feminists can do without being addressed as 'charming sex' and 'the more divine half of mankind'. And they want everybody to be free of chains. But then so did Citizen Sade.

Period Pain*

Stella Tillyard's *Aristocrats* has set out from its publishers with claims beyond even what one expects of conventional hype. There is much to admire in the book, particularly the industry that must have gone into its compilation: the examination of huge family archives which contain, apart from what one might expect in the way of letters and journals, everything from death certificates to poems. There is much to enjoy too, as there would be in any lively historical novel, past or present. But the eulogy pronounced by the great Simon Schama, author of *Citizens*, calls for comment: 'A dazzling achievement,' he writes, 'an extraordinary story told by a phenomenally gifted writer.' This strikes me as over-ecstatic.

The Schama connection is a matter of natural and wholesome professional sympathies. Stella Tillyard is married to historian John Brewer who helped Schama with *Citizens,* as the author warmly acknowledges in the introduction; and there is further scholarly harmony in the fact that Tillyard, in her preface, shows that she agrees with the views of Schama, and, increasingly, others, about the presentation of historical subjects. He decided to put forward his concept of citizenry in the form of narrative, opting 'to bring a world to life rather than entomb it in erudite discourse' and emphasising his preference for 'chaotic authenticity over the commanding neatness of historical convention'. Tillyard has seemingly followed this lead, describing her own work as 'a marriage of biography and history', and explaining that she employed narrative 'so that commentary intrudes as little as possible'.

The subject of aristocracy is of course highly topical. The publication of *Aristocrats* has more or less coincided with that of David Cannadine's *Aspects of Aristocracy: Grandeur and Decline in Modern Britain*, which follows some of the themes of his earlier book, *Decline and Fall of the British Aristocracy*. Tillyard's modishly-titled contribution is an enormous account of four eighteenth-century female aristocrats, from which we may draw as many inferences about aristocracy as we can or wish to. The women are Caroline, Emily, Louisa and Sarah Lennox, daughters of the second Duke of Richmond, the grandson of Charles II and his mistress Louise de

* From the *London Review of Books*, 9 June 1994. Review of *Aristocrats* by Stella Tillyard.

Kéroualle. The main story starts with the birth of Caroline in 1723 and ends with the death of Sarah in 1826.

About these four sisters and every single thing connected with them, one comes to feel, *Aristocrats* is relentlessly informative. It is as if the deliberate avoidance of commentary means the space has to be filled up with facts, significant or not. The book is not only a biography-cum-history but becomes an encyclopedia as well. Tillyard seems to think that her readers know absolutely nothing about anything, especially the eighteenth century, and that they lack the experience and aptitude to have amassed, in however relaxed and piecemeal a way, any store of general knowledge; whereas, surely, anybody actively wishing to tackle this book – few people pick up a blockbuster lightly – would be prepared for it by the usual means: stately homes of the appropriate date, novels, biographies and films set in the right period, possibly even schoolwork. They would, for example, almost certainly have a working idea of Bath, perhaps from Jane Austen. Tillyard supplies a four-page passage which starts: 'At the beginning of the eighteenth century Bath was still a small town largely dependent on a moribund wool industry. But it had two natural resources', and goes on to explain about Beau Nash, the Assembly Rooms, the Pump Room and John Wood's Palladian buildings. It is a competent slice of guide-book but dispensable in this case. After all it is only there to flesh out the fact that one of the characters went to take the waters.

Tillyard's kind of sustained instruction can have a weird effect. When I was reading her description of the birth of one of Emily's children, with full details naturally (the accoucheur, the expectant wet-nurse, the caudle the attendants were drinking, with recipe, all kinds of obstetric theory and speculations as to what room the Duke of Leinster, Emily's husband, might be in, waiting for the news), I could not rid myself of the notion that she was about to tell us where babies come from. Perhaps the high spot of unnecessary information is her account of Sarah's wedding to Charles Bunbury, in which after letting us know that the chapel in Holland House where it took place 'was two storeys high with round arched windows down the east side and an Inigo Jones ceiling', she quotes, entirely verbatim, substantial parts of the marriage service, the best-known parts, including 'I will.' There can be few of her readers who are not familiar in some capacity with a traditional Anglican church wedding or have not at least watched one on TV, whose serials so often end with this event, though, to be fair, the cameras sometimes move on after 'gathered here together in the sight of God' unless someone is going to forbid the banns or get shot.

There could be a practical reason for this expansiveness: the wish to satisfy markets other than British. But I suspect that the customers of these markets – those among them attracted to the book in the first place, that is – would be quite equal to the occasion and might even know about Bath. There could be an ideological reason as well. I have noticed that writers who share Stella Tillyard's principles about bringing warmth and accessibility to what they would call academic history (meaning 'academic' quite nastily, as people do when talking about a certain type of poetry or painting) often go on record with statements that are recognisably *de haut en bas* about wanting to reach out to a wider audience whom they manage to make sound educationally deprived; challenged, I mean. Obviously tyros have to start somewhere, and they do, but I think it would not be with *Aristocrats,* or at least they would not get far.

'I think many people are more interested in period pains than they are in acts of Parliament.' Thus spoke Stella Tillyard in an interview at the time of the publication of *Aristocrats*, enthusiastically stooping to the level of those people who cannot get excited about politics. I had already deduced that this is what she thought, from both the hype which had held the subject of period pains before us as a lure and from the index: 'Lennox, Caroline and menstruation' and a similar entry for two of the other sisters. I was rather surprised to see Emily included. Knowing by this time that she had had twenty-two children and many miscarriages I felt that her experience of period pains must be limited.

Obviously I am not suggesting that a prolix work of 426 pages should be extended; on the contrary. But I do wish that at least some of the exhaustive accounts of domestic life could be exchanged for something less claustrophobic. From the point in the story where Emily and Louisa (who married Tom Conolly, said to be the richest man in Ireland) settled in their new homes, Carton and Castletown respectively, we get reports of everything that went on in these two houses and their parks. Nearly twenty pages are given up to what, in content, could be a talk to the Women's Institute about the running of a large country house in days of old, but in style is more of a cool textbook providing minutiae of matters from what the staff wore and were paid to what exactly their duties were: not what the butler saw but what he did. Improvements, outdoor and indoor, were constantly taking place at both Carton and Castletown. Emily did up an old cottage on the estate as a shell-house; the Duke improved the park according to the principles of Capability Brown; and both the Duke and the Duchess were involved in redecorating the house itself. At Castletown, Louisa actively directed such drastic alterations to both its structure and its decoration that they took more than two decades to complete. All of this is chronicled with such attention to minute particulars as to be almost obsessional. In the case of Emily and her shell-house, for example, Tillyard gives us a picturesquely-worded list of all the shells that were used: 'huge conches from tropical seas, corals with a myriad of tentative fingers' and so on for several paragraphs. The whole of this section of the book sounds as though *Private Eye* was doing a parody of *House and Garden*. And all the time, unmentioned, Ireland was boiling up around the aristocrats, with agrarian unrest, complaints from the Catholic tenants about giving tithes to the Church of Ireland and other resentments.

In much of the book the narrative shuttles quite gracefully between the family lives of the sisters and their historical background. But sometimes the marriage between biography and history arranged by Tillyard is not as happy as she planned. As in the chapter just discussed, history does not always get a proper say. But when it does shake itself free from the oppressive paint-and-wallpaper, crib-and-wet-nurse sequences, the interaction between the two genres can be truly enlightening, as in the chapter which deals with the Irish rebellion of 1798. In France, just before the Revolution, Lord Edward Fitzgerald, Emily's son, converted to Republicanism. It was called 'the levelling movement' by Lady Emily, the last person one can imagine being levelled, who placidly remarked: 'I think it charming to hear talked of but I fear they will never realise it.' This was before Edward came back from the Continent and joined the United Irishmen. His mother's placidity was quite broken up, as well it might be. Violence took over and poor Edward never got home to see his picture of Tom Paine and the fancy uniform that he had put in a chest ready to wear on the first day of the Irish Republic. Lady Louisa suffered too, apart from her grief at the death of her nephew. She had been roused out of her long dream of improvements and doing good to her dependents and tenants, whom she had treated all her married life with resolute maternalism. When many of them sided with the rebel cause she thought of it as disloyalty, even betrayal. The way in which Tillyard writes about the rebellion recalls Schama's remark about 'chaotic authenticity'. I am not qualified to speak of the authenticity of Tillyard's treatment of the situation but I can vouch for its being chaotic. This is not only in keeping with her principles of no commentary but entirely appropriate to what was happening. With so many diverse, conflicting allegiances in religion, politics, class and family alliances, every person capable of thought or feeling must have been energetically leading a multiple life. It would have been not only impossible but wrong to make order out of it.

It is very natural that Tillyard should be infatuated with the sisters. If all her hard work had not become a labour of love she could hardly have continued with it. But it is misleading to speak of them as exceptional women – which she and the hype do – for they were very much products of their time and, given their heredity and environment, they are exactly what you might expect. It is rhetorical, too, to say that they lived in remarkable times. So did and does everybody. But they certainly move dashingly along their appointed tracks. Their biographer's enthusiasm makes them glow. Particularly enjoyable is the story of the second marriages of Emily and Sarah, which is a comedy in the best sense of the word. It hangs on the concept of marrying for love rather than by arrangement, which, so people say, was becoming more and more fashionable as the century advanced. As early as 1744, Caroline Lennox had eloped with Henry Fox, later Lord Holland and father of Charles James. It was a sensible move as he was far more exciting than his three future brothers-in-law, one of whom – Mr Conolly as a matter of fact – was so boring that the other two noticed it. There was little scandal; Fox was not a highly unsuitable match, and indeed he became as wealthy and influential as his new relatives. After a display of routine fury on the part of the Duke of Richmond, everything blew over except the marriage, which was a great success. But there was considerable scandal when, some decades later, Emily and Sarah made love matches the bliss of which they never tired of describing. Though by this time the age of Jane Austen was dawning, I do not think we are hearing the middle-class voice of Jane Bennet: 'Oh, Lizzy, do anything rather than marry without affection.' It seems to be a more robust voice altogether, as if the high-born sisters were saying to themselves: if in faded middle-age, widowed or disgraced or both, you find an attractive, eager second husband, rejoice. And, engagingly, they did. But of course a love match usually meant that the woman was marrying beneath her; had it been otherwise somebody would have arranged it. Emily and Sarah were afraid (but not very) that these new husbands, though far from boring, would not be acceptable to their family and to society. Sarah's, a Napier, was at least an officer and a gentleman and though poor the younger son of a baron, but William Ogilvie was the tutor of Emily's children.

The sisters, however, managed beautifully and with considerable ingenuity raised their husbands up to more or less their own station. Louisa helped by fossicking about and finding, or pretending to find, a peer with an improbable name in Ogilvie's family tree. Emily, who went on calling herself Duchess of Leinster, invented a new hierarchy, that of learning and scholarship, at the top of which shone William Ogilvie. Sarah posed as a sort of Marianne, a gallant woman who shared with her gallant mate the hardships and perils of a soldier's life (unspecified and largely imaginary in her case except for a drop in income) and set about convincing society that patriotism and valour in the field should be respected and perhaps emulated by the highest in the land.

Stella Tillyard writes best when she is in her straightforward, unaffected vein. Her heightened style lets her down; she becomes self-indulgent. Some readers may like it, of course.

But as their grief died down, Emily and Caroline, still daughters in their minds, began to hear their parents speak. So began a colloquy that would go on until they in turn left the world to their grieving children. Caroline and Emily joined in the huge mute conversation humanity carries on with the dead that stretches back through the ages as, with silent self-justifications and voiceless wrangles, children whisper to parents and they, children in their turn, lisp confidences to lost mothers and fathers.

Her principles of biographical narrative allow her to include imaginative passages but her flights of fancy (based on strong probability) tend not to turn out well.

Sarah lay in a bath. Her belly rose like an island out of warm water... Soon afterwards her labour began. . . When they said push, she began to push, sinking her mind into her abdomen, becoming a great muscle, forcing the baby out.

Tillyard's natural verbosity often works against her. She has consulted so many documents that we cannot ever be sure she is giving us particulars she really knows about; for example: 'The Duke of Richmond slammed the door and hurried back to his library.' Probably not in this case. It is all part of her individual style to leave nothing to our imagination. 'Fox sat down to write a letter.' 'Caroline sat down in her parlour, dipped her pen into the well of grey-black ink, and began to write.' This is harmless, though we would hardly have supposed that Caroline and Henry Fox ran about writing letters with dry pens, but she sometimes pushes the habit too far; not as far as the immortal 'St John of the Cross bit his lip' but quite near it, surely, with 'Ogilvie breathed a sigh of relief.'

The book is handsome, with a great many very pretty illustrations. It also has some very irritating spelling mistakes. Its forbidding size can be combated by means of a quick run-through followed by selective reading. It may seem odd to suggest dipping into a blockbuster, but that would bring out the real strength of *Aristocrats*.

For a Lark*

We have just lived through nearly two years of vox populi. The fiftieth anniversary of VE Day and, to a lesser extent, VJ Day, provoked a massive assemblage of what people had actually said in the course of the Second World War. It was as though these voices had been held back for half a century and were now bursting out. Martin Gilbert in *The Day the War Ended*, a recent account of the year 1945, has shown how inexorably this could happen. In appealing, as he had rashly done, to the public for material from those times, he had imagined that such replies as he might receive 'would provide an interesting if essentially minor element to the book: a sideline to history'. He was wrong. In the end he had to change the balance of the whole work to accommodate the hundreds of relevant contributions sent in.

Jenny Hartley, compiler of *Hearts Undefeated*, did not pause to feel her way. With no frippery about sidelines to history, she set out to quote the voice of the people, the whole voice and nothing but the voice, except for a few editorial passages. She saw no need to canvass but simply helped herself from the glut of autobiographical material produced during the Second World War and accessibly preserved in the Imperial War Museum, the archives of Mass-Observation and the publications of presses great and small over the years. She has surveyed the entire period of the War (starting as early as 1938 in order to include Munich) and so has constructed a substantial anthology. It is substantial in spite of the fact that inclusion was limited: a few exceptions were made but, in general, to qualify you had to be British, middle-class, apolitical and, of course, indomitable. Above all, you had to be female.

As can be seen from Hartley's scrupulous seven-page list of Acknowledgements and Sources, there was a great demand for female writing during the War. Women readers enjoyed having women writers pass on wheezes about how to cope. On the other hand, literati, illuminati and eggheads could not bear it. After four years of war, Cyril Connolly, editing *Horizon*, printed a comprehensive explanation of why he (and other editors) did not welcome contributions from women. There was a strong

---

* From the *London Review of Books*, 21 March 1996. Review of *Hearts Undefeated* by Jenny Hartley.

tide running against them. According to him their subject matter was too familiar, usually petty in itself and seldom presented with any degree of skill. It is surprising that Hartley should quote his remarks. She cannot have been hoping to refute them. Any reader of this anthology is bound to admit that he had a point.

With regard to subject matter, the journalists, both professional and occasional, represented in *Hearts Undefeated* were totally exempt from Connolly's strictures. Martha Gellhorn wrote about Dachau, Mavis Tate about Buchenwald. Laura Knight and Rebecca West covered the Nuremberg trials as Fleur Cowles had covered the Nuremberg rally, eight years previously. But the women who described themselves, persistently and irritatingly, as ordinary, unimportant, even simple, did tend to write as though they really were. For a lark they went to tea at the Dorchester ('So garbed in my best I stepped forth'), but the filling of the sandwiches had no flavour and the cakes (only two each) were awful. At the big stores they went up and down in the lift enjoying 'the flash registering the progress of its journey in rapidly changing lighted figures'. Nobody then or now would grudge them such recreation. Today in the mid-Nineties, however, so many books are being published to coincide more or less with the anniversaries – books of the calibre of Eric Lomax's *The Railway Man* with its account of wartime torture – that we are in no mood to hear about inferior sandwiches, fun in the elevator or Barbara Cartland fussing about finding secondhand wedding dresses for brides (who were of course 'pathetically grateful') so that on the great day each one might be 'a woman, lovely, glamorous and enticing, a woman to be wooed and won'.

In everyday life women had to be regular sunbeams, as some of them ruefully admitted, but in their writing when they could have taken liberties, they rarely shone into the deepest social and political corners. There were exceptions, of course: Nesca Robb, a temporary civil servant, wrote a strong piece about the difficulty of finding serious employment in wartime for middle-aged, middle-class women who, in keeping with the convention of the time, had never been trained for anything and now needed the money; Margery Allingham chatted her way through an account of the evacuation of town children to the country, which was usefully perceptive about class. When it came to politics, hardly any of them seemed to notice that at times of the country's greatest danger the British workforce, producing armaments and ships, repeatedly went on strike or to have spotted that when Churchill delivered his VE Day speech he was being blatantly economical with the truth about the contribution of our allies. The Hearts remained staunch about what side they were on; guided by popular comedians, they referred to Hitler as 'Old Nasty'. But they rarely discussed the reasons for the war or the possibilities of its outcome. Notably, one of them did. To Beatrice Webb the question of who was going to win the current war was immaterial. Her tone was both royal and prophetic; it catered for what might go on beyond the tomb. 'As we happen to believe in the rightness and eventual success of Soviet Communism, we are not despondent about the future of mankind.'

Connolly's disparagement of women's style could also be backed up by this collection. Jenny Hartley has presented us with a great deal of thoroughly bad prose. It was obvious from the start that her principles of selection had nothing to do with literary standards. The theme was the thing and it over-rode all other considerations. But there was more to it than that. She genuinely believed that in the outpourings of the Hearts she had come across a cache of 'extraordinary literary talent'. In fact, the best that could be said of all too many of them is that they would have done well in the days when Composition was a school subject. Letters and diaries do not constitute formal genres, I suppose, but if they did, the following extract describing Churchill's speech, mentioned earlier, could be regarded as representative of the diary. 'A Glorious Day... What a squash!... That voice... What a lad!... He was cheered to the echo, God bless him! We were glad to get to the flat for a cup of tea!'

Apart from the journalists whose skills put them into a category of their own, the professionals – novelists, biographers, travel writers, playwrights – did not set much of a standard. This was not entirely their fault. They gave themselves airs, certainly. Virginia Woolf considered her musings about the war a 'whiff of shot in the cause of freedom'. Elizabeth Bowen was even more grandiloquent: 'Wartime writing is in a sense resistance writing.' But in fact their subject and the attitude they were required to adopt forced them along paths which were not familiar to them, and often not congenial. E.M. Delafield could not be at her best when exhorting us, in *Time and Tide*, to display a sense of humour in wartime. By the nature of her brief she could not be too funny herself, and she was nothing if not funny. Dorothy Sayers was clearly ill at ease in advocating forgiveness of the enemy, as she did in the *Fortnightly*: she was happier with the implacability of Lord Peter Wimsey. In 1940 Virginia Woolf was asked to supply 'Thoughts on Peace in an Air Raid' for an American Symposium on current affairs concerning women. It could not have been an entirely welcome assignment; she had to fall back on rambling and padded reflections which she hoped might help in years to come the descendants of the men who at that moment were fighting to the death overhead: too long-term a train of thought, I would imagine, to be persuasive or comforting.

Virginia Woolf was not the only one who failed to write straightforwardly about the blitz, nor was Dorothy Sayers unique in stumbling over the concept of forgiveness. Many of Hartley's contributors showed comparable signs of strain, connected probably with fears that we might not win. But, once again there were exceptions. Lily Montagu, writing about forgiveness not as an assignment but as a matter of course to the members of her Jewish Girls' Club brought it off beautifully by her unaffected expression of her beliefs. Beatrice Webb, confronting the blitz in her eighties, endowed the cups of tea drunk by herself and Sidney at the height of the bombardment with a sort of virility that eluded all the other cups of tea which with almost satirical frequency slopped through the letters and diaries of *Hearts Undefeated*. The majestic common sense which came naturally to her made her comments, if perhaps not edifying, irresistible. She saw no need for look-outs or patrols anywhere near her property. 'If a fire bomb falls on the house and goes through the roof, we should hear it.' Occasionally the editor herself sabotaged her writers' work. Stevie Smith's article 'Mosaic' which came out in *Eve's Journal* in 1939 was not given the title for nothing. It consisted of small pieces meaningfully put together. Hartley, however, insensitive to everything but her point that at the time of Munich nobody knew where Czechoslovakia was, cut out and used that piece; not a good way to treat a mosaic, it ruined this particular one.

It is significant that no poetry has been included in *Hearts Undefeated*. The popular outcry for suitable poems during the War must have heaped up an absolute Parnassus of it to pick from. The editor was certainly not against poetry. She turned to it for her epigraph of which her title was part: lines written by a woman, F. Tennyson Jesse.

> Here there are homes, burnt homes
> But hearts undefeated to meet each day.

She did not, though, look to poetry for anything other than comfort, consolation and support; she linked it specifically with prophecy and prayer; and as she had no wish to comfort and console us, the current readers, but to inform and enlighten us, it was natural that she should leave it out. It is relevant, however, to quote the opinion of Philip Larkin about poetry in wartime as it throws light on the weakness of much wartime prose. He certainly did not mean to comfort or console us either. He speaks harshly of poets whom we may have admired in our time: 'A period which can laud the poetry of Keyes is no period for me'; but he does take care to explain: 'A war poet is not one who chooses to celebrate a war but one who reacts against having a war thrust upon him: he is chained, that is, to an historical event, and an abnormal one at that. However well he does it, however much we agree that the war happened and ought to be written about, there is still a tendency for us to withhold our highest praise on the grounds that a poet's choice of subject should seem an action, not a reaction.' This seems to me a very valuable comment. It certainly applies to the prose writers of this anthology.

In her introduction Jenny Hartley has discussed motivation, not her own so much as that of her contributors, and only a section of them: the amateurs. It was perfectly natural that those whose lifelong career had been to express themselves in writing should go on doing so when something happened. But why did women who invariably described themselves as nonentities and who had no reason to suppose that they had any literary talent suddenly expose themselves in such a wanton way? Hartley has not mentioned the wish to be published; indeed she rather suggested that her team thought they might disappear when the war ended, making them sound like the knitting-women who presumably went home when the guillotine was dismantled. I feel convinced, however, that the writing-women had their collective eye on being snapped up by publishers, and so sooner or later, most of them were. This explanation would fit in with that of their editor who emphasised that, for the first time in many cases, women could feel they were somebody. It is depressing to think that between the two World Wars a great many women endured lives of such pointlessness and invisibility that they cheered up at the notion of being targets for bombing, but they said as much themselves and unless we suspect they were being disingenuous we have to believe them.

Then there was the recording-angel syndrome which reached epidemic proportions at that time: a natural human instinct which could in the circumstances be comfortably regarded as a duty. Perhaps most significant of all (though Hartley did not mention it) there was the superstitious hope of immortality that had nothing to do with being published, a state of mind deftly explored – though only to be exploded – by Pat Barker's protagonist in *The Ghost Road*. His regiment was leaving for the front the following day (it was the First World War) and he and all the others were getting their diaries up to date. 'Why?' he wrote 'you have to ask yourself. I think it's a way of claiming immunity. First-person narrators can't die, so as long as we keep telling the story of our own lives we're safe. Ha bloody fucking Ha.' Unfortunately the Hearts, for obvious reasons, could not benefit from these vigorous comments.

Jenny Hartley's motivation as compiler was both straightforward and creditable: to show how marvellous women could be, given half a chance. At points she seemed to be exploiting the War to get her message across, but in fact things did not turn out altogether as she intended. In her introduction she pointed out that many people 'hoped the war would break down class barriers'. In that case, many people must have been disappointed. It did not, and this anthology shows how thoroughly it did not.

And but for this book we should never have known the extent of the failure. Most of the Hearts were appalling snobs. Barbara Pym's image may now have been dented by her gale-force sighs of relief at finding when she joined the WRNS that she was sharing a cabin with a girl of her 'own class'. The next few days, however, did not go so well: 'I don't think there are really any of our own kind though there are one or two pleasant ones'. On going out to drill she was shaken to see 'a curious crowd of women'. One toys with the riposte Aunt Ada Doom eventually got: 'Did it see you?'

The contributors obviously thought they were dab hands at rendering the speech of those less fortunate than themselves. A mere corporal addressed Vera Brittain as she was seeing her children off to America: 'I'm sending the wife and kid. She don't want to go but I tells her... ' and so on. Hilary Wayne of the ATS made the preposterous statement: 'Before I joined up I took my voice for granted and I suppose I did not give the question of Class a thought from one year's end to the other.' She was enlightened when she heard another recruit say 'Naow' when she should have said 'No', and from that moment started evolving a code (for use among equals) 'to differentiate those whom former generations would have labelled upper and lower classes respectively'. When Marghanita Laski offered to lend her landgirl a book, the girl replied: 'Oi'm that fond of reading. 'Ave yer got one about spois? I don't want no politics nor jography.'

Snobbish criteria often included physical appearance, especially when kindness was being shown. Esther Terry Wright, hearing that her husband had been shot down, was ungracious to her 'little landlady' who offered sympathy with 'a nervous grin', and scathing about the officer at the hospital, 'a little bald North Country man with protruding eyes and a grocer's confidential manner'. Had they been tall and imposing, one feels, she might have responded differently to their concern.

It was quite the fashion to be supercilious about the Women's Land Army. (I should mention my own interest here: a student for most of the War, I spent all my vacations as an auxiliary landgirl on a large farm in Devon.) The doyenne of the detractors was Vita Sackville-West. She organised a large area for the Land Army and had a wider knowledge of it than Sissinghurst alone could provide but that did not stop her from being patronising and inaccurate. I was intrigued by her account of 'us'. Apparently before the War we were shop-assistants, hairdressers and short-hand typists. We had worn high-heeled shoes, dressy blouses, costume jewellery and jaunty hats. Under the healthy influence of the country we tossed back our short curls and laughed as we picked plums, looking prettier than ever in our lives before. As we have been described en bloc I can only say that 'we' were not, had not and did not; and I cannot help wondering how many of the other accounts in this volume were equally unreliable.

At least *Hearts Undefeated* shows that there *was* a Second World War, which I gather will be news to some young citizens; and the brief introductions to the various sections will, where read chronologically, give a clear, if sketchy, idea of what form it took. But I feel that a really good novel set in the period would have been more illuminating. Philip Larkin was right. Simply being there at the time, reacting rather than acting, does not make a writer. The feeling of immediacy which Jenny Hartley was hoping to present has never meant going round with a diary strapped to your wrist. In Larkin's excellent words: '"The Wreck of the Deutschland" would have been markedly inferior if Hopkins had been a survivor from the passenger list.'

Slaves in Love*

A man's definition of a feminist is likely to be more interesting than a woman's. Two very readable biographies of women, by men, have just appeared: John Fisher's *That Miss Hobhouse* and Glen Petrie's life of Josephine Butler, *A Singular Iniquity*. Both authors speak of their subjects with considerable feeling but seem confused as to the degree of feminism they displayed. Mr Fisher refers to Emily Hobhouse on the cover as a Great Feminist. True, at times in the text he appears to be using the word 'great' as one might speak of a great nuisance or a great bore, but he thinks of her as a feminist all right. Yet Emily Hobhouse's main work was to help sufferers who happened to be women rather than to promote any sort of equality. By 'feminism' Mr Fisher seems to mean little more than female annoyance at male incompetence. Speaking of her humanitarian struggles to improve conditions in the concentration camps of the Boer War, he comments: 'A strong streak of feminism became apparent and she raged against the hopeless confusion created in the camps, as in the world at large,

---

* From the *Listener*, 9 December 1971. Review of *That Miss Hobhouse* by John Fisher, *A Singular Iniquity* by Glen Petrie, *Woman's Estate* by Juliet Mitchell, *Woman on Woman* edited by Margaret Laing, *Mary Wollstonecraft* by Edna Nixon, *Woman's Hour* edited by Mollie Lee and *Jolly Super* by Jilly Cooper.

by men in their ignorance and stupidity.' And for him feminism involves being woman-like – that is, cunning, dishonest and illogical. Miss Hobhouse's attempts to end the South African War by means of supporting the Conciliation Committee were activities that she denied to be politically motivated – 'nevertheless, woman-like, she was ready to make use of politicians after her own fashion; and on one of her later visits to South Africa, 'woman-like, having talked herself into the trip, she now upbraided Smuts for having urged her to risk her life by coming so far.'

But if Mr Fisher sees feminism where, strictly speaking, there was none, Mr Petrie doubts whether Josephine Butler was really a feminist at all: 'She never demonstrated much interest in the legal rights of married women, and absolutely no interest whatever in the question of female suffrage.' The fact that she devoted her life and health to attacking the double standard of morality which condoned the sowing of wild oats by gentlemen and blamed prostitutes for their reception of the seed, apparently did not qualify her.

A very clear definition of feminism, both actual and ideal, springs from Juliet Mitchell's analysis, in *Woman's Estate*, of the oppression which Women's Lib is currently struggling against. She shows how this oppression cannot be assessed or combated without a close survey of other oppressions, and especially those of race and class. This analysis and this survey she vigorously and on the whole persuasively carries out. Even when the argument is not new, it is energetic. And it calls for a great deal of energy from women. 'The spider's web is dense as well as intricate,' whatever the exact identity of the spider may be; and if there is to be any breaking out, the fly has to do some much harder thinking than most strugglers for freedom are capable of.

It is not at the moment fashionable to hold men as a sex responsible for the misapprehensions and injustices that women suffer from and we are constantly being told, by almost every writer on the subject, not to accuse only capitalism, or religion, or babies, or Freud, but also ourselves. Marina Warner, one of the essayists in *Woman on Woman*, quotes, though with reservations, Christopher Logue's apposite verse:

> The slave who likes to be a slave
> No power in all the world can save –
> And slaves who love their slavery
> Can be the death of you and me.

This is true, and among women there are as many slaves in love with their slavery as in any other oppressed class.

Take the question of husbands, for example: that is to say, the social obligation to have one. Most men still think that women justify themselves by marriage. Glen Petrie gives Josephine Butler full marks for being beautiful, even in her forties, and married. Emily Hobhouse had no husband, though, poor dear, she did her best to catch the highly unsuitable Mr Jackson, tradesman and small-town mayor, and her biographer is surprised that she didn't bring it off, with someone or other, as really she was quite presentable, even at thirty-five. But it is not only men who feel that no spinster can be wholly admirable. Look at all the women critics who perpetuate the myth of Jane Austen's suitor, met only once but the great love of her life, struck down by death before he could propose, a character so vague that her closest relatives could not agree about what he was called; or those who ferret around to find curates for Anne and Emily Brontë.

Even the superb Mary Wollstonecraft – whose story is told warmly though at times repetitiously, in Edna Nixon's book – with all her spirit and brains and independence and sexual honesty, wanted a husband. She called herself Mrs Imlay when she wasn't, though most of her circle were free-thinking people who would have considered this concession to morals a rather feeble-minded deception. And why did she marry Godwin? It is easy to see why she loved him and lived with him: contrary to many other reports, he sounds a dear. But given her principles, why *marry* him? Still, even George Eliot, after a lifetime of liberated behaviour, finally became Mrs Cross.

The triumph of owning a husband is apparently as great as ever it was, a trumpet blast that rallies the columns of the daily and weekly press. The perpetual and usually pointless references of Jilly Cooper and Katharine Whitehorn to their husbands suggest that they feel as though their status, their femininity and their very existence depend on their being married. (Glenda Slag is made of sterner stuff.)

And take the question of reading material: women certainly love their slavery as far as this is concerned. Mary Stott of the *Guardian*, in her chapter in *Woman on Woman*, speaks as interestingly about 'the ghetto of the women's pages' as one would expect from her wide experience. She acknowledges their limitations – they exclude 'the whole field of politics, industry, local government, planning, transport, finance'; and their dangers – 'where men excel is in *exploiting* the women's page': Miss X is hired to write a column because she can be projected as a sexpot or a purveyor of her 'true confessions'. Miss Y, whose talent is relatively tiny, will get a build-up because 'of course we must have a woman on the features pages'. But she still feels that it is justifiable for serious newspapers to have women's pages: because of the advertising, because of the loyalty they inspire in women readers and because they are 'a platform where women can say their say – not just to one another but to men'. The first two points are perfectly reasonable, if you are at all responsible for the circulation of a paper: the ideological excuse is less convincing. But what Mrs Stott does not say, and she has no need to do so as far as her own pages are concerned, is that most of what is written specifically for women – women's pages, women's magazines, women's radio – is dreadfully bad. And women like it.

Mollie Lee in her foreword to the third *Woman's Hour* anthology assures us that the reactions of listeners are the daily guide of those producing the programmes and that the audience includes all grades of ability from 'JPs and Oxford degrees to those' – as she tactfully puts it – 'whose writing betrays the fact that their formal education almost doesn't exist but who display as much intelligence and character as their more lettered co-listeners'. She also informs us that 'nowadays there is an infinitely more vital response to items on national and world problems than to queries as to what to do with cold porridge'. This selection must be unrepresentative, then. Almost the only concessions to national and world problems are simplistic memoirs of Lord Northcliffe and Hitler. The cold porridge school is much better represented, with, for instance, hints about reconstituting tired pots of foundation cream with a few drops of rosewater or, in desperate cases, with a dash of almond oil.

If the JPs, Oxbridge degrees and less lettered co-listeners really find such activities absorbing and self-justifying, then so they are. No one person and no society can live on the heights all the time. But I wonder if they really like being addressed as follows: 'My goodness, how wet a wet day in Venice is!' Do they enjoy the husband-and-wife badinage, or the tight-lipped comments on permissiveness, especially coming from a teacher who admits to preparing her GCE class for the Milton questions by means of dictated notes? Do they warm to the missionary zeal of the Raj in hearing of an attempt to introduce the Christmas spirit into Iraq with sixpences in the pudding and tinsel on the date palm? I think they do. Mollie Lee has done her homework. They like it.

They like Jilly Cooper, too. I am not saying, of course, that Mrs Cooper is necessarily like her column. I realise that journalists, like creative writers, can, for some good reason, invent personae that are unlike their real selves, but it is saddening to find the aren't-I-awful prattle that she does so successfully is as widely acceptable as it presumably is. Mary Wollstonecraft, thou shouldst be living at this hour, though I very much doubt if thou wouldst sell anything to the women's pages unless thou didst a piece on where Godwin ('my husband') bought his underpants.

Rope for Debs*

'You cannot loll and wilt while supporting the family jewels.' No, indeed, or rather, no, I imagine not. *Dance Little Ladies*, an extremely well-illustrated history of debutantes from the nebulous and implicit beginnings of 'the season' to its virtual cessation in the 1970s, presents a subject which is, statistically, outside the immediate experience of most people. We, the disadvantaged, know all about it, however, from twentieth-century novels and autobiographies. An *Evening Standard* man, reporting a debs' dance in 1959 where people brought their teddy-bears to meet their friends' teddy-bears, commented, 'It would have been so amusing if we hadn't read it all in a book somewhere.' He was right; we *have* read that book and several more like it. This was a risk that Margaret Pringle must have taken deliberately, and her book, though it could do with a tuck here and there, succeeds.

The factual account Ms Pringle gives us gains its momentum not only from the photographs but also from a series of well-chosen statements from ex-debs down the ages: Lady Diana Cooper ('I came out at the Belvoir Hunt Ball which couldn't have been drearier'); Joyce Grenfell ('It was the only way of meeting Reggie, who turned into my husband'); Margaret, Duchess of Argyll ('There were the girls who came out who promptly went in again'); the Marchioness of Tavistock ('That afternoon in Harrods I heard somebody say "Look, there's Henrietta Tiarks"').

There are other comments too: from the debs' delights, from able bandleader Tommy Kinsman, who knew his place and never made a date with a girl he was working for, and the Astor's butler, who know his too, and 'fled upstairs howling with laughter' after announcing a Labour MP.

One fact that emerges again and again from these accounts is that, by normal civilised standards, many people behaved very badly. Mark Chinnery is particularly outspoken about this, though at the same time complacent in tone. It was not a question of morals. Certainly sexual

* From the *Listener*, 8 December 1977. Review of *Dance Little Ladies; The Days of the Debutante* by Margaret Pringle.

morals, as nearly every contributor is at pains to tell us, were impeccable. Nobody admits to having slept around or even to knowing people who did. True, there was what a cavalry officer's daughter, unnamed, who came out in 1960, refers to as 'everything but' and this, it seems, was accepted practice. There was a considerable amount of theft, as Anne Griffiths and others reveal, especially of spoons: 'People used to pinch them, thinking they were from Buckingham Palace, but they were Jo Lyons'; this apparently made it all right.

The bad behaviour was nothing to do with morals; it took the form of insensitive, arrogant rudeness. Throwing bread and squirting champagne at each other, or fighting with rhubarb sticks, may be nothing other than high jinks when indulged in by consenting adults in private, but when the public has to suffer, the pranks seem less amusing: playing Hare and Hounds on the Circle Line in the Fifties ('people couldn't get on the trains') and emptying boxes of cigarettes on to tramps from the balcony of Londonderry House, again in the Fifties ('I say, hooligans is a bit strong. It was more, you might say, a spontaneous gesture to the poor.')

The abundance of quotation means that Ms Pringle can keep her satire subliminal. There is little need for her to do anything but hand out the rope. Certainly she need not comment on the savagery of the set-up ('People *could* be a bit cruel'). It's a battlefield: pretty against plain, Gentile against Jew, stinking rich against very comfortably off, upper class against middle class ('the middle class ones usually tried harder'), downstairs against upstairs ('There is no charge, Miss. This is the Jockey Club.')

The not-so-stinking rich would go to extraordinary lengths to disguise their shortcomings. Those who could not afford to leave London in August might buy up a month's supply of food and board themselves into their houses. One deb's mother told Tommy Kinsman, 'Tommy, I'm going to book you but I'll cancel you right away because I can't afford to have a dance.' Her party got into the list.

The bitcheries, pretence, and ruthlessness, declared as they are by those who took part and not by disgruntled onlookers, leave one feeling sad rather than indignant. The golden girls, according to the accounts of the other golden girls, came so thoroughly to dust. 'You should see the ones who were the successful debs today,' writes a deb. 'They knew all the catch phrases – "isn't it amusing, my dear?" and they did the Lambeth Walk. Now they are all rather fat crippled old ladies with jerseys drooping round the edge.'

Deaths in Devon*

If Emily Brontë had been a journalist of limited imagination and uncertain purpose, *Wuthering Heights* would have sounded much like John Cornwell's *Earth to Earth*. This book announces itself as 'a true story of the lives and violent deaths of a Devon farming family'. And so it is, as far as it goes.

In 1975 three middle-aged siblings, Frances, Robbie and Alan Luxton of West Chapple Farm near Winkleigh in Devon, were 'found slaughtered in strange circumstances'. Whatever would normal circumstances have been? The newspapers came out with predictable headlines, from 'Tragic Farm Where Time Stood Still' (*Observer*) to 'Night of Horror at Winkleigh' (*Express and Echo*). And 'a few days after the killings,' says John Cornwell, 'I went down to mid-Devon in the hope that there might be a book in the story of the case.' This is it.

It is a short book, though every effort has been made to spin it out. We are spared no detail, from the name of the maker of the Luxtons' grand-father clock to a list of bar snacks available at the local pub. The most egregious example of padding is the story of rape and murder told to the author by Proven Sharpe, the CID man in charge of the Luxton case, and repeated here in full. It concerns a Falmouth girl who was killed in circum-stances so totally different from those in which the Luxtons died that even Cornwell seems to have felt that its inclusion needed some justification. He explains that Sharpe was so reluctant to discuss the West Chapple killings that he had to approach the subject in this roundabout way, and adds that the story became the prelude to his own renewed interest in the Luxtons.

It is significant that Cornwell should have taken six years to write the book and that his inspiration was intermittent. It kept appearing and disap-pearing. It was probably trying to tell him something. During these years he was not the only person to exploit the killings, There was a film called *The Recluse*. And a novelist, Susan Barrett, produced a work of fiction called *The Beacon* which drew on some of the Luxton material. Neither the film nor the novel made Cornwell feel there was nothing left for him to do. I can see what he means when it comes to the book; the passage he quotes reveals a style which is hardly adequate to its theme. 'Birds are heartless; they sing through every human tragedy.' Well, birds are not the only ones.

---

* From the *Listener*, 28 October 1982. Review of *Earth to Earth* by John Cornwell.

Unfortunately John Cornwell's style is hardly adequate either. It is an undemanding blend of journalese and cliché, and is reminiscent of the average historical romance. Streams murmur, rivers brim, and beyond lush meadows we glimpse the blue haze of the moors. The Luxtons come straight out of Jean Plaidy: 'proud and physically strong with high fore-heads, broad shoulders and steady blue eyes.' And here is Catherine Cookson, perhaps: 'The company sat down to a gargantuan dinner, the consumption of which was in itself a notable feat.'

The construction of the book is frail to the point of collapse. The first section, all too accurately entitled 'In Pursuit of the Luxtons', shows Cornwell attempting to mislead both the inhabitants of Winkleigh and Luxton relatives. All of them already had good cause to be suspicious of journalists (who at least declared themselves) so part of his cover story was that he was thinking of buying the house. Well, certainly, one could think of buying a house while travelling through the Gobi desert, but the state-ment was meant to deceive. I would guess it did not succeed, knowing Devonians and judging from the superficiality of the information he got by these means.

The mid-Devon Luxtons were descendants of Robert Luggesdon, a yeoman farmer in the fourteenth century, and in the central section, 'A Family History', Cornwell traces their farming methods and their conse-quent degrees of prosperity through the centuries. His three protagonists were brought up to the practice of isolated self-sufficiency and the avoid-ance of all modern goings-on, from unionisation to the installation of electricity. None of this would have been thought particularly interesting if they had not died as they did. Yet this section does not, except in a limited environmental way, cast any real light on what happened.

After an unsuggestive interview with Fred Lyne, the farm labourer at West Chapple, we have 'The Inquest' which of course gives the verdict: 'In the case of the Luxtons, we have reached the following verdict this afternoon, that Mr Alan Luxton committed suicide and that Mr Robert Luxton first killed his sister and then himself committed suicide.' And finally to 'West Chapple Revisited', which ends with a knees-up at the farm, now under new management.

> We jived and rocked and drank in the farmyard and in the garden; we laughed and yelled in the barns and the outhouses. West Chapple had never seen anything like it and any lingering Luxton shade had surely fled by dawn.

Quite the best thing these dignified passionate ghosts could have done. May they rest in peace.

Doubtful Tale*

Books which have been suppressed for years because of possible scandal and at last safely presented to a supposedly eager world (T.E. Lawrence's *The Mint*, E.M. Forster's *Maurice*) almost invariably fall flat, in spite of a pious pretence at excitement by interested or charitable parties. The authors wrote in the knowledge that they were being daring, which necessarily affected their tone, and such a tone cannot but sound false when the need for daring has gone.

There are exceptions to this generalisation, of course, but W.H. Davies's *Young Emma* is not one of them. Quite apart from the essentially literary drawback just mentioned, there seems to have been an ambiguity, almost a dishonesty about the history of the book which, being caused by the author himself, is bound to be reflected in the text. C.V. Wedgewood gives a lucid account of the whole affair in a foreword.

In 1924 W.H. Davies, already known as a poet and the author of *Autobiography of a Super-Tramp*, sent his publisher, Jonathan Cape, the manuscript of *Young Emma*, which purported to describe the circumstances of his marriage, with the suggestion that it should be published anonymously. Cape showed the script to Bernard Shaw, who thought it should not be published at all, adding, however, that the decision must be left to Davies. At this point Davies, having consulted his wife herself – rather belatedly one would have thought – wrote to Cape again asking him to return the manuscript, destroy the two typed copies and let him know in writing that he had done so. He had, he said, irrevocably decided against publishing; at any time.

He did not implement this decision. When Cape faithfully returned the manuscript, Davies merely replied 'You can destroy the two typewritten copies as soon as you like.' And apparently from then on he made no enquiry whatever about the fate of these copies. The sound of the washing of hands is deafening. In fact the copies were put in a safe at the publisher's.

In 1972, more than thirty years after Davies's death, they were taken out of the safe and shown to, among others, William Plomer, who summed up the case for preserving and for having preserved the script with the masterly statement: 'The truth is that if authors of repute wish their unpub-

---

* From the *Listener*, 1 January 1981. Review of *Young Emma* by W.H. Davies.

lished writings to be destroyed, they should destroy them themselves.' After that, Cape had to wait only for the death of Mrs Davies, which occurred last year. And here we are.

The book is a literary curiosity and as such welcome. It can hardly be taken as straight autobiography. It has the ring of untruth throughout. The fact that Davies's version of his wooing is entirely different from the conventional patient/nurse romance proffered by his biographer does not mean that the biographer is wrong; and of course Davies's repeated protestations that he is being honest and frank – and without a thought of popularity, he stresses – actively suggests the opposite.

His portrait of 'Emma' is highly equivocal. In the first place, by perpetually referring to her as *young* Emma he is cutting down to size where ostensibly he wishes to aggrandise. Furthermore, as a writer he is no tyro and it cannot be his ineptness that frequently makes her sound cretinous rather than simple, and calculating rather than naive. All his negatives – she was *not* a prostitute; though pregnant when he first met her she was *not* promiscuous – add up to something like a positive. It is particularly significant that he should have suggested her as the source of his venereal infection (until the last page in fact when it is suddenly revealed to him without any evidence that it was another woman altogether), giving support to the item of folklore that in these circumstances men usually do name the wrong woman, on purpose.

His vaunted outspokenness operates in fits and starts. He is quite mealy-mouthed about sex, and in general often writes with an archness which obscures the story. If Emma did not have venereal disease what did she have? At the end she quotes the specialist as saying that 'women do not drink enough, and I must drink three pints of liquid a day', and Davies comments 'When I heard this, the whole truth came on me suddenly.' Did she have cystitis then, and if she did, why not say so?

In 1924 two interesting comments were made about the possibility of publishing *Young Emma*. One was by Davies himself: 'A book that is not fit to be published now can never be fit.' The other was by Bernard Shaw: 'I am always in favour of publishing genuine documents.' Amen to both sentiments, as sentiments. Both men would have been pleased at the outcome, and Shaw is right about *Young Emma* being a genuine document, though what it genuinely is I am far from sure.

Index of Names